Things
Reflections o

MW00440407

Essays on Matters from
Personal and Local
to Universal and Monumental

Richard Delong

Table of Contents

Preface

In October, 1986 Marvin Jones, editor of *The Chillicothe Gazette*, the oldest newspaper west of the Alleghenies, decided that the local paper needed more local flavor. He sought input from various segments of our community. I've said that he was looking for a butcher, a baker, and a candlestick maker. He invited representatives from many occupations, professions, trades, vocations, governments, and non-profits. Having been an English major in my undergraduate days at The Ohio State University and having taught English in the public schools of Upper Arlington and Zane Trace for three years, I responded to Mr. Jones' invitation on behalf of the local bar association. I'd been fascinated by words on paper since my childhood. My livelihood now being based upon the reading, writing, speaking, and interpreting of the verbiage known as "The Law," I felt a natural inclination to "try out my wheels."

Marvin accepted my application and began assigning my expected publication dates, three or four per year. I assumed that my contributions were expected to focus on legal themes, so I generally stayed that course for the preponderance of my essays over the first few years. Thereafter, I gradually expanded the subject matter to treat issues touching on modern culture, including some benign political comment, topics of local interest, family and personal concerns, and themes relating to various holidays. As time passed and I felt more confident, I strove gently to insert a spiritual perspective somewhere in each piece.

Here follows the results. I wrote to meet deadlines and to respond to current events, but I trust that at least some of the content reflects timeless values.

Acknowledgment

Only by the initial invitation and the continuing sufferance of *The Chillicothe Gazette* and of its parent corporation, Gannett Company, have I been privileged to share my drivel with the newspaper-reading public. Furthermore, only by permission of those entities are the contents gathered here authorized to be reprinted. I thank those publishers. I am especially grateful to Mike Throne, long-time editor of the *Gazette*, for his cooperation, guidance, leadership, understanding, patience and, most of all, friendship.

Only by the insistence, skills, and determination of Jay Wise, Dean of Off Campus Library Services, Indiana Wesleyan University, and Wesley Seminary Librarian, has this collection found its bound book form. Thanks is due Jay for his devotion to this project and to its author.

Dedication

To my wife and personal cheerleader, Beth, without whose presence and encouragement my life would have been drear, my motivation would have been nil, my daily view would have been far less beautiful, and this collection would not have appeared.

I.   Living Life in Modern Culture (Pre-9/11)

When I began this writing experiment in 1987, the readers of the world were not bogged down with blogs. Today, any seventh grader with a cell phone and a working battery can enter the wonderful world of blathering on about any topic, whether or not the writer knows a single thing about the subject at hand. When I commenced, only people like me, with the stamp of approval of the publisher, could do such blathering. I did believe, and still do, that a newspaper columnist has a special privilege and duty to provide serious and thoughtful comment and perspective on subjects of general interest to the community. Thus, many of my early pieces centered on testing my new "megaphone." Whether successful in meeting that aspiration or not, here are some pre-2000 columns in that vein.

February 7, 1987

Pressure: Too Much, Too Soon on Our Young People

"See Dick. See Jane. See Spot."

"Run, Dick, run. Run, Jane, run. Run, Spot, run."

Reading these words from an old first-grade reader reminds many of us of the peaceful unhurried pace of our lives as children. God was in His heaven, Andy Griffith was in his Mayberry sheriff's office, and Opie was home eating Aunt Bea's cookies. If today's first-grade reader reflects the pace today's children must live, the following might be an excerpt:

"See Dick. See Jane. See Spot."

'"Run, Dick, run. Run, Jane, run. Spot – GET!"

"Run faster, Dick. Get the lead out, Jane. Get that dog out of here; it interferes with your concentration. Now get back out there and run until you drop!"

The stresses formerly reserved to adults are being forced on youth at increasingly earlier ages. The pressure upon children to achieve much and quickly may be overwhelming many of them. We want to motivate kids to succeed without overburdening them with pressure. Evidence exists that we are pushing too hard.

Academic innovations reveal the trend: ballooning attendance at pre-schools, teaching of reading to preschoolers, teaching of languages in elementary schools, and the lack of recesses in nearly 20 percent of the elementary schools in this country. While these techniques may be individually defensible, the trend toward pressuring the young is obvious.

Pressures of participating in sports programs are building. Organized competition with the emphasis on winning is offered at ever-decreasing age levels. Soccer toddlers abound. Little leaguers get treats only if they win. Midget footballers must be mean to get victory. The time demanded from high school athletes is tremendous. Practices and games occur six days a week in season. Out of season, summer camp, open gyms and conditioning programs are mandatory. Total dedication is expected.

The burden of pleasing adults by winning is heavy. When young athletes see the fervor with which adults not only cheer their team, but also jeer the opponents, the game officials and the coaches, the message is clear. Winning is the only worthy outcome; i.e., the only way to please.

In some instances, the parents' will to win via their child's activities results in direct participation. A few years ago my son Douglas, then a first-year Cub Scout, was to participate in the Pinewood Derby. We understood that the scout was to carve and assemble a small car for participation in a race. I simply observed Doug's preparations and accompanied him to the race. On race day, the course was surrounded by father-son racing teams of the Trueman-Rahal variety. Doug's clunker was, predictably, beaten in the first heat. As the competition wore on, we noticed that the real competition was between the fathers. Some dads were calculating the weights to add or subtract from the racers. Others were busily greasing axles with graphite and silicone. The business of winning the Pinewood Derby was too important to be left to the scouts.

The need to learn to survive in a tough adult world is one justification offered for pressuring kids. Many kids, however, cannot cope with or survive growing up Kathy Ormsby, now paralyzed, is an outstanding example of pressure to win leading to a suicide attempt. While running in the NCAA 10,000-meter championship race last June, she realized mid-race that she would not win. She ran off the track, out of the stadium and jumped off a bridge in an attempt to end her disappointment and herself. Suicide is the second leading cause of death among teen-agers in our country.

Teen-age and even childhood criminal activity has become commonplace. Teen-age and even childhood sexual activity, with its effect upon illegitimate birth rates and sexually transmitted diseases, is threatening the fabric of our society. Teen-age and even childhood drug and alcohol abuse is a modern phenomenon. We condemn our youth when they turn to the pressure-release valves of drugs, sex, crime and even suicide. We tell them to "just say no," but we do little to relieve the tensions which force them to say yes.

I submit that all of us would benefit by giving youth more space to mature at their own pace. Revise the first-grade reader once more.

"Relax, Dick and Jane. Prepare for the future, but enjoy your youth at the same time. Lighten up a little."

"Here, Spot."

December 10, 1988

Reflections: Society Scurries from the Simple, Natural

On a frosty mid-November morning recently, I was at my usual pace. Living in Kingston and practicing law in Adelphi. I usually, and did this day, begin by visiting my client-bank in Kingston at its 8:30 opening bell. The cold click of the lock of the bank door's latch could as easily have been a starter's pistol.

After my quick rounds in the financial realm, I wheeled my little Chevy onto the straight-as-a-pin County Line Road, which leads across the prairie once covered by 12-foot-high virgin grass, but now a bare slate awaiting Ceres' next blessing. With any luck, i.e., without braking for trucks or deer, each fattened by the farmers' ripe fields, I could cover in about nine minutes flat the same nine miles that 17,000 years ago the Wisconsin glacier flattened in maybe 500 years.

My mind raced faster than my flywheel. If I could make it to my office by 8:50, I could instruct my secretary on her morning chores, could give a send-off to my paralegal as he set sail for Logan, could make the essential phone call to the client who called late yesterday, could proofread the papers for my 9:30 real estate closing, and could still navigate the Chevy the 15 miles to Circleville where borrowers and bankers were probably already approaching the table piled with closing papers.

Now my mind came back to driver's attention as I approached the dangerous Wissler Road intersection. The fall harvest had cut the blinding walls of corn on all four corners to mere stubble. Great! With an unobstructed view North and South, I could continue my flight into the rising day at the same mph and rpm to which I had already attuned my chariot.

Just then, just off to my right, I spotted a relic from another time. I let up on my car's accelerator and on my accelerator to breathe in the site of a solitary black buggy pulled by a single black horse and guided by a lone Amishman. As the sun shone over the Appalachian foothills and illuminated the mist shooting rhythmically from the gentle beast's nostrils, I was, even alone in my machine, somehow embarrassed.

In that moment, my mind flashed back to a business meeting I had a few weeks earlier with a young Amishman who was, with his family and friends, moving from eastern Ohio to establish a new settlement in southeastern Pickaway County. Most striking was the calm and serene nature of this gentle man. With the world whizzing by, he did not seem to be in a hurry. The memory of that conversation and the observation of the carriage's slow, steady progress along the road jolted me.

This vague sense of shame was both personal and cultural. The backward migrants, locked in the wrong century, for that instant seemed more sensible than we moderns. They keep things simple. Our Amish friends do not live by the clock, digital or analog. Nature provides their pace. Sun rises, work begins; sun sets, labors cease.

We, though, have left the simple and the natural behind. We invent and employ labor-saving devices, such as appliances, automobiles and computers, yet life becomes more frenzied. To borrow a phrase, "The hurrieder we go, the behinder we get." We educate ourselves fully, yet, in our wisdom, treat ourselves and our world most unnaturally, to-wit: drug abuse, pollution, spousal abuse, divorce, child abuse, suicide, alcohol abuse, crime, ozone depletion and stress.

I am sometimes defensive when describing to a client the laborious path the law must take to resolve the problems just enumerated. Oh, for a simpler way! Yet, now I see that my uneasiness in this is the same I felt when contrasting the Amish ways to my own. Our laws simply mirror our society's development. Complex problems require complex laws.

Nostalgic though I have sounded, I do not suggest we exchange our computers for hand-plows or our cars for buggies. Modern hardware is not the problem; modern attitudes are. Some of the Amish values are well known: the importance of work, however humble, well-done; devotion to family; due regard for the Maker and the world He has made; cooperation within a community.

During this season of reflection, we would do well to examine ourselves and our institutions, yes, even our laws, to be sure our pace is not detracting from our peace.

November 11, 1989

Maturation: Autumn of Life is the Period for Harvest

Thanksgiving approaches and I feel much older than I did at Labor Day. Mid-September brought my birthday, but my sense of aging seems to have little to do with the accelerating rush of marks against me. Seasons and circumstances change. So with the years does my vantage point.

The gap between 41 and 42 years was minuscule compared to the chasm I noticed between life the day before and life the day after my first-born left home for the university. Leaving the nest is a normal part of nature's cycle; I simply had not considered it beforehand. The successful parent guides the child to independence. Success can be painful.

Aging's pace continued gaining momentum. My slightly younger second (and last-born) recently experienced the thrill of finding the girl who likes him as much as he likes her. The yard where he and I annually recreated the World Series stands empty. The room where Mick Jagger and Stryper assaulted our tranquility lies strangely silent. The silence is rather deafening.

Some say being old is not all bad. Getting there, however, requires endurance. Family, friends, clients and associates are breaking down or breaking up in escalating numbers. A mystery disease strikes a friend my age inexplicably. An aging client goes under the knife three times in two weeks and emerges less a limb and struggling to survive. Friends strive to keep marriages alive or to regroup and continue after marriages have yielded to divorce.

Even the earth itself is not exempt. The Charleston, S.C., coastal area is a place where centuries of culture and beauty had accumulated and, temporarily, been preserved. In one night, Hugo turned a grand Southern lady into an old bag of bones. On the unlucky 13th, the "next-to-the-big-one" put more than a few wrinkles into the young, tanned landscape of California. The Golden State may be reaching for its Golden Buckeye Card.

The sky may be depreciating, too. Authors predicting the death of nature as we know it have begun to sound realistic rather than alarmist. Irreversible global warming, ozone depletion, and greenhouse effect may signal the planet's demise as surely as continuous fever, anemia and hardening of the arteries might for an elderly patient. A difference exists though – no strong, middle-aged children or eager-eyed grandchildren wait by earth's dying bed. If earth expires, it leaves no offspring.

We are all maturing at the same rate. So, must we slide together into the dark pit of maturity with frowns? No! The commercial said we're not getting older, we're getting better. Ben Franklin wrote: "An old man in the house is a good sign." Maurice Chevalier said: "Old age isn't so bad when you consider the alternative."

Human ripeness has its compensations. Autumn is not the time of death, but the time of harvest. The payback for the aches and pains of human aging is, ideally, wisdom and perspective. The independence of maturing children is the harvest of attentive child rearing. Even the sickness or death of loved ones is somehow comforting evidence of the never-changing grand plan, a plan bigger than the greatest of us, yet encompassing equally the least of us. The environmental changes are, indeed, a bitter harvest of the youthful gluttony of this planet's inhabitants, but one that may yet force maturing homo sapiens to make some needed adjustments to "this old house" we all inhabit.

So this aging may not be so bad. Bring on Thanksgiving. We'll be grateful to have come this far and reaped such a harvest. Then we'll watch for the beauty of winter, nature's final cycle, knowing that spring will soon confirm the hope of the aging: renewal.

September 15, 1990

Selfishness: Personal, Public Gratification Out of Hand

"Share your toys."
-Statement by all mothers from time immemorial.

"He who dies with the most toys wins."
-Saying on bumper sticker in the 80's.

All agree that our country and its citizens face many problems. Solutions for these problems have been elusive. For the purposes of discussion this morning, let me propose a simple (and admittedly probably a simplistic) prescription for our maladies: "Be less selfish."

The critical reader may first ask: "What's this? A lawyer writing about selfishness? Isn't that similar to a prostitute writing about purity or a politician about honesty?"

I can understand that attitude. Attorneys appear to be acting selfishly when insisting that their clients' rights be enforced. Really, however, our legal system seeks to prevent selfishness. The law of the jungle, i.e., survival of the strongest, promotes selfishness. Our system prevents the selfish, strong few (the government leaders, the corporations, the super-rich, the bullying neighbor) from overrunning the weak.

Our culture is, though, weakening itself by confusing the enforcement of rights with the gratification of desires. Mothers know that children may "own" their own toys, but wise mothers encourage sharing. Mothers realize their children might someday be the ones without toys. Besides that, mothers try to teach that sharing is just plain right and that selfishness is wrong.

Has society bought instead the message suggested by the bumper sticker – the message that getting and keeping are the only virtues in life? Possibly.

Self-interest prevents our government officials from acting on important issues. Nineteenth Century British theologian Benjamin Jowett said, "The way to get things done is not to mind who gets the credit for doing them." Our politicians, always looking for the credit, have turned this on its head. They say: "We do not care if nothing gets done; we simply will not risk condemnation for unsuccessful attempts to cure problems." Consequently, Congress and the president fiddle while our economy burns.

For example, the budgetary problems are well known. A balanced budget is not necessary or even desirable every year, but ours is as out of balance as a centipede on a unicycle. Taxes should go up some; spending should come down some. Enter selfishness. The politicians will not vote for either because they want to keep their jobs. Their constituents (we) never forgive them for any vote which hits us in our own pocketbook. They and we are selfish to the point of national and self-detriment.

Our nation has selfishly abused the environment. For a while, our unthinking treatment of the world stemmed from our ignorance. Our present inability to change our behavior stems from our selfishness. We are too selfish with our time and with our comforts to learn to develop and practice suitable ways of disposing of our waste.

Selfishness hurts also on an individual level. The advice given by some professional and many amateur psychiatrists for the past couple of decades has been to love oneself so that one can then love others. The first part of the lesson is getting through, I'm O.K.; you're O.K. Look out for No. 1. Unfortunately, the second part of the lesson, treating others better, is not getting through. Examples abound.

In the name of self-realization, many spouses trash any hope of marital harmony. Only spouses who can subordinate themselves to each other and to the larger concept of the marriage unit will find contentment.

In the name of personal independence, parents by the millions have practically abandoned their children. The short-term happiness of these parents will yield the long-term pain caused by their confused children.

In the hope of finding joy for themselves, people bury themselves in their addictions, food, smoke, drink, drug, work, sex. The ironic harvest of these desperate attempts at self-pleasure is nearly always self-destruction.

Jean Paul Richter said: "For sleep, health and wealth to be truly enjoyed, they must be interrupted." When we become a Japanese economic colony, we may attempt to compromise a bit politically to get something done about our economy. When we are up to our ankles in slime and trash, we may change our selfish, wasteful ways. When even more of our families disintegrate and the criminals who are a product of this domestic anarchy infest every street corner, we may renew the art of self-sacrificing parenthood. But we would be stupid, as a country and as individuals, to wait so long.

In neither the national nor the personal sphere has toy collecting been beneficial. It is time for each of us to remember our mother's admonition: "Share your toys."

July 9, 1994

Grandma Not the Only One Confused by TV

Television arrived long after Grandma Carney's birth in 1879. By the time she left this world in 1973, though, TV had become a very real presence in her life. Too real.

Poor Granny. In her twilight years, Mrs. Carney talked back to the TV. A quiet, yet polite person, she thought it only courteous to respond to those people speaking to her from that bright little box in her living room. She was horrified when she inadvertently appeared less that fully dressed in front of those people peering at her from behind the frosted glass Philco.

I point out Grandma (my cousins', not mine) Carney's trouble distinguishing the real from the Memorex not from any lack of respect for her suffering during her final days. No, I raise this image because it highlights nicely the difficulty our society now experiences. The line between truth and fiction, between real and imaginary, between fact and fantasy, is fading faster than full-time employment with benefits.

Tell me where news ends and entertainment begins. When TV newscasters began, they were all business. They dictated the pure, unvarnished news, more or less. When Walter Cronkite signed off by telling us, "And that's the way it is," he really had done just that.

Now the evening news reminds me of "Sesame Street." Assuming that the attention span of the audience equals that of the average preschooler, the networks have decided to encourage us to stay tuned by having the co-anchors act as if they are best friends and the weatherman and sports anchor as if they are fraternity brothers, and juvenile ones at that. That's bad enough, but then the reenactments of the way things might have happened at the murder, rape, or robbery scene begin. Interviews of the spouses and parents and children are then conducted at the gravesites of the victims. If we are especially lucky, we can get Barbara Waa-Waa questioning (glorifying?) the aberrant human who actually committed the acts.

Whoa! I'd better get off my soapbox and back to my thesis, which is: The increasing inability of our citizens to distinguish and evaluate real life situations from make-believe ones diminishes our society's chances of maintaining a certain level of civility.

We're having as much trouble as Grandma Carney separating the visitors at the door from the visitors in the tube.

You knew it had to be coming, so here it is: the O.J. Simpson case. Now I have watched less TV coverage about this case than anyone I know. You might conclude that I know less about it than anyone I know. I will not concede that point. The hyperactive news coverage appears to have provided so much about everything even remotely concerning the personalities involved in the case that viewers trying to learn about the case may well be totally distracted.

As an attorney, an officer of the court, this disturbs me. Of course, courts must be open to public view. Secret justice will nearly always disintegrate into no justice. But public trial should not be interpreted to mean trial by the public.

Flip on a camera and people strive to become something they are not. Get out your family videos. You'll see that everyone wants to be a comedian or a star or a hero. I worry that this tendency may be stronger that the tendency of a person under oath to tell the truth.

So, although I do believe that we can go too far in giving the media totally free access to the courtroom, I nevertheless believe in the freedom of the press as protected by the First Amendment. I am sure the judge will balance the interests of the state, the defendant, and the media, and a fair trial will be delivered---even to Mr. Simpson.

What really concerns me is the increasingly apparent practice of people treating life as if it were a mere game. Whether Mr. Simpson is guilty of murder is yet to be determined. But we do know that O.J.'s fabled freeway fleeing was with police in pursuit. Fleeing an officer is illegal. Yet dozens of onlookers were cheering the one fleeing. The bystanders were out of touch with reality. They could as well have been watching a game on the screen of their home computer.

"So what," you say? I'll say what. So what if you or your family member is the next victim of a drive-by shooting—a shooting conducted by one who thinks life is merely a game and that the one being killed is somehow less that truly living? So what if you're the next one to have your head bashed in by whatever person near you who is stronger than you?

"So, Mr. Smarty," you ask, "what's the solution?" I certainly do not claim to have "the" solution. I do not believe in censorship. I believe my political hero, Thomas Jefferson, who said he would rather have free press with no government than government without a free press.

I do humbly submit, however, that a voluntary weaning from the more sensational aspects of the free press might be helpful. Begin skipping your nightly fix of "A Current Affair." Pass up your weekly purchase of the National Enquirer (Did you know that Jackie O. and Elvis were spotted at the 7-11 down the street from O.J.'s place on the night of the crime?) Watch one less made-for-TV movie per week about another extremely personal tragedy.

David Frost said: "TV is an invention that permits you to be entertained in your living room by people you wouldn't have in your house."

Grandma Carney, even if she could distinguish the real from the fictional, would be aghast at the characters we are allowing into our homes and our lives today. Let's get real.

December 10, 1994

Good Manners Replaced by Vulgarity

My dad possessed many worthy characteristics, but he couldn't cuss worth a . . . worth a darn.

His mild manner manifested itself even in his manner of speaking. Only in the direst of circumstances did anything resembling profanity escape Dad's lips, and even then, the words were not vivid enough to inspire much awe in a little guy with big ears.

If little Richard was to learn to swear as a "real man" swore, where was he to look for guidance? Television was a fledging and offered no instruction in the act of foul speech. Milton Berle was no shock jock. Newspapers did publish four-letter words, but none were indecent, for indecency was all private back then. *Boys' Life*, my sole magazine subscription, described nothing dirtier than fish cleaning. I didn't even have a big brother to imitate.

Then one day I found my mentor of mature speech. I'll call him Roger, the manager of a local merchant's office with whom my Dad dealt regularly. Boy! Could Roger swear! I had no idea what some of his pronouncements meant, but I never missed a chance to hear more of them. I guess I've always been interested in getting an education.

My lawyer's mind was set to rambling upon these memories when I recently read about the effort of Raritan, New Jersey, to ban public cursing.

My fascination for foul words had faded long ago, I never learned to swear well, and I didn't regret my deficiency. Now I am repelled by, rather than attracted to, the massive vulgarity which confronts all of us along our daily way. My aversion comes not from a belief that I am somehow above all which is unclean. I have plenty of habits of which I am not proud.

And it's not that I have virgin ears. My college dorm room discussions and summers of factory employment provided opportunities to observe obscenity that made Roger's sound like Mr. Rogers.

I simply believe that our society has mastered the art of vulgarity all too well. Each day's deluge of degradation threatens to overwhelm us.

Where does the law line up on this one? Would we be better off if such speech were outlawed?

Enter the well-intentioned Raritan town council. Also, enter the U. S. Constitution. One man's junk is another man's treasure. One man's useless vulgarity is another man's spice of speech. The freedom of speech guaranteed by the First Amendment prevents the government from composing a list of words forbidden from use by its citizens.

So, much as I dislike admitting it, decent speech cannot be legislated. Just as prohibition of alcohol consumption failed, legislative efforts to ban certain words are doomed as illegal and, no doubt, ineffective.

Still, I am uncomfortable, especially with minors in my car, when facing the barrage of bumper stickers such as the one credited to that paragon of American virtue, Forrest Gump, (S---happens). I know it does and I believe in the right of each citizen to publicize his or her philosophy of life. I'd just rather not have to drive through the smelly stuff to go pick up a quart of milk.

Who cares what offends that old fogey, you may say. I agree with you. My personal preferences concern no one but myself.

Can we agree, however, that to be civilized, a society must maintain some minimal level of civility, i.e., manners? Can we agree further that good manners dictate that we sometimes refrain from doing or saying certain things, which, although legal, may offend those within our range of seeing or hearing?

The wife of Samuel Clemens (Mark Twain), it is said, was aggravated by the crusty writer's salty vocabulary. To register her point, she peppered her own speech with a few profanities. He responded: "My dear, you've got the words right, but not the tune."

I am not so concerned about the words America is using as about the tune it is singing. Unbridled vulgarity precedes the fall of a civilization. Legislation won't help. A new tune might.

July 29, 1995

Changes Will Continue

Have you seen "Bridges of Madison County?" Or, maybe you read the book.

I resisted reading the novel. Possessing a bachelor's degree in English, I had convinced myself that any book that was popular with the masses must be a no-brainer. So, don't ask me why I accompanied my wife to a recent Sunday matinee to view the Iowa version of *The Dating Game*.

The movie was not as bad as I had imagined the book to be. Except for the implication given in the movie that a four-day fling can be more rewarding than a lifetime of commitment (a theory with which, I sadly suspect, most people today have come to agree), I found the film, to be entertaining and, in a strange way, uplifting.

But one feature of the script galled me a little.

The people of the small Iowa town in which the action was set were depicted by Francesca and her Romeo, f.k.a. Dirty Harry, as permanently provincial gossip mongers who were judgmental, hypocritical and narrow-thinking know-nothings. The royal couple went on to implicitly equate those who failed to welcome change with Neanderthals.

The movie conveys the impression that those who voluntarily live in less than urban areas are moral midgets. If only the rest of the Hawkeyes could be as liberated and conscientious as these adulterers!

This attack on my small town sensibilities reminds me of the recent exchanges on these pages about the impact of growth in Chillicothe and Ross County on the quality of life here.

Some believe the coming of Wal-Mart and a wider Western Avenue portends doom. Others believe that lack of progress would seal our doom to wallow in the stagnant pool of the past as surely as Iowa swine marinate in the mud.

What will bring or keep joy here in Mudville – progress or paralysis?

I'm forced to admit that Harry . . . er Robert, did dispense some wisdom to frisky Francesca. When she stated how resistant to change her Iowa neighbors were, the Honorable Mayor Eastwood told her how he had come to view and treat change. Since change is inevitable, he had decided to embrace it as something he could count on, i.e., a constant. Thus, in a life in which few things could be counted upon, change could be, paradoxically, a comfort.

Change has occurred here in Mayberry. The township roads upon which I helped my dad drive cattle and combines in the 1950s are now sped upon by thundering herds of hard-driving suburban types racing to and from their homes in the new strip subdivisions.

Whereas in that yesteryear Harry Sims' hole-in-the-wall was the only place in Kingston open on Sunday to get a little bread and milk, today Sunday commerce cannot be distinguished from any other day. Change has come and will continue.

Which changes should our community endorse and implement? Which should be prohibited or resisted? I am not sufficiently informed to judge. I do hope, however, that the verdict passed upon us small towners by the King and Queen of the Corn Festival will be ignored by us. That we live in small towns does not have to mean that our brains are small.

Reactions to changes can be rational. Solutions to problems caused by change can be found. Ross Countians can disprove the stereotype that rural people are those whose waist size exceeds their IQ's.

Bridges doesn't have a happy ending. Not all are able to get what they wanted. But it does have a proper ending. The pain caused by change was minimized because the parties involved determined to honor previous commitments made.

Those who long ago established our community committed to create a place to work fruitfully and live comfortably, all in a manner consistent with nature, the natural qualities of this spot on the earth.

Can we manage to change while honoring that commitment? If Francesca could, certainly we can, too!

February 24, 1996

Excess Leads to Defect

What did you get for Christmas? Quick now – can you name two presents, let alone all of them?

Don't worry. More gifts are coming your way. Many are readying for Christmas 1996 already.

Every day is Advent, always leading to the next Christmas.

Christmas, it seems is always to be with us. Just check your February credit card statement. If gluttony is a deadly sin, we would have all been dead by Dec. 26.

I've heard our Christmas routine described as the process of spending money we don't have to buy for people we don't necessarily like things they don't need. That's not a pretty picture, but excessive indulgence never is.

Ash Wednesday sneaked by this past week. Hardly anyone noticed. Ash Wednesday marks the beginning of Lent on the Christian calendar. Lent is the period leading up to Easter. Tradition calls for believers to deny self and to reflect more during this season. Some choose to engage in partial fasting or in sacrificial giving.

Both Advent and Lent are religious observances. The contrasting ways we celebrate each may reveal an underlying cause of many of our culture's increasingly evident difficulties.

Pick a problem – any problem. Then apply the principle my wise old mentor, Fred Orr, expresses this way: "Any excess is a defect."

Take sex, for example, (Ha! I gotcha. I'll bet you won't skip ahead to the sports page or comics now.) Excessive repressiveness regarding sexual matters is unhealthy and unnecessary.

Families and schools have a right and a duty to educate the young on this subject.

We have erred, however, in flooding the eyes and brains of our youths with information and with opportunity to use that information inappropriately.

Richard Foster, a Quaker and one of my favorite authors makes a great analogy. A river within its banks is a beautiful, powerful, useful thing. When it overflows its banks, though, it produces ugly destruction.

Similarly, sex, when bounded within appropriate channels, is beautiful and, of course, useful. Perpetuation of humanity is pretty practical. But when running loose, this natural gift can wreak unnatural havoc.

Isn't it fair to state that unbridled sexual freedom is causing more pain than joy? The excess is revealing a defect.

Want another example? Let's try "Freedom Without Responsibility" for $500 a la *Jeopardy!*

First, let me affirm my belief in our Constitution and the Bill of Rights. Our personal freedoms are precious; I would not retract even an iota of them.

For instance, regarding freedom of the press, I agree with my political hero, Thomas Jefferson. He said he'd rather have newspapers without government than government without newspapers.

Unrestrained government would soon become a dictatorship.

What I'd prefer is media that volunteers to use some discretion and good taste. Having the freedom to do an act does not mean that exercising the freedom is wise.

Why must grieving families be filmed at funerals? Why must gruesome crimes be realistically reenacted by news folks? And was there ever such a wretched excess of reporting as during the O. J. trial?

I know that sensationalism sells, but I think it also stinks. I would fight to preserve freedom of the press, but I would beg to see it used responsibly.

Allow me to take a gamble on one more. I believe government is wrong to encourage gambling.

Billboards flash the latest Lotto line. At nearly any grocery counter, our daily lottery ticket appears with our daily bread. I'm not a prude. I know life itself is a gamble. My bank may fail. The stock market may crash. But my government actively attempts to prevent that.

The entertainment value of gambling assures that it will always be present in some form.

Government cannot eradicate it. But doesn't it seem excessive for government to encourage it?

I wonder if as many citizens would participate if the sign on the counter contained the truthful label: Lottery Tax.

I'm sounding like a dreary drudge. I'm not suggesting we have no fun. No. I do not suggest that we abandon Christmas. I love and need the sense of wonder and joy of that celebration.

I am suggesting, though, that we all need to engage less in gluttonous attitudes and more in the self-sacrificing spirit of Lent. Remember that excess leads to defect.

December 6, 1996

Put Play Back in Sports

"WORK BALL!"

I suggest opening all sports contests with this revised command.

"Play Ball" misses the mark. The time-honored phrase is passé', out-of-date, washed-up, and, well, just plain inaccurate.

Sports have ceased to be play.

Certainly professional sports have become just that, a profession – mere employment. A day existed when both players and fans could forget the vocational element once the game had begun. Not now.

Take Albert Belle, (In the classic words of comedian Henny Youngman, "Please.") The uninformed reader must learn that Mr. Belle spent several formative years toiling in the outfield of the Cleveland Indians baseball club. His talents developed at a pace exceeded only by his foul demeanor. He would be a perfect "before" in a before and after ad for the Dale Carnegie course on how to win friends and influence people.

He could certainly afford tuition for the course. The Chicago White Sox have rewarded Prince Albert's higher than average talents, while ignoring his lower than average behavior, by employing him to "work ball" for the kingly sum of approximately $11,000,000 per year.

To misquote Joshua, the Israelite, who could have bought two promised lands for $11,000,000: "Choose for yourself whom you shall cheer, but as for me and my house, we'll stay home and be bored to tears rather than spend a penny that in any way could help pay Big Al $68,000 per game."

Watching adults work for outlandish profit is not my idea of recreation. Would I pay to sit in Donald Trump's office to watch him conduct the deals that make him his millions? Never! Neither will I transfer my cash to Albert's hand for the privilege of watching him perform his job for an employer even richer than he.

More disappointingly, I'm convinced that all sports are becoming professional. Collegiate sports operate to build treasuries for the colleges and pro careers for the athletes, not to build character for the well-rounded student. I exaggerate less than I wish when I say that many college athletes spend more time in jail than in class. School spirit and sportsmanship are as archaic as the fox trot at the school prom.

Watching children work at playing is the saddest spectacle. In the first column I was privileged to contribute to this space, nearly ten years ago, I suggested that we need to give children more space to mature without so much pressure so soon. At least in the sports arena, my suggestion has created as much response as Ralph Nader's presidential campaign. It's been received as Miss Manners would be at Roseanne's dinner table.

Amateur athletics has ceased to have anything to do with play. Play means recreation. Play is light-hearted. Play has an element of spontaneity. The play I am observing in our youth today is as serious as a heart attack.

When I hear of the tremendous practice schedules for high school athletes, when I learn of the year-round devotion required from student athletes just to be allowed to participate, and when I see how far tiny-tot soccer players travel for games and tournaments, I wonder. Can we really call this play? Kids today don't play sports; they work sports.

Now don't call me an egghead. I have excellent "sports nut" credentials. My dad, Wayne, kept the basketball scorebook for Kingston and Zane Trace teams for nearly forty years. I accompanied him to nearly all of those games. I lived to play (now work) high school baseball and basketball. I was a red-hot high school sports fan for many years as an adult. Now my zest has evaporated.

I am not coach bashing. Coaches are just trying to do the job they are assigned by the schools and parents. I'd recommend that the school boards and parents simply change the coaches' job descriptions. Make clear that character takes precedence over championships. Specify that family time is as important as floor or field time. Insist that respect for authority (i.e., game officials) must prevail over the victory-at-any-cost attitude.

A recent article in the *Gazette* reviewed the career accomplishments of former Paint Valley High School coach Oral Crabtree. Descriptions of him and his method seem the antithesis of what athletics is becoming today: "modest...a gentleman...calm...never yelled at a referee...hardly ever raised his voice... a stickler for grades."

I know all players, coaches, parents, and fans will not, cannot, and need not adopt Coach Crabtree's style. I only plead for the return of some balance and maturity in the amateur sports scene. Let's not make sports participation a job.

So, what'll it be: "WORK BALL" or "PLAY BALL?"

November 15, 1997

We Still Need a Day of Rest

As a child, I spent most Sundays with my extended family at Grandma Hartsock's farm. Of course, at that time, I didn't know my family was extended. And I didn't know I was being deprived of my right to shop or eat out. I doubt we could have afforded either regularly, even if stores and restaurants had been open on Sunday. I accepted Sunday as the day to worship and then watch the men snooze, the women talk, and the kids play.

Harry Sims' hole-in-the-wall was the only place in Kingston to get bread and milk on Sunday.

Those traveling by necessity and those who failed to plan ahead could, with persistence, find a solitary gas pump in each community to quench the thirst of the "machine." Most commercial establishments stood dark and silent as the losers in last week's elections.

This newspaper in its editorial of October 27, 1997, spoke against an enforced "Holy Day." I can agree with that, but I question whether we are better off living, as the editor put it," . . . in a world that is never at rest."

Robert Frost wrote: "By working faithfully eight hours a day, you may eventually get to be a boss and work twelve hours a day." Our nation, by going full tilt 24 hours a day, 6 days a week, has now moved its way up (?) to 24 hours a day, 7 days a week. Are we really prospering in the long run by "maturing" to the point of running full steam, every day, day after day?

I do not speak in this essay to the religious aspect of a Sabbath. As a Christian, I do believe God commands an observation of a weekly day of rest. God created for six days; then He rested – not because He was tired. He was setting the example for us. I have endured personally the fatigue, which plagues one trying to contradict for a long period this God- given principle.

I must also confess my hypocrisy. I appear in church, but also in restaurants and shops, nearly every Sunday.

While holding this opinion, I nevertheless concur with the erudite editor of this epistle who wrote: "(B)ut in the multicultural world we live in now, enforcing a holy day for one religion with laws seems unfair and unconstitutional."

Agreed. I would not want to be prohibited from practicing my profession on Tuesdays because the members of the New Orleans Society for the Weekly Celebration of Fat Tuesday amassed enough congressional support to pass a federal law requiring such observance.

This discussion leads to a couple of tougher issues, one legal and one personal.

First, what are we to do when good sense happens to match the Good Book? Who would argue that we must abolish all laws against homicide just because the Sixth of the Ten Commandments states: "Thou shalt not kill?" Shall we abolish all laws against stealing because such laws coincide with the Eighth Commandment: "Thou shalt not steal?"

Of course not! Unfortunately, though, that's where we're headed. Because of such super sensitivity to avoiding the appearance of government endorsing religion, we are slowly adopting a body of law, which is detached from good sense.

In arguing that Ohio should abolish all laws regulating the sale of liquor on Sundays, the editor is separating the law from good sense, not from religion. The editor complains about local control of liquor sales, e.g., the right of a community to vote to be "wet" or "dry."

Democracy does not grant each citizen the right to expect his or her every whim to be fulfilled at any location and at any time he or she chooses. Groups of individuals, called communities, also have collective rights, which at times legally override certain individual rights. That makes good sense.

Second, why don't we exercise good judgment and do voluntarily what the law would have required if it existed?

One of Parkinson's laws is that work expands to fill the time available for its completion. In a similar vein, our activities expand to meet the time made available for these activities.

Retail establishments operate 24 hours a day because customers come 24 hours a day. Kids practice and play team sports seven days a week because parents and schools provide the opportunity seven days a week.

If the grocery were open only 20 hours per day, we would not stop eating. We would shop when the stores were open. If school sports were not played on Sunday, the programs would not vanish. The coaches and players would simply do what they could on six days.

Ben Franklin said: "Wealth is not his that has it, but his that enjoys it." I recall a statement in *The Town Mouse and Country Mouse*, a children's book I read over and over to my children: "But what good is elegance without ease or plenty with an aching heart?"

When I recall the good Sundays I experienced as a child, I don't thank the legislature of the 1950s for the Blue Laws. I thank family and communities who had the good sense to discipline themselves to schedule time to do essentially nothing.

Time for that is missing today. Can time for restoration be restored?

By law – not entirely; but by good sense – yes, I believe so.

February 4, 1999

Children Need Training

I read in a recent newspaper article that "potty training" has become a dirty . . . oops, I mean an improper word.

A pediatrician named T. Berry Brazelton and others are advocating a kinder, gentler approach toward toddlers' acquiring that basic function of life, (dare I say it), "bowel and bladder control."

The new approach begins with changing the language applied to the process. "Potty training" has fallen from favor. The preferred terms, it is reported, are now "toilet teaching," "potty learning," or even "toilet education." The experts seem to feel that training is for animals or plants, not for children.

Before going on, let me make known that my apparent stance against postponement of such training is not passionately held by me. I'm not hung up about the issue. It merely serves as a good vehicle for my real point. I'm not advocating forced potty training at an early age. If my grandchildren are not trained by nine years of age, I'll probably be offering typical grandpa stuff, such as: "No need to rush it."

The dictionary indicates that to train is to direct growth, to form by instruction, discipline, or drill, and to teach so as to make fit. Education, at least in the mind of these experts, seems to be merely providing schooling and information. They apparently find the pressure involved with training to be objectionable.

To the contrary, I am thankful for the training I have received. I am glad my parents trained me to cross the street only after the light had turned red for traffic. I am happy my parents trained me to keep my hands off the cooking stove's burner.

Until now I thought the proper job of parents was to provide that through the repetition of a good, but unnatural behavior, their children would develop appropriate habits for existence in a community. This learned pattern of behavior was formerly called manners.

As an adult, I would rather have dinner with friends who have suffered under harsh parents who "trained" them not to burp at the table than to eat with a group of belchers who were only "educated" about proper table etiquette. Training puts education into practice.

Brazelton's bunch advocates a "go at your own pace" plan, so to speak. In explaining why accomplishing toilet training by the age of two and a half years is no longer necessarily attractive, the experts say: "There is no reason to rush it. This is a child-centered activity rather than a parent-imposed achievement." The experts go on to say, "We've backed off anything negative or coercive."

Well, excuse me!! I have thought all along that maturity was synonymous with "other-centered." I understood that the idea of civilization included subordinating one's own desires for the good of the whole community.

Imagine applying this theory to other learning activities of the childhood years. Do these folks advocate teaching a child to play piano by simply placing the child before the keyboard and telling the child to strike whatever key looks attractive at the time and in the order that the child feels led? This would truly be "child-centered" piano teaching.

Fundamentals always come first. Sound coaching requires training in the fundamentals before learning the finer points of competition.

Imagine again. Apply Brazelton's concepts in the field of law. I believe this may be happening. Obeying and respecting the laws of our nation and communities is fundamental to the existence and continuation of a civilized society. Law-abiding is not a self-centered activity. The freedom of individuals to do exactly what they want is restrained by the need to maintain an atmosphere allowing the general good of the whole, a community. Ignoring that bedrock concept leads to anarchy. Every person then decides when the time is right to obey the law.

Maybe this is part of the difficulty our citizens and our nation are experiencing. We are living in "self-directed" times. Translate this as "self-centered" times.

"Save MY Social Security."

"Lower MY taxes."

"Give me MY rights."

Now, education is good. I'm all for it. I've even participated in quite a bit of it, both as teacher and as student. It is indispensable.

We should be learning, however, that education alone will not establish maturity. We have inundated our children with sex education, both formally at school and certainly informally in our media; but confused sexual behavior among us reigns.

We have produced the best-educated generation regarding drugs, alcohol, and other substances that are prone to being abused, but substance abuse prevails.

I fear that toilet "education" may be destined for failure. Education is indeed good, but merely supplying education and opportunity alone is not sufficient. At least a touch of training is a necessary part of the recipe for maturity. In order to resist our urges, we must develop, by training, certain habitual responses, whether to the call of nature or to the invitation to obey the laws.

Biblical wisdom had it right: "Train up a child in the way he should go and when he is old, he will not depart from it" (Proverbs 22:6).

June 15, 1999

When Will We Learn . . .

I'll never forget the terror in those eyes.

Betwixt Columbus and Kingston on that late Sunday afternoon in January twenty-odd years ago, a typically dreary Ohio winter day turned wicked. By the time our little Chevy Citation had made it to the Kingston Pike, visibility had vanished. I could glimpse only a faint glimmer from the glassy, snow-slickened road. Uh-oh!

Anxious to get home, I didn't drive with proper respect for the elements. Attempting to negotiate an ever-so-slight bend in the road, I lost control. I involuntarily executed a perfect doughnut.

About 210 degrees into that 360 maneuver, I sneaked a glance into the rearview mirror. My young daughter's terrified eyes silently spoke these words that no responsible father wants to hear.

"Daddy, I thought I could trust you to protect me. Now look at the mess you've gotten us into. How could you have betrayed us?"

By the grace of God, no other vehicle was near ours. We stayed on the roadway and slowly, very slowly, crawled on home.

As I garaged the Chevy, I felt guilty, but grateful.

The eyes of the youth of Columbine High and, in fact, of children everywhere today remind me of daughter Amy's in the mirror that inclement day. Today's youth are fixing their gaze on us adults and crying out, maybe silently: "We thought you were protecting us. How have you allowed this?"

Lawyers love Latin. Maybe a little of the dead language could help us as we continue to sort out where we are. Let's try "in loco parentis." Contrary to most teenagers' belief, this does not mean, "My parents are crazy."

"In loco parentis" didn't die until recently. Latin for "in place of the parent," these words until the past 20 years or so denoted a legal principle that aggravated the dickens out of young folks, but gave parents a sense of peace.

The doctrine allowed institutions, e.g., schools, from grammar schools to universities, to control the behavior of their students as if the institutions were the parents of the students. For example, university rules barring women from the living area of men's dorms seemed oppressive to me while at OSU in the mid-60s. In retrospect, however, I appreciate the guidance I would not have applied to myself. Freedom is good; so is discipline.

The social realignment of the 60s weakened most forms of authority. "In loco parentis" didn't survive the assault. The winning argument went: "If an 18-year old is old enough to die for his country, he's old enough to decide when he should get back to his dorm at night." The rights of young citizens overtook now have mostly obliterated the "right" of children to be honored by being protected.

The swing of the legal pendulum away from "in loco parentis" leaves a void at this critical time.

Masses of our children are now being raised essentially without parents. Absent fathers have nearly become the norm. For this and other reasons, many mothers are not around to raise their kids either.

Daycare centers attempt to fill the void, some admirably, most not. Grandparents often assume the parental role. The U. S. Bureau of the Census estimates that in our country grandparents, without either parent present, are raising 1.42 million children.

Today's children are bewildered, and their immoderate behavior demonstrates it. They are looking with frightened eyes at the world that is thrust upon them. They may ask for independence, as any self-respecting younger generation does, but they really want, need, and deserve our protection.

The pendulum of law swings slowly. Many years, maybe many decades, will pass before the law again allows institutions to stand "in loco parentis" to young people. Until then, we need to do individually and voluntarily what the law formerly enforced institutionally. I'm not sure it takes a village, but I believe community can make a difference in the lives of its young people. As individuals, whether in or out of family, we need to look for chances to connect with children and offer, maybe even force, some guidance. As members of institutions, e.g., the church, the service club, the school, and yes, even the legal system, we need to find more ways to befriend youngsters, teach youngsters, and then benevolently hold them accountable to an appropriate standard of behavior.

Amy is a parent now. She knows that parents are not perfect, but that a good, loving parent always has a child's best interest at heart, even when he negligently loses control of his car.

With to without the help of the law, we adult Americans and our institutions need to reassume our role of "in loco parentis" to the terrified youth of this nation. We cannot comfortably continue to behold those terrified stares from the backseat.

II.   Law

I attended night law school at Capital University and concurrently taught school in the daytime. Mine was a rather practically oriented legal education. Harvard and Yale may have been teaching jurisprudence and legal philosophy, but Capital was leading us to draft effective deeds, wills, and divorce documents. Finally, thirteen years after passing the very practical bar examination, this author's opportunity to write essays on broader legal topics afforded both his readers and him the chance to reflect on the rule of law and the role of lawyers, too, in our social fabric.

June 27, 1987

Generic: The Un-Brand U. S. Constitution is a Bargain

The trend in our supermarkets toward offering generic products began a few years ago. The cost of advertising name-brand catsup and canned corn across the country was pushing the price of food staples so high that many families were unable to afford some of the basic foodstuffs needed to nurture a family.

Eleven years ago, in 1976, our nation celebrated the 200th anniversary of the signing of our Declaration of Independence. July 4, 1776 is customarily considered our nation's birthday, but that was merely the day our nation was conceived. The nation's actual birthday was Sept. 17, 1787. On that date in Philadelphia, the delegates to the Constitutional Convention adopted and signed the Constitution of the United States.

When our Founding Fathers met in Philadelphia 200 summers ago, the high cost of name-brand government services was preventing the common person living in what later became these United States from deriving much good from the system. The Revolutionary War had been fought partly to throw off the yoke of government by royalty, but the disorganization of the fledgling government of the victorious patriots, The Articles of Confederation, was threatening to exclude once again the common man from deriving meaningful benefits from the government.

The Constitution came to the rescue. To be sure, the original Constitution had its faults, the major one being the endorsement of slavery. Nevertheless, more than any other document in history, especially after the amendments were added, the United States Constitution created an enduring government by making sure that people's basic, daily governmental needs were met. Just as the offering of generic, un-brand foods allow all shoppers to secure the necessities of life with a minimum of sacrifice, our Constitution allows citizens to obtain the daily, minimum requirements of governmental assistance without great effort. Let's check the grocery list created for us by the Constitution and its amendments:

The Meat – The Right to Vote

"Where's the Beef?" In the new Constitution the beef, the substance, was in the vesting of power in the people by granting them the right to elect representatives. The King could do wrong, but the hearty citizens of the New World insisted on the right to turn the rascal out if he committed too many wrongs.

Article I of the Constitution provided for direct election of the House of Representatives. The Seventeenth Amendment extended direct elections to Senate members. Of course, women, racial minorities and those too poor to pay poll taxes had to go meatless until later amendments and court interpretations of those amendments opened the meat counters to all who wished to partake.

The Potatoes – A Representative Government

The potatoes, the starch that holds the body of the government together, were offered by the creation in the Constitution of a representative government. Monarchy was abhorred, but total democracy was out of the question in a country with diverse citizens and seemingly endless geographic boundaries. The idea that citizens could install in positions of power representatives to act in the best interest of the citizens was the reason for the Boston Tea Party. The Constitution joined with the tea that basic staple – the potato, i.e., representative government.

The Bread – Freedom of Religion

Man can survive on bread and water. Many believe, however, that life can be lived meaningfully only in a religious context. Religious repression had spurred many to risk crossing the wide ocean and risk pushing into the wilderness. The First Amendment guaranteed the right of each citizen of our country to make and consume the bread, the religion, of his choice: white, wheat, rye or pumpernickel.

What's more, this amendment even protected those who didn't feel like eating any bread at all.

The Vitamins – Freedom of the Press

The generic vitamin has been widely accepted. The "one-a-day" habit supplements the diets of many. The First Amendment guaranteed that the citizenry would always be able to supplement its knowledge with another "one-a-day" habit: the reading of a newspaper, the listening to a radio news reporter, or the watching of a television news presentation, all uncensored by the government. This supplement often provides the extra energy needed to prompt governmental change, to-wit: Viet Nam and Watergate.

The Liver – The Income Tax

"Eat your liver," mothers have been saying for centuries. The Sixteenth Amendment provided the liver for our governmental diet. "The Congress shall have power to lay and collect taxes on incomes…"

Potatoes and bread are much more attractive elements of our diet, but we must build strong bodies to survive. The liver of income tax may be distasteful, but the Constitution, like the good parent, must provide for the continued growth of its children.

Many of the great protections of the Constitution can be picked up in the aisles of your local grocery store. It's time we all recognized the great bargains we are getting.

Lawyers: Perception of the Profession Way Off Base

Question: "What's brown and white and looks good on a lawyer?"
Response: "I don't know. What?"
Answer: "A pit bull."

My friend told this joke to a group of lawyers and provoked a few good-humored chuckles, but I am sure almost any group of non-lawyers would have received the joke with more relish. Lawyers are one group people love to hate.

In this column on Jan. 31, 1987, a contributor stated that he respected the legal profession least of any – even less than television evangelists. Centuries ago, Shakespeare's character suggested "The first thing we do, let's kill all the lawyers." Today's opinion polls never list law among the most admired professions.

As a member of the maligned multitude, I am disconcerted. Our society has striven in recent years to erase the stereotyping of women, handicapped persons, minorities, and others. On a personal level, therefore, I resist being judged by my label rather than by my content. As a proud member of the profession, however, I worry even more that the public has a false image of the legal profession. Although I am a biased observer, permit me to list some common perceptions and then review some of the corresponding realities regarding lawyers.

PERCEPTION: Hired Gun Syndrome

Lawyers have no values to which they will cling. For a fee, they will support the position of any client. They may argue one side of an issue this month and the opposite side next month.

REALITY:

What appears to the public to be insincerity is to lawyers the adherence to duty. The oath taken by new attorneys requires them to assure all citizens the opportunity to have their views articulated when parties to a legal proceeding. Lawyers representing those who have acted or spoken in ways generally unacceptable do not necessarily agree with their clients, but enabling all views to be stated is the only way to insure that freedom will flourish. Otherwise, the state would accuse, the rich would sue, and the rest would lose. Shakespeare's character wanted to kill the lawyers so that his group could obtain absolute power over a new society. Then and now lawyers speak to protect individual rights.

PERCEPTION: Shyster Syndrome

Lawyers are cheaters and liars. They will use all methods, even unethical and tricky ones, to win a case.

REALITY:

I wish this perception were wholly untrue. Alas, it is not. Too many attorneys do resort to improper means to accomplish their goals. A favorite quotation of mine states: "Lawyers are no more dishonest than any other people – that's the trouble." Lawyers should be held to a higher standard of character and conduct because they deal so personally with people's lives and property. Through admission policies and disciplinary proceedings, the system attempts, not always successfully, to keep out and kick out the shysters.

The full reality is, though, that most attorneys are honest. They are each officers of the court and are pledged not to defraud the court. Most honor that pledge. But lawyers are adversaries with a responsibility to argue diligently for their clients. Since cases deal with such intense issues as crime, violence, divorce, accidents, and death, losing is not usually accepted gracefully. The loser can more easily blame shysters than face the facts.

PERCEPTION: Ambulance Chaser Syndrome

Lawyers have stirred up this litigation that chokes our society. Lawyers profit from protracted court battles, so lawyers want to make a federal case of every little alleged wrong.

REALITY:

The agrarian society of the 19th Century did not spur much lawyer contact for most people.

No cars wrecked. No airplanes crashed. No prepared foods soured. Grandma did not often sue Grandpa for divorce. The simple life may not have been easy, but it was relatively lawyer-free.

Now life is more complex. The complexity gives more chance for injuries. Injuries give rise to litigation. Resort to courts has increased, but not necessarily because lawyers have orchestrated it.

True, legal advertising may prompt some to seek redress in the courts; but in my experience, clients are often hungrier for lawsuits than attorneys are. We could all profit from the advice given by Thomas More circa the year 1500: "Go not for every grief to a physician, not for every quarrel to a lawyer, not for every thirst to the pot."

PERCEPTION: Buddy-Buddy Syndrome

All the lawyers are in a "club." Their main loyalty is to their friends in the club. They all get together before a trial to decide who will win this time. The judge goes along with their decision since the judge is a former lawyer.

REALITY:

Lawyers are independent and proud. Wanting to win cases and build reputations, they do not intentionally lose cases. A more believable allegation is that their compulsion to win sometimes prevents them from accepting reasonable settlement offers.

The buddy idea may stem from seeing the friendly way attorneys treat each other, even in battle. This mannerly treatment is essential to prevent the courtroom from becoming a wrestling ring. Attorneys do have an obligation to maintain decorum and civility when trying cases. If attorneys treated each other with hatred and contempt, their egos would be on the line. No case would ever be finished without trial and appeal. Professional etiquette signifies that attorneys care more about clients' cases than about their own egos.

I am not naïve. I know that many of my number stray from the ideal. Also because I am not naïve, however, I know that the stereotype of lawyers is inaccurate. Hold the pit bull.

October 1, 1988

Probate: Settling of an Estate Need not Provoke Panic

Fred and Nellie were good folks. They married a little young, but they were hard workers. They raised three kids on their own.

Fred got on at the factory when the kids were still young. The family was not rich, but neither was it poor. As the kids grew, Nellie took a full-time job at the store. The family became a two-wage earner home – part of the new American dream. Before long, the kids were grown, the 30-year mortgage was paid, and the retirement income was quite comfortable for people with modest tastes.

Now, without warning, Fred has died. At least Nellie thinks she has the home ($50,000), the car ($5,000), some jointly held stock in Fred's old company ($5,000), the joint account at the credit union ($5,000), a small nest egg in a joint certificate of deposit at the bank ($7,500) and a life insurance policy ($10,000). With $85,000 worth of property and with her Social Security checks to continue, that should keep her going quite a while.

But wait! What about probate? What about estate taxes? What about attorneys' fees? What about administrator's fees? After all that, Nellie will be lucky to have half her assets left. She may have to sell her home to pay the bills.

The probate process need not unduly frighten Nellie and those in her shoes .... Let's examine the facts.

Probate is simply the process of settling the property affairs of a deceased person.

Probate has many legitimate purposes. The probate court serves as a place for creditors to press claims against the decedent's assets, for the government to determine, and if due, collect estate taxes, and for persons to litigate issues, including will contests.

Most importantly, probate court assures that assets of a decedent are transferred to the persons entitled to them. We know that people do steal and that some people would even steal from Nellie.

We would not be so naïve as to conduct an athletic contest without officials; neither should we believe one's assets could invariably be transferred to the deserving parties without the firm, guiding hand of the judge and the law.

Handling a decedent's affairs does consume some time and money. The normal estate administration, without business or tax problems, takes four to six months to complete. A will must be admitted to probate, a fiduciary (e.g., executor) must be appointed, and an inventory and appraisal must be made.

Estate settlement expenses may be divided into three categories: debts, estate taxes, and administration costs. If lifetime debts of the decedent exist, they must be paid. Estate taxes threaten only the largest estates today. Generally speaking, assets passing from one spouse to another can do so free of federal or Ohio estate taxes. Even without the spousal deduction, federal estate tax generally applies only to estates exceeding $600,000 while Ohio estate tax may apply to estates as small as approximately $30,000. However, the Ohio tax brackets range from 2 to 7 percent.

Administration expenses include court costs and appraiser's fees (usually around $150), attorney's fees (normally 4 percent or less) and fiduciary's fees (usually 4 percent or less.) If the fiduciary is a family member, this fee is often waived.

People usually try to avoid probate altogether. The only way to avoid the need for any death transfer planning or action is to accumulate nothing or die at the instant of spending the last penny.

Some good techniques exist, however, for minimizing the time and dollars expended at death. In many instances, parties may wish to place ownership of their assets into a form that will allow transfer to a named beneficiary without intervention by the probate court. These forms usually do not reduce estate taxes. Neither are they self-executing, i.e., some action is still required at death to trigger the "automatic" transfers.

Common examples of property owned in non-probate form are: life insurance policies with a named beneficiary; bank accounts, stocks and bonds registered in a joint and survivorship form; real estate owned as survivorship tenants; and gifts made prior to death with the giver retaining a life estate.

An absolute warning is in order regarding non-probate forms of ownership. Do not employ these devices without receiving advice from your attorney, accountant, tax advisor or certified financial planner. Sometimes ownership in the non-probate form may aggravate rather than simplify probate problems.

Now, what about poor Nellie? Since she and Fred had not converted ownership of their home to the survivorship form, Fred's one-half interest in the home will need to pass through probate. The automobile in Fred's name can be transferred to Nellie upon the mere presentation of an affidavit to the auto title department. Since Fred and Nellie held their bank accounts and stock in the survivorship form, these items can be transferred outside of probate upon direct presentation of a few documents.

The likely settlement expenses for Nellie are as follows:

Court costs - $150.

Attorney fees - $650.

Executor's compensation – waived.

Federal estate tax - $0.

Ohio estate tax - $0.

The settlement expenses of $800 amount to 1.7 percent of the value of the assets being transferred at Fred's death.

With a little planning, Fred and Nellie could have reduced these expenses even more. By spending a little time and a few dollars to write a will and possibly re-register the ownership of some assets, normal people can provide for a relatively quick and inexpensive death transfer of their hard-earned assets to their loved ones. The fear of probate is needlessly exaggerated.

March 18, 1989

Decaying: The Legal System is only as Good as its People

I must be getting old. Besides the obvious indications of a balding top and a bulging middle, a sure sign of advancing years is the tendency to inform younger people how good things were in former times.

Lately, I catch myself saying: When I was your age (pick one):
A. Boys looked like boys.
B. Heavy metal was iron or lead.
C. My parents allowed me to go out only once a week.
D. People respected the law.

The aging glorify the past and lament the present. Those of us currently serving our time as the older generations are no exception. We see the carnage of modern life around us (the drug usage, the pollution, the divorce rate, the hunger, the illegitimacy rate, the violence), and we envision how straight things were during our youth. We remember a society in which tough laws, stringently enforced, and generally respected by a rather polite citizenry made living safe, predictable, and enjoyable.

Our greening years were not really so serene and orderly. The '30s had the Great Depression, the '40s the Great War, the '50s the Korean Conflict, the '60s the assassinations and Vietnam War, and the '70s Watergate. The call for a return to law and order rings a bit hollow. Nevertheless, most observers agree that our society is sliding, if not downright declining.

Cultural institutions are established by the consent of a people to provide a framework within which individuals can exist in a civilized manner. Our institutions include school, family, church and government. Our laws are generally arranged to protect these institutions.

When these institutions appear to be fading, as they now appear to be, many blame weak laws or law enforcement. I submit that decency has declined not because of lack of good laws, but because increasing numbers of citizens do not want law and order applied.

Most want law and order applied to the criminally accused, but not to themselves. If strict adherence to the tax law costs us money, let's fudge the figures a little. If we own a little too much property to qualify for government aid, let's hide a little. We are being hypocritical.

We say we want strong schools to straighten out our youth, but we do not vote for taxes to support schools and we do not help our kids with homework. We say we want stronger family units, but we divorce as soon as we realize the personal sacrifices needed to keep a marriage going. We say we want more ethical politicians, yet only a pitifully paltry percentage of eligible citizens even vote. We say we want churches to inculcate stronger morals in our youth, but we would rather read about fallen evangelists in the National Enquirer than read about fallen angels in the Bible.

My wisest friend, Fred B. Orr, a farmer-philosopher with eight and one-half decades of experience, recently reminded me of the thin line between order and chaos in the world of science. For example, a properly functioning heart is the picture of order. Its regular beating allows the organism to live and function beautifully. If a heartbeat becomes irregular, however, the organism cannot function normally.

The individual citizens are the heart of our legal system. So long as the citizens pull together for the common good, the legal system and the institutions it protects operate very nicely. If, however, the majority of citizens will not voluntarily conduct themselves in a manner consistent with the aims of the system, the system will collapse. Order will cease; chaos will appear.

If the majority refuses to obey the tax law, government could not hire enough agents to keep the system going. If parents do not work to keep families together, no amount of domestic relations court orders will save the family unit.

Dean Acheson said, "In the search for ways to maintain our values and pursue them in an orderly way, we must look beyond the resources of law." The legal system is not blameless. Judges, lawyers, and legislators must work to improve our laws, but the basic truth remains. Our legal system is only as good as the people being governed by it. Our legal system cannot often improve people, but improved people will greatly enhance our legal system.

August 12, 1989

Law: Accepting Old Wives' Tales as Facts Can Cause Trouble

Webster defines "old wives' tale" as a silly story or superstitious belief such as might be passed around by gossipy old women. Break a mirror and have seven years of bad luck. See a falling star and know that someone has died. Open an umbrella indoors and prepare for showers of misfortune.

Lord Byron wrote:

"'Tis hard to venture where our betters fail,

"Or lend fresh interests to a twice-told tale."

The law is a fertile field for the growing of old wives' tales. Law is composed of mere words. Since most people can talk and read, many think they understand the law. It must be simple. "Everyone" knows that. "Didn't you ever hear that?" Even in the face of Byron's warning, this article attempts to debunk a few common misunderstandings about our laws:

A common law marriage exists if a couple has lived together seven years.

WRONG.

A civil marriage results from following the letter of the law: A license is obtained and a ceremony is performed. A common law marriage may exist merely as a result of the actions of a couple. A couple may be married at common law if they have agreed to consider themselves husband and wife, if they hold themselves out to the public as such, and if they live as husband and wife for a period of time. No set duration is required. Some may live together for years and never be considered husband and wife. Others may live together for a short period as pals, yet face divorce-like problems upon termination of their relationship. Just ask Lee Marvin.

Oh! Remember. While our system recognizes common law marriage, it does not recognize common law divorce. If persons are married, whether civilly or under common law, their freedom must be earned the old-fashioned way – by decree of divorce.

Land cannot be landlocked in Ohio.

UNTRUE.

To find truly landlocked land in Ohio is rare. Access is usually provided by public highways or by private easements granted in deeds. If neither exists, courts often find that easements of necessity should be implied. Nevertheless, courts will not simply force an easement. If conditions do not exist which will permit a court to establish an easement, helicopter may be the only method of reaching the lonely parcel.

All documents must be notarized to be valid and legal.

OFF BASE.

Many documents must be notarized to be effective: e.g. motor vehicle titles, deeds of real estate, and affidavits. Many other basic and very important documents need not be notarized: wills, contracts, and court pleadings. Many documents are notarized unnecessarily, but when in doubt, err on the safe side. Unneeded notarization doesn't hurt, but omission of needed notarization is fatal to the instrument.

All contracts must be in writing to be valid.

NO WAY.

Life is full of little oral contracts. The consumption of food at the restaurant table and the bid and gavel at the auction are two examples. These contracts are just as binding as the four-pager used to buy that new automobile or the 14-pager to insure that automobile. Try leaving the restaurant or the auction without paying: cries of "breach of contract!" or other epithets will ring out.

Certain contracts must be in writing to be valid: e.g., contracts to purchase real estate. My late mentor, Don C. Patterson, often reminded me that a contract was about as good as the other party to the contract. So, ironically, whether oral or written, be sure to contract only with good people, people who are so trustworthy that contracts really would not be needed. Still, get it in writing whenever possible and practical.

Every business transaction has a "cooling-off period."

SORRY.

A few transactions may be voided without reason within a few days after being entered. The outstanding example is the home solicitation sale, e.g., the signed paper that remains after the encyclopedia or cookware salesmen leave. Aside from these rare instances, however, if you buy, you pay.

The law usually makes sense, but does not always coincide with common sense. Before taking any actions of consequence, check with your attorney to be sure you are not relying on old wives' tales. After all, ignorance of the law is no excuse. Well, that even depends on the situation.

If . . .

March 3, 1990

Trump's Prenuptial Contract May Not be Worth Anything

Finally a topic with some glitter. Columns designed to enlighten the public on legal issues do not tend to be glamorous, but the Donald-Ivana Trump affair provides me the perfect opportunity to compete with the *National Enquirer*.

The item getting most attention in this, America's divorce, is the Trumps' antenuptial agreement.

Antenuptial? Sounds like it may have something to do with a poker game in a flower shop. That is not a bad analogy, but an ANA is actually a contract entered by two people prior (ante) to their marriage (nuptial). This premarital contract modifies the rights each party usually has in the other party's property by virtue of being a spouse.

Most couples ready to enter that institution Sir Alan Herbert called Holy Deadlock never consider an ANA. Most couples begin married life with no assets to protect. Furthermore, asking the beloved to enter, before the wedding, an agreement that will severely limit that beloved's property rights upon the eventual termination of the marriage does not bespeak much confidence in the relationship.

Besides, such requests just are not very darned romantic.

Sam Rogers said, "It doesn't much signify whom one marries, for one is sure to find next morning that it was someone else." Cynical, or possibly realistic, people who believe this and who have riches to protect often opt for the ANA. ANAs can protect one's assets from being snared by a new spouse in a divorce proceeding or from being snared by a surviving (second) spouse in a probate proceeding. If no ANA is entered, divorce courts tend to require equal division of marital property.

If no ANA is entered, a second spouse often is able to acquire a large portion of the deceased spouse's estate even if the deceased's will left the estate to children of a first marriage.

Mr. Trump is no chump. The master dealer apparently approached Van prior to the ceremony with this proposition: "If we split, you get $25,000,000." That figure was probably chosen because it matched what he held in his Christmas Club account at the time. Mr. T. wanted an ANA, and, for whatever reason, Ms. I. agreed. Point for Don! (And point for Ivana, too, it seems to me.)

The Queen of Trump now wants to renege. She says the ANA is invalid. Donald says a deal is a deal. After all, are not contracts sacred? Surprisingly, ANAs are often not sacred; many do not hold up under attack.

Before entering an ANA, each party must make a full disclosure of all assets owned. Each party must have an independent attorney. The ANA must be fair under the circumstances. If these conditions are not met, the ANA may be voided later. Careful, Donald.

The Trumps' ANA came only after the fullest disclosure since Father Washington saw the wood chips in George's pants cuff. Don's lawyers told Ivana's lawyers everything. So, one would think, point for Don. The ANA stands. But not necessarily.

If conditions change so much that enforcement of the ANA would be unconscionable, Iva may be allowed to get more than the $25,000,000. Conditions have changed; Don has accumulated more assets than some countries. $25,000,000 now looks like spare change. Point for Ivana.

Who will win? Stay tuned. Nobody knows. I just hope more circumstances arise which allow exciting treatments of otherwise dry legal topics. Maybe Elvis will be reported to have been spotted kidnapping the septuplets born to a prior incarnation of Shirley MacLaine and a space being so that my column can explain the inheritance rights of children adopted by a presumed decedent.

June 15, 1991

Consequences: Bad Judgment, Evil Not Synonymous

You baby boomers remember the early television game show "Truth or Consequences." A contestant who failed to answer the host's question correctly paid the consequences of ignorance by the public undertaking of some demeaning and embarrassing act. Our legal system operates in a parallel fashion.

Our laws, whether criminal or civil, set a certain standard of conduct for our citizens. The citizen who fails to adhere to that standard must pay the consequences. Sometimes the consequence is jail time or a fine; other times it may be payment of a civil judgment or subjection to an injunctive court order. (Do this. Don't do that.)

A recent and relatively simple breach of the standard appears to have taken place in Circleville. The alleged perpetrators were students of the local high school, most on the brink of graduation. Some evidence exists that, in a fit of teen-age euphoria, as commencement day approached, a couple of dozen students trashed school property late one night.

Any reader of this paper or watcher of local TV news knows with some specificity the type of deeds performed: property was destroyed, graffiti was painted, manure was spread. (By the way, some may say that this writer, by virtue of his former position as a farm boy and his current position as a lawyer, has excellent credentials to comment upon the spreading of manure).

In the beauty shops and coffee shops, the banks and barbershops, the battle lines quickly formed across our territory. Should the kids be banned from commencement exercises? Should the kids lose their scholarships? Should they be made to clean up the mess themselves? Should they be prosecuted? Should they be excused because their acts were mere "pranks" carried out almost as a tradition?

The accused students have been and will be paying the price for their fun. The consequences have begun piling up for the offenders: suspensions from school, exclusion from graduation ceremonies, and possible criminal penalties if police and prosecutors can prove their cases.

I am satisfied to allow the school and court officials to answer the first four of my questions based upon the facts of each case. I would like to concentrate, though, on whether these actions, if proved, should be excused on the basis of age or circumstances.

Many acts, which in themselves appear to be illegal, are granted an excuse under the law.

Self-defense is the prime example. Violence upon the person of another is normally outlawed; but if such act is undertaken for the purpose of self-protection, the behavior is legitimized under law.

Being age 17 or 18 years does not constitute a valid defense to a criminal charge. An infant or a minor of tender age and obvious immaturity will often be found incapable of understanding the nature of his otherwise criminal act. Students who have spent 13 years in school learning everything from civics to calculus cannot argue that they did not have the capacity to judge right from wrong.

Certainly, the status of "student" does not magically pardon the conduct. A 16-year-old student may drive a vehicle upon the public highway. An 18-year-old student is entitled to vote. The granting of the diploma has no bearing on the issue of responsibility.

Some students felt that they were only disciplined because they were honest enough to confess their roles. This is a classic "shift the blame" argument. The discipline is being administered as a result of the actions, pure and simple. Lying out of the punishment would not erase the initial poor behavior, but would merely supplement and aggravate it.

That numerous persons engaged in the act is not a suitable excuse. If such were the case, the mass hysteria which has led to racially motivated lynchings would be an excuse for murder. Cheating on taxes would be forgiven since so many citizens revel in this activity. Speeding on the highways would be ignored since so many motorists join that sport. Laws are not invalidated simply because the masses ignore the laws.

So it appears that the manure-slinging students will have to face the music. "Give them what they deserve," you say! Let's not get carried away. Let up a little on these kids. They used poor judgment, but they are not evil people. The evil students had probably dropped out of school long ago to sell drugs on the street.

And let's not be hypocritical. If you are clamoring for their severe punishment, remember the same standard when your fuzz-buster fails you or your tax preparer lets you down. If the truth be told, even you might have to suffer some consequences.

August 9, 1993

Family Respect Can Help End Lawlessness

Manners!　Who needs 'em?　So says most of any younger generation.

As a child, I failed to grasp why Mom kept at me to close my mouth while I was eating.　As she offered me delicious, bounteous meals, she stole my pleasure by parroting every night: "Don't chew with your mouth open."　How could I stuff my pudgy body fast enough if I had to chew and swallow with my mouth closed after each bite?　I preferred the conveyor belt style of dining.

The rules to be obeyed in polite company, or even in the supposed ease of our private home, were many in the 1950's.

"Take your hat off inside buildings."　(Don't tell Garth Brooks about that one).

"Stand when your elder or a lady enters the room."　(No. I'm in the middle of Nintendo).

"Bow when you are introduced to someone."　(When's the last time you were actually introduced to someone?).

The list seemed endless to an impatient young man.

I was not much rebellious, but I would have obeyed more happily if I could have seen the reasoning behind the rules.　My parents instructed me, though, that the rules of the game were already set.　I was just expected (and required) to play the game by them.

Mark Twain, with his odoriferous cigar smoke and crusty language, was no exemplar of good manners, but he was insightful.　He wrote: "Good breeding consists in concealing how much we think of ourselves and how little we think of other persons."　Here is the essence of manners: caring more about avoiding hurt to another person's sensibilities than about fulfilling one's selfish desires.　I wonder how old I was before I yielded my need for speed to my tablemates' right to a decent sight.

People with eyes, ears, and brains know that the practice of basic manners is passing from our culture.　If the majority has agreed to abandon these customs, so be it.　The rules can be changed if most of those playing the game agree.

Laws!　Who needs them?　So our whole population seems to be saying today!　Laws are just manners important enough to be enforced by the power of government.　Not only is it impolite to hit, rape, rob, or kill, it is illegal.　A breach of etiquette brings a stern look from Mom; a breach of law draws a stern gaze from the judge.

One needn't possess a PhD in sociology to recognize also the decline in our country of respect for laws. Documenting the lawlessness of our nation is not difficult. Approximately 10,000 people each year die in our country from gunfire, 4,200 of which in 1990 were teenagers. (See *Time*'s cover story in its Aug. 2 issue.) Countries as big as Canada and continents as big as Australia have only a dozen (as in 12) or so gun deaths each year. On a given day in the U. S., it is estimated that 100,000 students carry a gun to school.

As we were made painfully aware by the high-profile seminar in Chillicothe last week, sexual abuse and incent are rampant even in our little corner of the nation. Political scandals, banking rip-offs, and church debacles send our institutional leaders to jail. (Cf. Mayor Barry, Mr. Keating, and Rev. Bakker.) Or, just check the News of Record section in today's Gazette. Disregard for law is epidemic.

While the decline in manners may be lamentable and make daily living less pleasant, lawlessness is downright dangerous. If the majority care more about acting out their own desires than about obeying laws which protect others' rights, safety, and sensibilities, government by law fails and the law of the jungle prevails. Before we reach that point, causes and cures need to be found.

Many would lay the fault for this lawlessness at the door of the statehouse and/or courthouse. As I have admitted in this space before, the system could stand improvement. But believing that our problems can be solved simply by passing harsher laws or enforcing them more rigidly is naïve. We have more laws than ever, and we have more of our citizens behind bars than ever. Yet the lawlessness rages on.

To paraphrase Caesar, leader of an earlier debauched society, the problem is not in our laws, but in ourselves. We have very little "breeding." We no longer conceal our greater regard for ourselves than for our neighbors: we glory in it.

It is comforting to blame this condition on the legal system or the schools or the churches. It is uncomfortable, but realistic, to blame the family or, more accurately, the lack of family. Only in the intimate setting of family life can manners be taught MTV would never have taught me table manners. Similarly, I believe respect for law can best be instilled by a family. And, let's admit it, family does not exist in a positive, meaningful way for most youths today.

And how can the institution of the family be rebuilt? Certainly not by new legislation, but maybe by old-fashioned manners: that is, by placing the welfare of family and children above our own selfish desires.

March 25, 1995

Good People Better Than Good Contract

"A verbal contract isn't worth the paper it's written on," according to the late Hollywood mogul Samuel Goldwyn. One must wonder if even a written contract is worth anything today.

Shortly after I began my law practice, an unsuspecting client hired this rookie attorney to prepare a complex contract. I do not recall the client or the subject matter. I do recall the energy I expended in drafting and redrafting the agreement. I also remember the best advice given in that case. My father-in-law, with whom I was associated in practice, gave me that advice.

When I presented my masterpiece to Father for comment, he patiently reviewed the document. Then he gently led my brain from the ivory tower to the street corner. After complimenting my draftsmanship, he illustrated the difference between knowledge (mine) and wisdom (his).

"Yes," he said, "you have set down a wonderful contract, but always remember this. Your client's contract is about as good as the person with whom your client is contracting." And then he added the stinger: "I would rather have no contract and be dealing with an honorable person than the best contract in the world when dealing with a scoundrel." Father always did know how to deal effectively with overeager, slightly arrogant young lawyers.

Now, written contracts are useful. A good written agreement has prevented many lawsuits and many more disagreements. One should always strive for a solid written agreement when purchasing real estate or entering upon any business arrangement. But the best of both worlds would be: a good contract with a good person.

This principle also applies in our personal lives. Marriage, for example, is a civil contract. The parties to be joined procure a license and then pronounce their respective vows in the presence of a government official and witnesses. The contract is sealed. If only the substance were as pure as the form! Marriages founder on the rocks of life not because the contract was defective, but because at least one of the parties turned out to have been a scoundrel. To be sure, remedies for breach of the contract exist, (to-wit: divorce court), but the damage, in human terms, cannot be remedied.

The rule holds good in our business dealings, too. Consider landlord-tenant relations. The world's best lease cannot prevent a troubled or troublesome tenant from staying on after the lease has expired or from trashing the premises just before leaving. Likewise, a tenant's contract does not provide much warmth if an unscrupulous landlord has decided to terminate electric service in order to speed up a tenant's departure. Yes, Municipal Court will sort out the issues and make a fair decision, but after the fact and in many cases after irreparable harm has been done. The contract was fine; the humans were weak.

I believe this fundamental pertains even to the affairs of our nation. The resurgent Republicans have promised legislation billed as the "Contract with America." The terms of the contract sound good: budget balancing, spending limits, welfare reform, tougher criminal laws, income tax cuts, and more. Wow! How could one speak against such a splendid contract?

I'm concerned that the Contract may be another case of knowledge over wisdom, of short-term politics over the long-term effectiveness.

Let's review, for example, the provision in the Contract for the federally funded school lunch program. As I understand it, the new program would get the federal government out of the business of feeding school kids. As a substitute, the feds would send "block grants" to the states. The states could then decide how to expend that money. Now let's apply the good contract vs. good contractee test.

People my age and older may remember when each state was responsible for administering its own programs for providing health care to the poor, elderly, and infirm. Some states did an admirable job; many did practically no job. Medicare probably has more fat than lard-fried potato chips, but our nation's elderly do receive high-quality medical care now. If we are merciful, we must be careful not to sever a muscle when we cut the fat.

Remember those glory days before the federal government began using America's real contract, the U. S. Constitution, to guarantee that no state denies civil rights to its citizens? Does anyone believe that block grants to Alabama in the 1950s would have been used by Governor George Wallace to integrate the public schools? Who believes that elected state officials today, subject to political pressures, will uniformly assure what appears to be a basic goal of government – that all citizens, including schoolchildren, have enough to eat?

Lincoln had it right. Government should be of the people, by the people, and for the people. Government is the people. Our contract of government will be about as good as the people who are parties to the contract, i.e., us! If we as a people have lost our goodness, our desire to care for each other, then the Contract with America may as well be written in invisible ink.

October 7, 1996

Law Protects All Citizens

Soon after my lawyering days began, my father-in-law and office associate instructed me that I would need to have broad shoulders.

"Nobody likes lawyers," he said.

I've found him to be largely correct. I've tried to carry the monkey on my back gracefully, but some days I feel the weight more than others.

"One who is his own attorney has a fool for a client." So goes the old proverb. Defending oneself may be dangerous, but, in today's climate, defending the legal profession may be downright foolhardy. Nevertheless, one suffering my affliction cannot resist a challenge. Lend me your ears.

In this space a week ago Saturday morning, Lorna Abbott contributed a column conveying a simple, powerful, important message: lack of personal integrity and refusal to accept personal responsibility for our lives threaten to sink our country. I commend her.

Buried in the middle of the essay, however, was this line: "If an attorney gets a guilty person an acquittal, we say that he is a good lawyer." Even one such as I, who always favors mercy be extended to those brave enough to contribute their humble efforts to this space, detects a bit of animosity. I safely assume that columnist Abbott is not the president of the F. Lee Bailey fan club.

Words are slippery fish. If my co-columnist meant to say that an attorney who allows or assists a client to lie to a court is reprehensible, I fully agree. Attorneys are officers of the court; they are sworn to uphold the principles upon which courts of law operate. One such principle is truth-telling.

Ethical standards exist to prevent such conduct. I move that we enforce those standards. If my predecessor means that it is a shame when one who commits a crime is acquitted, I can still agree. I remind her, though, that such occurrences are rare, but inevitable when dealing with feeble human institutions, including our system of justice.

But if my colleague in print means that she believes we would be better off with a system which does not afford each citizen the assistance of counsel to defend against allegations of criminal conduct, I must respectfully, but vigorously, disagree.

I'd think even the most dedicated lawyer-haters would agree that a society governed by the law of the land is preferable to one governed by the law of the jungle. Lawyers exist to assist citizens in assuring that the biggest gorilla does not rule all in the land. Without lawyers, the most giant gorilla, the government, would simply crush the people.

The law of our land happens to be the U. S. Constitution. One important portion of that document guarantees all citizens – not just the rich, not just the popular, not just those who are probably not guilty – due process of law. In other words, the big ape of government may not squash a citizen like an overripe banana unless it first follows the rules – the law of the land. Lawyers exist to prevent the goon of big government from terrorizing and eliminating little chimps like you and like me without first proving its case. The law provides a framework to determine if the case has been proved.

And if my neighbor means to condemn proceedings which result in acquittals when the evidence proved overwhelmingly (beyond a reasonable doubt) the guilt of the accused, I concur. I would gently suggest to her, though, that the citizens of the jury, the non-lawyers of the system, are the ones who determine the guilt or innocence of a defendant. Lawyers cannot vote in the jury room. Many thoughtful observers of our system believe that the refusal of juries to do their duty and convict when guilt has been proved beyond a reasonable doubt (O. J. in LA?) is causing the loss of confidence in the system, the same loss that is expressed by author Abbott.

Yes, I certainly agree that all of us – lawyers, politicians, media persons, journalists, teachers, care givers, office workers, factory workers, home workers, and all other citizens – need to develop personal integrity and live by the dictates of that integrity. I simply offer this supplement: personal integrity requires that all of us, lawyers and non-lawyers alike, strive to honor and maintain the system which, according to Lincoln, is the last, best hope for humankind.

Thanks for letting me get that gorilla off my back.

April 3, 1999

In Defense of Lawyers

Ouch! That's hot!

I could be speaking of the blistering coffee McDonald's formerly served or of the flaming rhetoric appearing in an article written for this space recently by my fellow amateur columnist, Paul Campbell. Either could scald.

As a member of the legal profession that Paul burned in his well-written column, I thank him for reminding me and my brother and sister officers of the courts that common sense should be a major ingredient in the recipe for our system of laws and justice. I agree.

I realize that one cannot lose when attacking lawyers. On the other hand, defending lawyers and the realm within which they operate is a tough assignment. On the day I was admitted to practice, my father-in-law and soon-to-be senior associate in law practice warned me bluntly: "Dick, you're going to have to have broad shoulders. Nobody likes lawyers except the other lawyers."

So, I know I'm probably arguing a losing case; nevertheless, our system holds that everyone deserves a defense – even lawyers and the legal system.

My journalistic colleague highlighted a couple of damage awards granted in civil cases that seemed ludicrous to him. He was particularly steamed by the now famous (infamous) "too hot" McDonald's coffee case. I believe Paul innocently gave you the decaffeinated version of that case.

Yes, the plaintiff ordered hot coffee at the drive-thru window. Yes, she spilled it into her lap. Yes, she filed suit against Ronald for her damages. And, yes, the jury (I repeat, the jury) granted her a very substantial judgment.

Now, let's inject the caffeine – the rest of the facts required for that full-bodied understanding of this case.

Common sense does reveal that one who orders coffee should expect it to be hot and not suitable for pouring into one's own lap. Common sense, however, also allows the purchaser to reasonably anticipate that the seller of the coffee would not be handing over to a driver of an automobile a boiling liquid more suitable for scalding feathers off a dead chicken than for drinking.

The jury, having common sense and applying a very solid rule of law requiring one who sells a commodity to promise that the commodity is suitable for the purpose for which it is sold, decided that McDonald's breached its duty to its customer.

The jury then took leave of its common sense and awarded the plaintiff a huge sum, nearly enough to buy half the coffee beans in Brazil. Note – the java jury did this – not the lawyers and not the courts.

In fact, the system that my well-meaning friend castigated is the system that later repaired the injustice wrought upon McDonald's. Upon appeal, the court granted a remitter, i.e., reduced the plaintiff's damages award to a realistic level. Somehow, the press did not do a good job of reporting this to the nation, so Paul can be forgiven.

Paul alleged that our citizens have the sense and intelligence to know the difference between right and wrong. He wondered when the courts, lawyers and government will catch on, too. I respectfully suggest that the laws and lawyers understand well. The "good" citizens are the ones who sometimes leave common sense in the cup.

Our worthwhile correspondent concluded by encouraging folks to take responsibility for their own actions and mistakes and by lamenting that untrustworthy citizens who want to bring false suits can find "expertise they need to trump up all those phony charges."

Could he be referring to attorneys? If so, I object. I politely resent his implication that lawyers routinely assist clients in manufacturing lies and false evidence in order to defraud the system. The coffee Paul is serving up is too hot. It's boiling over with unfounded accusations.

I'm not naïve. Of course, I know that attorneys occasionally succumb to temptation. They ignore their duty to the court and participate in dishonest schemes with their clients. This is the exception.

The courts, the government, and the bar association themselves police the profession and punish, suspend, and disbar attorneys who fit Paul's flawed vision.

The overwhelming majority of attorneys will promptly dispossess any client of the opinion that making up stories or fabricating evidence is allowed. An attorney will portray facts and law in the best light for the client, but that's how the system works. Then the jury, we hope, determines the facts and applies the law in a common sensical way.

So, there! We have reached the bitter dregs of this cup. I'm sorry to have spoiled the pleasure of stereotyping lawyers and the legal system as corrupt, but that theory just won't hold coffee. . . er, water.

December 24, 2000

Glimpsing the Bedrock of Law

Most people never get a chance to bite their landlord. I did, and I did.

Dr. Clarence V. Yaple practiced dentistry on the second floor of the building still standing at the southwest corner of Paint and Main streets, Chillicothe, Ohio. My family lived on and farmed his farm southwest of State Route 159 and Blackwater Road in Green Township, Ross County.

This connection apparently enabled my folks to arrange for my dental care at a tender age. I must have been around five years old in the early 1950's, when old C. V. put in his thumb and pulled out a plumb masticated thumb. I took offense to his archaic and aggressive dental style and nearly detached one of his digits with my incisors. In other words, I bit him hard.

Our relationship improved thereafter. Over the years, I grew to sense and appreciate the substance of Dr. Yaple as a man.

Occasionally, I visited what I then considered to be Dr. Yaple's mansion on West Fourth Street. After passing by the lead-glassed front door and sliding through the cool, darkish recesses of a dining room and kitchen, we emerged into the Doctor's wonderfully warm den. Books lined the walls, more books than the Kingston library held, more books than I had seen in one place.

They were "real" books. I saw lots of newspapers and schoolbooks around my humble farmhouse, but not many "real" books: literature, fiction, biographies, or histories. Doc Yaple's books carried strange, yet inviting names. I remember seeing boldly printed on the spine of one heavy book: *The Day Christ Died* by Jim Bishop. I still haven't read it, but Dr. Yaple's ownership of this and so many other "real" pieces of literature impressed me mightily.

Those tomes carried more clout than any groupings of words I'd seen to that date. Leather bound them. Mahogany held them. And Dr. Yaple had read them. I began thinking of C. V. and those who read books as people of gravity, of substance. Newspapers would blow away in a light breeze. Textbooks would be out of date in a few years. But those volumes and the people who read them were anchored, solid, and somehow immovable.

Maybe that foundation sensation attracted me to the study and practice of law. My friends and family do not see in me much of an urge to experiment. I'd rather build a modest house on a solid rock than a glorious one on a hunch.

For centuries . . . no, for millennia, cultures have inscribed their laws on their heaviest receptacles. God inscribed His Big Ten on two large stone tablets. (Imagine carrying those books in your backpack). In 451 BC the Romans placed their code on twelve bronze tablets, the Twelve Tables. (Could this be why Pizza Huts, even today, are equipped with exactly twelve tables?). We strive for durability in law.

Our nation's Founding Fathers wrote the Declaration of Independence, the Constitution, and the Bill of Rights on mere paper (20 lb. bond, no doubt) but my, don't we protect those originals! Visit the National Archives in Washington, D. C. and ask to thumb through the pages of these tender legals. You won't come close. We protect our laws as written.

Can you imagine the original copy of the Magna Carta on a floppy disk only? Can you imagine issuing the Code of Hammurabi via e-mail? Can you generate much sense of awe for the law by viewing the whole result of two hundred years of Ohio jurisprudence on a single, dusty compact disk which has been rattling around in your drawer? Matters of gravity deserve means of substance.

Law connotes heaviness. What citizens have labored for centuries to establish should not be able to be lightly or inadvertently deleted. Images on a monitor fall short of stones in the desert.

So, what's my point?

Our recent electoral agony has shaken many citizens' faith in law as the bedrock of our society. The "Supreme Court Shuffle" between Washington, D. C. and Tallahassee, Fla., did not instill a sense of security in the legal process; nevertheless, the peaceful resolution proves that the anchor has held.

We do not all agree that the outcome was appropriate. Apparently, half agree and half disagree. But, we should not expect the imperfect machine of law to render perfect results.

I regularly remind clients that the law does not have to make sense; it's just the law. In a similar sense, the rules of, let's say golf, do not always create fair results, but they are the rules.

Only by having and obeying rules can the game be played meaningfully. Only if we agree to abide by the rules of government can our public lives be lived civilly. The "consent of the governed," i.e., the acceptance by the people of the results of legal process, even if imperfect, is the true bedrock upon which the law itself rests.

Lasting law is rooted in the solid character of good people. That's a rock upon which to build a future.

Dr. Yaple, I'm sorry I bit you.

Lady Justice, we're sorry we chipped you.

October 10, 2003

Estate Planning Uncomfortable, but Necessary

The carpet cleaners come tomorrow. Tonight, I am toting all manner of tangible personal property from spot to spot around my office. A kind of melancholy heaviness tugs at my heart.

I'm devoted to separating from the surface of the carpeting all items which I can handle and move. I place some chairs and waste cans on tabletops. I transport other chairs, chair pads, and the like to the uncarpeted back room. Soon the rooms begin to look like skeletons.

So, big deal! So, why this uneasiness within me?

By tomorrow night, the cleaners will have cleansed and departed. The furniture will have reappeared in all the customary locations. Day after tomorrow the office routine will again be humming along.

But tonight . . . tonight, as I labor to vacate the space where so much activity has occurred and, presumably, will occur again, I have caught a glimpse of that day down the road when I'll ply my profession here no more. The accouterments of trade will move not only up or back, but out. The shingle will come down. The door will close. The lock will turn. And no turning back will occur.

In the shadows of this evening, the end of this law practice is foreshadowed. The grim reaper comes tomorrow . . . or, if not, some tomorrow.

Again, so what?

Before I tell you what, let me apologize. This beginning sounds mostly morbid. I don't write to depress the reader, but death is just not a very lively topic.

Some, though, have found a sunnier side to dark death. British writer J. M. Barrie said: "To die will be an awfully big adventure."

Some anticipate death. The great, but deaf composer, Beethoven, exclaimed: "I shall hear in Heaven."

Optimists see the good even in death. Author Kingsley Amis joked: "Death has got something to be said for it: there's no need to get out of bed for it."

Some actually long for death. St. Paul spoke for all Christians in Philippians 1:21: "For to me, to live is Christ and to die is gain."

I don't pretend to prescribe your attitude towards your death. I only remind you that your death and mine are certain. Only you and I can plan effectively for the consequences of our respective deaths.

I have spent a major portion of my practice advising clients whose assets one day will pass to others and assisting those beneficiaries whose day has come to receive. But tonight I have come to recognize something. Having seen the "melancholy heaviness" on the faces of those signing their wills, trusts, deeds, and other documents which will guide the eventual disposal of their precious earthly assets, I now understand that carrying out the duty to plan the end of our days brings uneasiness.

Nevertheless, prudent people clean their carpets even though the process is inconvenient. Not to do so invites uglier stains, smellier odors, and more expensive cleaning bills in the future.

Reasonable people also plan for the orderly passage of their assets at their deaths even though the process requires an investment. Not to do so invites, nay assures, uglier, smellier, more expensive legal processes after a person dies. Failure of one to plan ahead will saddle the survivors with a messy cleanup job – inside or outside of probate court.

So, what? Here's what!

Get your head out of your deep-pile carpet. Call your investment adviser, your family attorney, your CPA, your insurance agent, or all of the above and just do it – the planning, that is.

Brendan Behan is quoted: "I'd rather be dead than think about death." A significant number of my clients, usually male, apparently subscribe to Behan's plan. The lucky ones have finally lost the argument with their spouse and eventually make their way to the planner's table, sometimes pulled by the ear. The unlucky ones pridefully win the battle. They avoid the unpleasant planning process. They never get around to completing the job. Their families, however, lose the war, and they must "clean up" after the stubborn one has died.

As the modern saying goes, "The hearse does not pull a U-Haul-It." Again, St. Paul instructed us in 1st Timothy 6:7: "For we brought nothing into this world, and it is certain we can carry northing out." You cannot take it with you.

A little cleaning relieves a lot of smelliness. A little planning relieves a lot of heaviness.

The carpet cleaners do come tomorrow. Are you ready for them?

October 2005

Rule of Law Shouldn't Depend on Whims of Judges

"Because I said so, that's why!"

This rationale for an order does not strike most of us in most situations as a sufficient justification for the order. Kids like more than that from their parents. Employees yearn for a fuller explanation than that from their bosses.

In some contexts, however, the unvarnished order must suffice. A soldier has no right to question the rationale of a commanding officer's order. Allowing discussion would be foolhardy and could endanger the mission, the company of soldiers, and even the soldier receiving the order. Discipline and order lead to victory.

To a degree, the law rests upon a foundation of "because I said so, that's why!" The doctrine of *stare decisis* provides that courts generally abide by the decisions which have been rendered in earlier cases applying the law to similar facts. While the Latin name of *stare decisis* may sound like a newly discovered star or a rookie dancer in a Las Vegas revue, the legal doctrine is ancient. It may seem to provide a poor basis for decision-making, but it actually has one stellar quality: stability. The judge deciding a case by relying on principles set forth in cases decided earlier is basing the decision not just on the sand of personal whim, but upon the rock of years, decades, or even centuries of past experience.

My high school reserve team basketball coach would not have cared much for *stare decisis*. I didn't know the word at the time, but I now know Coach was capricious, i.e., unpredictable. He espoused one theory one day and an opposite the next. When any of us on the team were dumb enough to contest an inconsistency, he would quote an old proverb: "The wise man changes his mind, a fool never does." Being a former military man, he next ordered the ignorant offender to run laps to reinforce his philosophy that Coach is never wrong.

The just-concluded Senate confirmation hearings for Chief Justice John Roberts and the upcoming ones for nominee Miers' pinch hitter, have and will turn in part upon the nominees' statements of their allegiance toward this arcane doctrine of *stare decisis*. The senators want nominees to divulge how they will rule on future cases.

Nominees have an advantage over their inquisitors. The nominees can simply state they are true believers in *stare decisis*. They could quote Sir William Blackstone, the foremost commentator of the 18th century on English law, which we inherited in large part: "The doctrine of the law then is this: that precedents and rules must be followed, unless flatly absurd or unjust."

In other words, each candidate says, "I will not depart from precedent unless a compelling reason exists for doing so." Properly determining what reason is compelling enough to chart new territory separates the great jurists from the mere bench sitters.

This cagey answer trumps both the attackers from the left, who want a promise *Roe v. Wade* will never be distinguished, ignored or overturned, and from the right, who want a promise whatever the Founding Fathers said will always go. The wise nominee holds his or her cards close to the vest, preserving the option to make a turn in the legal road when the opportune case presents itself and justice at that moment demands a change.

Law must be predictable if it is to be valuable. It has been said we have a government of laws, not of men. It's a good thing, too! Imagine a sports contest in which the referee simply made up the rules which seemed fair to him on the day of the game. Chaos would reign, and the contest would become meaningless. Imagine judges who adopted Coach's philosophy. Law that depends upon the whims of the particular judge deciding a case is actually lawlessness.

Should our legal system ever descend to the place that each serving judge felt free to decide cases without regard to precedent, we citizens would have no chance to play the game of life in a fair, meaningful l way. We need judges who will apply the law as existing in a sober, detached, even-handed manner, not judges who will make law in accordance with their personal preferences.

So, why should loyalty to the old doctrine of *stare decisis* be insisted upon as essential in the makeup of any potential Supreme Court justice?

"Because I said so, that's why!"

III.   Local Interest

Editor Jones wanted to add more local color to the local newspaper, so I occasionally used my allotted space to highlight old buildings, new buildings, old people, new people, businesses, basketball, and even partially clothed people riding motorcycles on our hallowed fairgrounds. Extra! Extra! Read all about it!

June 30, 1990

Preservation: Are Only "Old" Buildings Worth Saving?

So long, Reese's Pieces Sundae! Hello, Burrito!

A few months ago the rumor mill commenced to cranking. Friendly Ice Cream, that checker on the board of who knows what conglomerate, had found Chillicothe to be unfriendly. The cozy café in the attractive, brick edifice on North Bridge Street would be closing soon. Could it be true?

The mill continued to churn. Taco Bell, Pepsico's swift slinger of hacienda hash, had been eyeing the First Capital. Hey! Maybe T. B. will stake its claim on Friendly's ex-façade. No! We are talking franchise food. Each chain needs uniformity, recognizability. Chimichangas just could not be sold in that Yankee setting. What? T. B. will demolish Friendly's building and put up its standard taco temple?

Preposterous.

The locals followed this little soap opera more closely than the flag-burning amendments, the most recent cracks in Streetscape, or even the daily reports of the number of traffic lanes open on Western Avenue. Issuance of the demolition and building permit to Taco Bell provided this drama's climax. The aroma of refried beans will rise from the ashes of Hershey's hot fudge.

Why did this little escapade fascinate us? Most of us do not protest upon the passing of greater landmarks. Few shed tears when the old Mt. Logan School disappeared. Fewer still whimpered when the Barrett Mansion fell to make room for Hart's. But threaten to pull down one of our early semi-fast food shrines and we become as watchful as a cat over a bird egg. We wonder what will hatch?

Possibly, this affects us viscerally. (A gut issue?) Cicero taught that one should eat to live – not live to eat. He did not anticipate the modern mind, stomach, or schedule. We want what we want, when we want it and where we want it. Many families get almost no nourishment anywhere besides restaurants these days. An interruption in a local food "chain" naturally grabs our attention.

Perhaps our curiosity is based on architecture, not gastronomy. As solid country folks, we are disturbed. We see a substantial, brick building with ceiling molding vanishing and contemplate an adobe, plastic, and glass hut appearing. The old building said, "Sit down. Be served with waiters and real dishes." We fear the new will say, as so many others already do, "Line up here. Bark out your order. Grab a paper plate. Find a plastic bench."

But this alone must not be the cause of our consternation. After all, we have not supported the full service regime to the degree needed to keep that concept profitable here. We do, however, support dozens of instant food vendors around town.

The primary reason for our special interest is found deeper in our psyche. John Ruskin said, "When we build let us think that we build forever." We strive for permanence. When ancient structures fall, their demise is impersonal. However, when we witness the replacement of a building which we saw erected and in which we sat when it was new, we are personally affected. This creates an unnatural feeling. Just as children are to outlive parents, buildings should outlast their builders.

Maybe this is where the preservationists should take a stand. They might be able to win one like this. John Q. Public does not seem excited about saving the grandeur of the 1870's, but protecting familiar landmarks of the 1970's might spark some popular support. Better yet, the preservers should work to convince the public that a bit of all of us dies when an outstanding or unusual building of any era expires.

Enough philosophizing. Ring in the new. Get ready for tostadas and guacamole. I just have one request of Ma Taco Bell. Please, beside the drive-thru lane, leave at least a small patch of real grass. It may be the last between Blue Gables and Massieville.

October 5, 1991

Uproar: From Moral Outrage May Come Accommodation

One would not expect an attorney to base a column partially on hearsay evidence, yet your writer has no choice. He has talked to a few witnesses. He has read the published letters and news articles regarding the event. But he did not attend the Easyriders annual get-together at the Ross County Fairgrounds on Labor Day.

Opinions are more tantalizing than facts. Still, a listing of the facts which are ascertainable is required for readers who live outside Chillicothe and its hinterland or who are natives but have been in a coma for the past month.

Fact: For the past few years, a group of motorcycle enthusiasts has rented the Ross County Fairgrounds for the Labor Day weekend. Here these cyclists and their admirers gather to share common interests in cycling and engage in other social activities.

Fact: More than 10,000 persons attended the event this year. As a result, the Ross County Fair Board, the on-site vendors, including some schools and service groups, and local retail establishments profited handsomely from the visitors.

Fact: The fair board and the cyclists' association have agreed to continue this arrangement for at least a few more years.

Fact: The Gazette's editor received and published a letter from a local clergyman condemning the activities reportedly occurring at the convention and questioning the wisdom of a continuing lease. An avalanche of letters and reports, pro and con, followed.

As Dorothy Sayers wrote: ". . . facts are like cows. If you look them in the face hard enough, they generally run away." The facts in the instant case rambled over the hill and out of view at about the same time the last Suzuki crossed the county line. Facts have been obscured; accusations, innuendo, and conclusion-jumping quickly replaced them.

Since this is a family newspaper, a full listing of the activities alleged to have transpired at the Honda Happening will be omitted. Suffice it to say that the goings-on complained of by the man of the cloth required very little cloth. Or, put another way, some of the celebrants supposedly showed more than the head, heart, hands and health exhibited by the 4-Her's a month earlier on the same hallowed grounds.

The battle lines thus drawn, the volleys continued for weeks. The attackers cast a broad net, suggesting that most of those attending engaged in reprehensible conduct, that the law enforcement officers "looked the other way," and that profits gained from vile conduct are tainted. The defenders accuse the minister and his supporters of making a Harley out of a moped. They say that only a few engaged in misconduct, that to forego easy profits would be foolhardy, and that the critics have violated one of their own basic principles: "Judge not, that ye be not judged."

As usual, neither army can claim total victory. As the smoke clears, a few truths do emerge.

Morals and the law are not synonymous.

Morals are a culture's value judgments regarding right or wrong conduct. Laws are simply agreed rules for behavior. Laws usually spring from morals, but the two do not always coincide. So, immoral conduct may or may not be illegal.

We should expect nothing less from our religious leaders than to condemn morally questionable behavior.

The brave reverend pricked the conscience of the community. True, as the pastor's opponents pointed out, Jesus said only he without sin should cast the first stone. However, after dispersing the crowd with that admonition, Jesus turned to the sinner and commanded her to sin no more. A minister should not be vilified for merely doing his job, i.e., reminding us to sin no more.

We should expect nothing less from our law enforcement officials than equal, even application of the laws.

The same standard should be applied to the cyclists' convention as would be applied to the county fair, a ballgame, or an outdoor drama. If the law of Ohio is broken, the violator should be charged – not because the moral code of a community might be breached, but simply because law is law.

Generalizing and stereotyping is almost always undesirable.

If those critical of the behavior at the assembly charge that all attending were of low moral fiber, the critics are exaggerating and, in the process, damaging their own cause. Some of the best Christian people this writer knows ride motorcycles. On the other hand, if the defenders dismiss as religious kooks all those who question the fairgrounds function, they too are unrealistic. The complaints merit investigation and, if necessary, corrections.

Our marvelous system often works out an accommodation. If the system works in this case, the moral outrage expressed by a few will result in adjustments which extend the benefits of the meeting, but bring it within the laws and a little closer to the moral tenor of our community.

July 12, 1997

Zoning Needed in County

"Head 'em up! Move 'em out! Rawhide!"

Echoing the cowboy shows from early television, I'd yell that kind of thing 40 years ago as a 10-year-old farm kid. My folks lived on and farmed Dr. Yaple's acreage which lay between Blackwater Road and State Route 159 in Green Township. Although a mere mile from Kingston, I felt as if I lived on the frontier. I reveled in the little cattle drives we conducted.

In order to move a herd of Herefords from the barn lot to an outer field of alfalfa, we drove the cattle on the county road and state highway. We did not need a permit. No vehicle drivers tooted or flashed hand gestures our way. All agreed that animal husbandry had its place and, at least on the days of the cattle drives, deserved priority. One segment of society, the travelers, yielded its desires to accommodate the needs of another, the farmers.

That farm has seen its final grazing calf. And the only corn and beans to appear after the current emblements (a real estate attorney's term for growing crops) are harvested will be the succotash fresh from the microwaves on the tables in the kitchens of the houses which will be rising inexorably upon the newly subdivided lots. The old farm is becoming Blackwater Acres or Fox Hill Farms or maybe Mortgage Note Subdivision.

A few weeks ago I spotted from Blackwater Road the first of these new homes. Right there on sacred ground, just west of the barn in which little Richard had pelted tough pigeons with weak BB's, just north of the creek on which he had floated boats made of leaves and bark – right there sat the silent shell of Home Number One. My frontier had vanished. A McDonald's in the middle of the burial grounds of Mound City would have looked no more out of place to me.

My emotions tell me to get mad. They're taking my playground – hallowed ground to a child and to the child in a man's memory. My intellect, however, tells me to get real. They're adding to the tax base.

I believe citizens all across our region share this schizophrenia. On the one hand, we want the beauty of amber waves of grain and purple hills' majesty. On the other hand, we crave the convenience of modern homes on lots with public utilities not far from work. The battle rages and we are living on the battlefield.

I'd like to sound the battle cry and rally the troops to defend good ol' Ross County. We all know that Columbus is marching right down U. S. 23 to gobble us up and change our culture. Yet, what a hypocrite I'd be to assume the mantle of leadership to resist growth and development. Look at the record.

I built my own house in 1979 in the middle of what had been Forrest Kreisel's cattle lot. My sister, my nieces and nephews, and many of my friends have placed their foundations on similar terrain. And I've not even mentioned those hundreds of clients for whom I have facilitated such activity by drafting deeds and examining land titles.

I surely don't have a monopoly on hypocrisy. All of us, even the conservationists and preservationists, live on land that formerly was someone else's farm or hunting ground. I guess we now know how Tecumseh felt when the Europeans overran this ground theretofore possessed by the Shawnee and other tribes.

So what shall we do? How can we manage the growing development beast without killing it altogether? How can we provide for the people and businesses who want to settle here while maintaining the beauty, livability and "frontier" atmosphere that some of us old natives remember and revere?

More bureaucracy is not a popular concept, so I'll call it "citizens helping citizens." All sections of our area need to adopt comprehensive zoning regulations. The efforts of our planning commission need to be supported. Commercial developers need to develop a conscience assuring that areas being developed are done so with a view toward quality of life as well as quantity of profits.

Many feel that more regulations will strangle us. Admittedly, procedural requirements slow results. If Tecumseh had convened a Chalagawtha Zoning Commission, the heirs of Nathaniel Massie might still be trying to get the plat for Chillicothe approved. As Mr. Eckert has portrayed, Tecumseh was a better warrior than a politician.

But just as strong fences make good neighbors, good land use rules, fairly enforced, increase the chance that members of a community can live in harmony. Nothing destroys neighborly spirit as quickly as sewage on the loose or contaminated water in the pipes. Land use planning contributes to peaceful and healthy living arrangements.

The cattle drives are over. I don't believe that our spirit of neighborliness must be though. We are a growing community whose face is changing from agricultural to residential. Only by proper planning and by preserving a willingness to accommodate each other can the transition be made bearable.

Contractors are waiting. "Head 'em up! Move 'em out! Rawhide!"
September 28, 1998

People Make This Area Great

Greetings, Ingstonians:

Whoops, sorry, I should have said Kingstonians. I'm really not upset that you changed the name of our little village. After all, I've been gone a long time. Even when I lived there in the little village I founded in 1816, I got pretty tired of explaining to people that "I" really was the first letter of the name of our hamlet, Ingstown. By the way, I am proud that you have chosen to preserve "Ing" as the name of one of your streets. It does my old heart good to see that I am remembered down there.

I have been amazed to watch the sleepy little wide spot in the road that I laid out develop into the thriving village it is today. When I was operating my tavern there, we thought it was a big month if a few dozen people passed through. Now you have that many people pass through in one cycle of your traffic lights. I surely did not need a drive-thru window at my tavern back then.

You face different challenges in old Kingston now than I did in 1816. Not many years before I bought my 40 acres from James Ritchie, the Indians, whom you now call Native Americans, were locked in a contest with us invading Europeans. I was still a little uncomfortable settling this area knowing that this general vicinity had been sacred ground to some of the tribes. In retrospect, from my new perspective, I have to admit that those people were outstanding in many ways. I'm sorry I missed it, but that speech given by Logan under that big elm tree a few miles up the road is still the most eloquent I have ever run into. Let me quote a little of it to remind you:

"I appeal to any white man to say, if ever he entered Logan's cabin hungry and I gave him not meat; if ever he came cold or naked and I gave him not clothing."

"During the course of the last long and bloody war, Logan remained in his tent an advocate of peace. Nay, such was my love for the whites, that those of my own country pointed at me as they passed by and said, "Logan is the friend of white men." I had even thought to live with you, but for the injuries of one man. Colonel Cresap, the last Spring in cold blood, and unprovoked, cut off all the relatives of Logan; not sparing even my women and children. There runs not a drop of my blood in the veins of any human creature. This called on me for revenge. I have sought it. I have killed many. I have fully glutted my vengeance. For my country I rejoice at the beams of peace."

"Yet do not harbor the thought that mine is the joy of fear. Logan never felt fear. He will not turn on his heel to save his life. Who is there to mourn for Logan? Not one."

But I am digressing. History is history, and you've made lots of it since I left your place.

It's funny how the history and development of our little village has paralleled the history and development of Ross County. I'm proud of my little development, but I never could keep up with that Nathaniel Massie. He was practically the first guy up the Scioto. He laid out Chillicothe in 1796, and he had savvy. He gave away numerous lots in Chillicothe to a pack of Presbyterians. Those thrifty, hard-working folks got busy and developed a little community. Then, Massie had lots of folks coming to whom he could sell his lots at a fair market rate.

By the way, I am sure you know that some of those Presbyterians were the same ones who set up a house of worship out on Mount Pleasant; you know out where the cemetery is. That was in
1798. Zane's Trace went right through there back then, I've been amazed to watch that congregation thrive and survive all this time. Two hundred years later and they are still worshipping at the corner of Church and Pickaway Streets in your village. Wow.

Anyway, I wasn't quite as smart as Massie. I sold my first lot, the one there at the corner of Main and Ing Streets (Gee, that sounds nice) where your school now stands, for $52.50. I guess I should have held onto it. I bet I could get twice that much now, huh?

When I bought into Green Township, Chillicothe was the capital of this State of Ohio. Being somewhat of a visionary, I envisioned Chillicothe remaining the capital city. I knew it might take a few decades, but I figured Kingston would become what Upper Arlington, Worthington, and Dublin have become to Columbus, the prime suburbs. Well, I laid Kingston out in 1816 and, sure enough that was the same year that confounded legislature moved the capital to Columbus to stay. What timing!

Still in all, I think we've done pretty well around here, don't you? The biggest plus for us was that the site I picked upon which to develop Ingstown turned out to be the same one Ebenezer Zane picked through which to run his trace. That meant everyone coming from the East out to the frontier and everyone on the frontier that wanted to travel back east had to come through our village. Since they all needed food and drink and a roof over their head at night and clothes, my professions of tavern-keeper and tailor were perfectly suited to the area.

Have you had any famous people through town lately? I'll never forget the day Senator Henry Clay from Kentucky stopped in. My, he was a talker. I wonder if politicians are still such good talkers. And we were all a little on edge when Santa Ana, the former president of Mexico, came through town. We didn't have any experience with Mexicans or presidents, so we weren't quite sure how to conduct ourselves. I suppose now with all your sophistication from cable TV and that thing called the Internet, you'd be okay even if the King of Siam came through town.

Ross County and Kingston were also fortunate in that they were in the middle of a rich agricultural area. Land has always been the base of a strong economy. I know one reason Kingston and Ross County developed well was the prosperity brought by the ability to market the farmers' crops and livestock.

And when the railroads came through town, this ability really took off. Of course, Ingstown started with just a few people, i.e., my family. By 1880, Kingston had grown to a population of 442. At that time, Adelphi was slightly ahead of us with 469 people. By 1890,

Kingston, with a railroad here or coming, was up to 751 population. In the early part of the 1900's, we kept growing until we hit and have stayed at 1200. Adelphi, without a railroad, still has approximately 450 population. The railroad brought some noise and some soot, but it also contributed to our prosperity.

So, as I see it, Kingston's location is what made it boom. As I see the future, though, location won't mean as much. Oh yes, I can see that location is important. In fact, Kingston and the surrounding area must be a pleasing location to lots of folks. I am shocked when I look down and see all of the residential development on the ground that had served as farmland for so many decades after I left town. It looks like you'll soon use up all of the farmland, and the population growth will then level off.

The thing that has really made Kingston and Ross County great, however, is not location. It has been the character of the people. I considered myself fortunate that those who bought the lots I had for sale were by and large law-abiding, hard-working, God-fearing people, who, yes, wanted to get ahead in this world, but not at the expense of their neighbors. We all pulled together to survive at the beginning. The following generations pulled together to help the community progress to the point it is today. As I close, I hope you will accept my recommendation that you strive to keep these qualities alive in yourselves so that the next century or two of Ingstown's (whoops, there I go again) I mean, Kingston's existence will be as pleasing as the first couple of centuries.

Yours very truly,
Thomas Ing

I couldn't have said it better myself.

A Revealing Chat with Gov. Thomas Worthington

You won't believe this!

While searching for a theme upon which to base a column celebrating Ohio's bicentennial, an extraordinary opportunity presented itself. My request for an interview with Thomas Worthington (1773-1827), one of Ohio's principal founders, was granted. The transcript of that exchange follows:

Question: Gov. Worthington, thanks for coming out of retirement to speak with us. What have you been doing since you died?

Answer: Well, to quote your Mr. Ray Charles, "Got nothing to do but roll around heaven all day." I'm rather glad to be invited back for this encore.

Q: Many of us now in the Scioto Valley were born here; but when you were born, Europeans had not yet subdivided Chalagawtha. How'd you get here?

A: I was born in Virginia. I was the last child my folks had. They died when I was quite young. When 13 years old, I chose Gen. William Darke as my guardian. Being a distinguished soldier in the Revolutionary War, he acquired lands in the Virginia Military Survey here. My brother-in-law, Ed Tiffin, (you may have heard of him, too) and I came up the Scioto in 1796 to check out the territory. We liked what we saw. In 1797, I visited again and bought a little real estate. In 1798, I brought Mrs. Worthington and my little girl here; and we "went to housekeepin'." The rest, as they say, is history.

Q: I'm sorry to tell you, but you did not come here from Virginia. The place you lived near Charleston was later declared to be part of West Virginia.

A: Well, whatever! I guess I'll have to trade my UVA Cavalier cap for a WV Mountaineer one.

Q: I was surprised to hear that you were an international sailor as a young man. Is that so?

A: You bet. I sailed on a British merchant vessel for a couple of years. I was nearly taken captive by some British rogues! That was scary! Once I returned to the states, I became a confirmed lifelong landlubber.

Q: I understand you brought some other folks with you as a part of your entourage when you moved here.

A: Oh, do you mean the workers?

Q. Well, Governor, some people called them slaves!

A: Young man, let me speak very directly to that issue. I may be old, but I'm not necessarily old-fashioned. To my chagrin, slavery, an abominable institution, was legal and customary in the Commonwealth of Virginia. Yes, my wife, and even I, to a lesser degree, held slaves in Virginia. But, I want you and your readers to know that as we brought these workers with us to the Northwest Territory, we freed them. Not only that, we tried to give them the means and motivation to provide for themselves. Many succeeded quite well. Later, I drafted the clause adopted into Ohio's constitution outlawing what was called in many states "Negro apprenticeships" – a polite synonym for slavery.

Q: Whoops! I'm sorry if I offended you, Mr. Worthington. Moving along, you clearly accomplished many great things during your lifetime: governor of Ohio, United States senator from Ohio, canal administrator, initiator of many public facilities and improvements, superb businessman, land baron, a leading citizen of your community, state, and nation, and a caring and devoted husband and father. What would you declare as your proudest accomplishment?

A: Sir, you just heard about it in my previous response.

Q: Let me ask you some quick-hitters. How do you like the restoration of Adena, your former residence?

A: They've done a beautiful job – very authentic.

Q: What's your favorite part?

A: The inside outhouses.

Q: How'd you get Benjamin Latrobe, architect of significant modifications to both the U. S. Capitol and the White House, to come out from Washington to design Adena?

A: That wasn't hard! Wouldn't you want to get out of that swamp and come to a place as nice as our town?

Q: Are you referring to the mosquitoes in D. C.?

A: No, the bureaucrats!

Q. Gov. Worthington, I can only say that you and Latrobe hadn't seen nothin' yet when you were there!

Q: A last architectural question: What would you change if building Adena today?

A: Again, inside outhouses!

Q: You met lots of famous people in your career. What'd you think of Thomas Jefferson?

A: Without doubt, Tom had the most inquisitive mind of any person I ever met. And what a writer! It's just too bad he couldn't manage his personal affairs (Is that the right word?) as well as his public ones.

Q: What about Tecumseh?

A: Now there was a man's man. Although, of course, we had a natural barrier separating us from forming a lasting, personal friendship. I'd like to think that I had the respect of Tecumseh and his people. I know he certainly had mine. I just wish I could stay around until summer to see that great drama I've heard about out at Sugarloaf.

Q: You were personally and politically hugely successful. What was the key ingredient to your successes?

A: That's easy – Eleanor Swearingen Worthington. My wife, with her talents and devotion, made It possible for me to accomplish anything you and history has judged as success. Who do you think managed my family and my considerable business interests while I was away so much? In your world today, she'd be the senator, not I.

Q: As you look around, what do you think of the old Scioto Valley today? It's much improved since your time, isn't it?

A: Are you kidding me? All I see is people, and all I hear is noise! And you all move so fast. These horseless carriages are ingenious; but please, they could be dangerous! Somebody could get hurt driving one of those.

Q: Yes, Governor, I suppose you are right. In closing, what advice do you have for today's Scioto Valley inhabitants?

A: First, take a Sabbath. I made sure that my household took Sundays off. We had church. We ate together. We rested. You people need to pace yourselves. Slow down and live. Second, buy land.

Q: Thank you, Gov. Worthington.

A: You're welcome. I'm feeling a little tired. After all, I am 230 years old, you know. I guess I'd better get back to heaven now. Good-bye, and have a great time celebrating this year.

Works of Public Art Make Ohio's First Capital Stand Out

I must have been about 4 years old when I got my head stuck between the rungs of the wrought iron fence at the Ohio Statehouse. My older sisters probably would have been happy to leave me there, but good old Dad freed me and took me back to the farm – or so I'm told.

I don't recall the details. Maybe I was a precocious political observer. Or maybe I was peering at the first statues I had ever seen.

I did not get much art appreciation training or opportunity while growing up in the 1950s on Blackwater Road. The only sculpture I saw regularly was the cow made of butter at the Ohio State Fair. The only poetry I absorbed was from the Burma Shave signs along the highway. Great painting was the occasional Mail Pouch ad on the side of a local barn.

So, I've had to pick up the knack of recognizing and appreciating the works of artists. I'd be a dunce in any school of art, but I know what I like. And I've noticed something I like here in our old first capital – the works of art which have been sneaking into public places in our town the last year or two.

Sculptures

Col. Richard Enderlin is the guy who has captured and focused my attention. Moving his stone likeness from its obscure position in front of the armory and stationing it in the intersection of Paint and Water Streets and Alexander Road works magnificently. Viewing the old boy as I head up Paint Street raises my spirits a little each time.

Then, turning onto East Water Street, I spy the World War I doughboy. I see the Mount Logan range behind him, and I think of the thousands of boys who saw that same beautiful range while training at Camp Sherman.

The soldier is signaling. I'm not sure if it's a sign to move forward into battle, a sign victory has been won, or a simple salute to his comrades and fellow citizens, even me, these decades later. I only know he looks better standing there than an abandoned grain elevator would.

In the midst of these military heroes now rises a clock tower. This is not exactly art, but it sure beats the digital clock on my dashboard. Even simple analog instruments approximate art these days.

Murals

As I bound down the steps of the Ross County Courthouse, a work of art in itself, I see the mural on the west wall of the Huntington National Bank. While I know Rembrandt's reputation is not threatened by this offering, I am inspired nevertheless. The mural reminds us of the importance of place, this place in particular, and of people, those who settled and developed this area into a stable, but progressive community. The mural lends dignity to our place and reminds us of our duty to carry on the traditions of our forbearers.

At the very least, it beats plain stucco.

Another mural has appeared on the east wall of the building at the northwest corner of Second and Mulberry streets. That wall, or one like it, looked out upon the Ohio & Erie Canal 15 decades or so ago.

Now, the wall projects a scene from our town's canal days. As I wait for the traffic light to turn, my blood pressure decreases a couple of points having been reminded by the mural that commerce, whether by mule pace or cyberspace, continues, slowly wending its way through time.

Architecture

Structures themselves can be art.

Our community is blessed by the presence of graceful buildings supplied by past generations and preserved by present ones. Examples abound: the aforementioned courthouse, the rows of commercial buildings across the face of our downtown, the Majestic (including its unique arch), the *Gazette*'s statehouse replica, the marvelous mansions of South Paint and of West Second, and the quaint residences of the Caldwell/Fifth Street neighborhood.

We tend to take these for granted, but only because familiarity breeds complacency. These beauties do not exist in other county seats. Enjoy them. So, what should the community do from this point forward to supplement and encourage its "public art?"

First, preserve what we have. That's not to say every structure no matter its lack of functionality should be protected, but reasonably compelling reasons should be demonstrated before "pulling down" begins.

Second, be alert to the opportunity to add even small touches that make a big difference. For example, the stylish post lamps on the new Bridge Street and Main Street bridges make a subtle, but noticeable statement about the taste of Chillicotheans.

Third, get creative. Devise additional artful embellishments of our cityscape.

Rio de Janeiro has its statue, Christ the Redeemer, on the mount overlooking and blessing that city.

Maybe we can come up with statuary of Rio scale: Nathaniel Massie with his surveying instruments, Thomas Worthington with his pen, Tecumseh with his tomahawk. Maybe we can construct an attractive landmark for our fair city (other, of course, than the towering Mead stack by which many Ohioans recognize us). Maybe we can find another building or two to serve as canvas for imaginative murals, of inspirational or even whimsical content. Maybe when building or renovating we can add a flourish to everyday architecture. The Carlisle Building, whether repaired or replaced, would be a great place to start.

Make this newspaper a forum by submitting your idea to its editor.

Go ahead and stick your head through the fence and take a good look at the possibilities.

You may like what you foresee.

January 24, 2005

The Mead's Smell Means Different Things to Locals

My nose first informed me.

Grandma Delong lived on East Seventh Street in the 1950s. The behemoth factory building of Mead Corporation, before, then, and now, hunkered a block southwest of Grandma's house.

Now, noses are notoriously fickle. If beauty is in the eye of the beholder, stench is in the nostrils of the smeller. On our little farmstead in Green Township, I had smelled manure up close and personal every day. That bothered me not. I could tramp directly from the hog pen to the dinner table without changing my shoes.

Although Mom had higher standards of manners than I, I could have happily eaten her wonderfully aromatic mashed potatoes while ignoring the mashed manure on my boots.

Yet the odor of Mead's recipe of wood chips and more nearly sickened me. The food didn't taste so good at Grandma Goldie's. My nose, an oblivious odor detector at home, became an extra-sensitive instrument at Grandma's. Experience made the difference. I'd had plenty with pork making, but none with paper making. In time, I gained experience, my perspective changed, and "The Mead" did not smell so badly.

My tolerance level probably began to increase in the summer of '61 when I began playing VFW baseball at the diamond in Mead Park located on company property just south of the factory. Corporate sponsorship of sports had not reached the modern level yet, but I had enough sense to know that the company had a lot to do with me playing shortstop on a grass infield for the first time. I loved baseball. The glory of being on a real ball field somehow neutralized much of the mill's odor.

In the summers of '66, '67, and '68, Mead gave me the opportunity to work, not play. Hiring college kids as summer help was a strong Mead program back then. Union power assured that even summer help received wages of $5 or $6 per hour – an astounding raise from my theretofore normal $1 or $1.25 per hour. Suddenly the mill smelled like tuition money to me. Poor though I was, Mead assisted me in obtaining a college degree without debt. I pledged never to complain about the smell again.

Later, I settled into my Ross County law practice. I'm happy to report scores of Mead workers have retained my services over the years, and they all paid me promptly with some of those funds Mead's payroll office handed them every Thursday. Believe it or not, the stench has vanished entirely, and not just because of the taller smokestack.

The news that soon, for the first time in decades, no Mead sign will hang on the factory on South Paint has rattled our community. We've tilted our noses to the air, sniffing for any new aroma we can detect. What odor will the Cerberus wind blow our way? Will it be a bitter draft of layoffs and cutbacks or a sweet scent of stability and prosperity?

Maybe we'd best withhold judgment. Just as I found when my experiences with Mead moved from my juvenile ones at Grandma's to my maturing ones with the opportunities Mead gave me, our community may discover over time that change doesn't smell so badly after all.

Do you smell something?

February 17, 2014

Passions Run Strong at Tournament Time

"It's cold outside, but it's hot in here! All for Kingston, stand up and cheer!" Ross County and environs loves its high school basketball and has for a long time. Cheers such as this arose from gymnasiums across our region during my growing-up years in the 1950's and 1960's as they did long before and have continued since. Some things never change. Some do.

The day after Thanksgiving my daughter and her family invited me to attend an OSU basketball game at Schottenstein Center. What an eye opener! Now I am not uninitiated when it comes to amateur roundball. My dad kept the scorebook for Kingston and Zane Trace teams for more than forty years, so I cut my teeth watching battles of the local boys during those early winters of my life. I played, with moderate success, but immoderate enthusiasm, during my junior and senior high school days.

And I had more than a little experience with OSU b-ball. Big Frank Howard and the prolifically scoring Robin Freeman were leading the Buckeyes at the Ohio State Fairgrounds Coliseum when I saw my first college game as a third grader in 1955. I observed games at St. John Arena in the late 50"s and early 60's when Lucas, Havlicek, Knight, et al. were dominating the hardwoods. I saw lots of games there during my OSU years since student tickets were cheap and available and since I lived across the street in Ohio Stadium in a dorm built under the concrete decks of Woody's House.

The contrasts I perceived then between the atmospheres of big time college ball and small-town high school ball were stark. Noise: OSU's approximated a funeral home. Ross County League's conjured a bar fight. Fashion: OSU's hinted of church or at least a "nice casual" social affair. Ours down home approached essence of cattle lot or paper mill. Attitude: OSU-mildly interested; local-win or die. Overall: genteel and well- heeled vs. raw and down-in-the-heels.

Well, I have now found out that the college atmosphere " ain't what it used to be" .We climbed to an altitude higher than a grain elevator to find our assigned seats in the next to highest row in the place. From there, we looked DOWN at the monstrous scoreboard, which exhibited more information and functions than my pre-digital age brain could process. In the next few moments, the behemoth attacked the audience. First came the smile cam. That was pleasant enough. Next came the kiss cam. The camera flashed the picture of a couple of fans, who were then expected to smooch for the audience. I'm glad my number didn't come up. I didn't even know the guy beside me. I doubt that Supt. George Armstrong (Centralia H. S.) or Pryor Timmons (Clarksburg H. S.) would have approved use of the kiss cam. Cheerleaders and dancing girls appeared and gyrated the whole evening on and around the floor. (Don't even ask George or Pryor for permission for this one.) Rap music, loud rap music, blared before and during the game, overpowering the pep band, a mere sideshow at this three ring circus .As for fashion, I felt downright Amish, being possibly the only attendee of the 20,000 without a logo stamped anywhere on my clothes or body.

The game eventually transpired. Some didn't let that interrupt their evening. Two ladies in the row in front of us were much more interested in each other than the game, but some of us even attempted to watch it. I did. Of course, being one of the very few without a hand-held device to allow me to multi-task, what else was I to do? The game didn't hold much suspense since the opponent, North Dakota State, couldn't have beaten Knockemstiff Elementary. The half time diversion of little kids going onto the floor to do flying dunks on the biddy-ball backboard was a little more entertaining.

All I could think of on the way home was the difference between that colossal arena and the humble, but personality-filled ball halls of my young years. Our own at Kingston had open staircases at three of its corners, which could have led to the death of any player dumb enough to execute an Aaron Craft-like headlong dive for an exiting ball. Unioto's floor had a confusing hollow section. Centralia's floor at Kinninnick was so inordinately wide that visiting players' shots from the corners would routinely fall wildly short. None of our ancient arenas beat Buckskin Township's...a true cracker box. It was so cramped that the foul circles intersected the center circle. The end walls constituted the boundaries of play. Some players could score from nearly any spot on the court. Just "turn and shoot." My last high school game there, Buckskin's Ed Schiller did that successfully 19 times on his way to a 40-point night. (KHS still won 92-89).

Not having attended a local high school game for a number of years now, I cannot testify as to how the atmosphere may have changed. I know the gymnasiums have improved, but have, no doubt, lost some of their quirkiness. I hope the passions and loyalties for our respective teams have not declined. I know, however, that they could not have increased beyond those of my dear, late mother. Nina. A wonderful, attentive, loving, mother who sacrificed much in life to assure that my sisters and I were raised properly, nevertheless did allow her passion for her Kingstonians to create a legend.

Witnesses have verified that one night in the mid-50's in that same Buckskin cracker box, she was positioned along the passageway through which the referees, coaches, teams, and spectators were forced to walk in order to exit. On this night, Mom had gotten the impression that the officials had not administered the rules of the game in, shall we say, a "fair and balanced" manner, thus resulting in a disadvantage to dear old Kingston High. In her determination to exhibit her support for the boys, she was able to remove her long, sharp hat pin from its secreted place and administer a jab to the posterior of the passing stripe-shirted official in an efficient manner. He yelped a profanity. The aggressor was never until this day identified or arrested, but she was often praised by the Kingston faithful.

Some things change, to-wit: big time college basketball and small-town gymnasiums. Some things don't: ardent partisanship for our local teams. So, as temperatures outside continue to decrease and the passionate yearnings inside the fans increase, with Heartbreak Trail, as broadcaster Grant McDonald termed tournament time, looming, control yourselves (Sorry, Mom!) and enjoy yourselves.

November 8, 2015

Building Renovation Bridges a Cultural Gap

How can one building mean so much? Think of your childhood home, your grandparents' house, your elementary school, Ohio Stadium, the U.S. Capitol, the World Trade Center. Whether related to family, education, recreation, government, or commerce, the very image of a structure, in one's eye or even in one's mind's eye, prompts reactions, positive or negative. Architecture matters.

Our ancient metropolis, the first and third capital city of infant Ohio, continues to experience this truth. Many, including your humble correspondent, despaired of ever seeing anything other than gravel or grass on the southeast corner of Paint and Main, the site of the Carlisle Building. The dilapidated dame stood forlorn for a dozen years after the conflagration which ravished the old girl. All the while, most locals nursed fond memories of her salad days, her heyday.

In the 1950's I accompanied my mom on her shopping forays to the downtown of the county seat. No shopping centers yet existed on Vaughn's dairy farm and environs on North Bridge Street, only Guernsey cows, not Guernsey Crossing. I looked forward to the clacking and sucking sounds of the pneumatic tubes in Schachne's Department Store, across South Paint Street from the Carlisle, magically transporting Mom's currency or her metal store charge account card imprint from clerk to office and back. Down the block, I gazed wondrously at the image of my metatarsal bones inside my wiggling piggies under the fluoroscope as we chose my new shoes at Hermann's Shoe Store. But I looked most wide-eyed and open-mouthed at the sundae glass being filled for me at the soda fountain at Central Pharmacy, just inside the corner door of the Carlisle. I cared much about appetite and none about architecture.

Fast forward a quarter century and find me, a budding young attorney, bounding up the long, steep staircase of the Howson Building, adjoining the Carlisle, to visit the offices of legends in the profession. Such star lawyers as John Scott Phillips, Richard Middleton, former mayor of Chillicothe, and William Burbridge Brown, associate justice of the Supreme Court of Ohio, maintained offices in the dark, spare, mysterious, high-ceilinged, spartanly-appointed, turn-of-the-century, i.e., 1899 into 1900, funereal spaces. Even former probate judge, Marshall Fenton, who was born in 1885, the same year the Carlisle was dedicated, somehow still struggled up those stairs to sit behind his shingle. I felt I had stepped back into a bygone era. To be in the presence of these luminaries in the rarefied atmosphere of such a venerable space….intoxicating.

And then back downstairs, tucked in the southeast corner of the Carlisle, the charming, unique Harvester Restaurant served up pretty fine, pretty fun food. I would pay dearly today for the recipe for those grease-drenched croutons that appeared copiously on the salad bar stationed in the wooden wagon just inside the sliding rustic barn door entrance. My adult appetite for the Carlisle's contents still greatly exceeded my appreciation of its architecture.

I do not consider myself to be a staunch preservationist. My wife and I did buy and bring the circa 1835 building at 1 North Main Street in Kingston from the brink of uselessness to daily usefulness to house my law practice. Practicality drove that decision. Preservation was a side effect.

Preservation for the mere sake of preservation can be proper and wonderful. The problem: that can also be a hard sell to investors. The "museums" resulting from strictly preservation-based rehabilitations draw in relatively few observers and even fewer "paying customers." The resurrection of a structure with an eye toward its future use adds a tasty element, attracting investors. Strawberries preserved are pretty in the jar, but the memory and the promise of these on my morning toast actually motivate me to buy the jar. The pleasing memory of past usage of the Carlisle and the delicious vision of the future usage motivated The Chesler Group and Adena Health System to invest.

Seeing a structure conveys factual information. Looking at the refurbished and improved Carlisle tells all that downtown Chillicothe has something big going for it. Remembering a structure adds emotional content. When we think of the stellar history of the Carlisle, we puff a little with pride. Using a structure brings satisfaction of a need. The new Carlisle bridges a gap a growing Chillicothe and Ross County had an awfully tough time crossing.

My wife Beth, one of the Carlisle naysayers for the past dozen years, now says she is glad to have been so wrong. Join the crowd, Honey. Our community applauds the rising of our phoenix from the literal ashes. May this legendary lady at the center of our town be consumed over the coming years only by the flame of good, satisfying service so that 130 more years on down the path of time, around 2145, this community can complete the next remodeling of the Grand Dame, our Carlisle. March majestically onward. Architecture does matter.

IV. Life/Character

Once in awhile, I'd see a person, internationally recognized or simply next-door neighbor, experience an event, or simply have an idea swim into my consciousness, which sight, experience, or thought geminated and then grew into a theme for a column. I often had no expertise relating to many of these topics, (remember the seventh grade blogger), but as my life progressed through the years, I began to claim some actual familiarity with these sometimes troublesome quagmires of life in this old world.

June 8, 1992

Death: Life, Properly Lived, Not Mere Statistic

Read John 14:1-4 (NIV)

Romans 8:19 (NIV): The creation waits in eager anticipation for the sons of God to be revealed.

The note informing me of the death of an acquaintance stated that my friend had died "unexpectantly" that morning. I hoped not. I hoped the writer of the note meant "unexpectedly." Those who have placed their trust in God can live and die with the expectation of spending eternity with God in the place Christ has prepared for believers.

St. Paul wrote in Philippians 1:21 (NIV), "For to me, to live is Christ and to die is gain." Those living in the light of God's love experience the very presence of Christ in their lives each moment. They also live in anticipation of the glories to come in an eternity with God. Whether vibrantly alive or nearly dead, those in God's family can trust that their heavenly rooms are prepared and reserved for their eventual triumphant occupation.

This report of the unexpected death of a friend prompted me to consider a question: "Am I living each day expectantly with the blessed assurance of an eternity with God?" We must live each day walking in God's light so that it will never be said that we died "unexpectantly."

Prayer: Eternal God, thank you for giving us your Word that you will stay close to us here on earth each day and your promise that we can spend eternity beside you in heaven.

Thought for the day: Walking with God today emboldens us to live in expectation of eternal life with God.

Prayer Focus: Those living without hope.

December 5, 1992

Gleaning: Maybe It's Time to Bring this Tradition Back

"You can't hit someone wearing glasses!" As a grade-schooler, I put that order right up there with "Thou Shalt Not Kill" and "Thou Shalt Not Steal."

Legislatures create some laws by writing them. Courts create other laws by interpreting the written laws or by establishing rules based on fairness. Society "creates" still other "laws" by simply adopting a common standard of behavior.

The law of gleaning began as a written law under the Jewish code; i.e., the Old Testament. Gleaning progressed to a point earlier in our American history that it had become one of those cultural norms, a part of every agrarian citizen's conscience. Gleaning may now have gone the way of the Edsel.

What is gleaning, anyway? An illustration is worth a thousand explanations. Picture a group of junior-high-aged youths in November 1959, burlap sacks in hand, slowly moving through a charitable farmer's corn stubble, bending to spy, grasp, and stash the ears the one-row corn picker had lost, missed, or smashed. My church youth group used the proceeds from the sale of the gleaned corn to support its projects.

Unlike his Hebrew predecessor (see Leviticus 19:9-10), that farmer was not required to allow groups or individuals to traipse his acreage panning for maize. Instead, he consented to the gleaners for the same reason we didn't think of punching the kid we affectionately called "Four-eyes." At the foundation of our culture was an unwritten rule of civility – an agreement that the strong would go only so far in profiting at the expense of the weak. A sense of responsibility existed among the relatively well-off for seeing that the relatively poor-off were able to obtain the basics of life.

In a capitalistic society, winners cannot exist without losers. Competition breeds the tendency to knock the other guy down and, if possible, out. Our laws foster that competition. Yet in our culture we have prized the notion that all people, whatever their deficiencies, are entitled to the necessities of life. How can our system of laws accommodate both principles?

In reality, the legal system, acting alone, probably cannot. If we balance the scales on the side of the free market, winner takes all, we create a subculture of have-nots. If we overreact in favor of those who cannot compete successfully in our system, we create a welfare state. A permanent balance has never yet been struck.

At present, evidence supports the view that the "haves" have it over the "have-nots." Recent studies show that more than 35 million Americans live at or below the poverty line. That is the equivalent of all the people in three states the size of Ohio. Drive through a city (Columbus), a town (Chillicothe), or even a village (Kingston), and you with ease will spot the homeless. Many families above the poverty line are there only by increasingly frenetic activity: two wage earners, multiple jobs, children working.

With the changing of the guard in Washington looming and with the season of good will toward men just ahead, could this be the time to reinstitute the law of gleaning? Government may tinker with the economic controls to adjust our balance. But the primary method of revising our downward spiral will be on a personal level. We, the people, must adopt an attitude that we are each responsible to allow the gleaners into our fields.

Note that gleaning is not simply giving handouts. The gleaners must participate to profit. But without a field in which to work and some guidance from the owner of the field and a willingness of the owner to allow a little of the grain to escape his modern reaper, even the energetic gleaner will not succeed.

Allowing gleaners is more than just allowing a few more tax dollars to trickle down to the needy. The needy must glean from the winter's time and talents also. Supporting the new local chapter of Habitat for Humanity, for example, is to allow gleaning. The disadvantaged work along with the advantaged to build, pay for, and maintain housing. This is no handout program. Work a little at the homeless shelter. Be a Big Brother or a Big Sister.

Allow yourself to be gleaned. In so doing, you may be moving toward restoration of the balance this country needs.

As John F. Kennedy said Jan. 20, 1961, at his inauguration: "Ask not what your country can do for you; ask what you can do for your country."

I submit that we all can contribute to our own welfare and to that of our nation by returning to the gleaning principle. And remember, never hit a person wearing glasses.

July 24, 1999

Live Life to the Fullest

Early on a bright spring morning in 1963, as best I can conjure, the same year John F. Kennedy was assassinated, I was walking to school. Kingston's Eastern Avenue fronted the home of J. P. Gardner, D.V.M. When Dr. Gardner was younger and stronger, he vigorously practiced his veterinary profession throughout our farming community. That morning he hailed me as he struggled to the curb.

"Young man," he muttered, "I've a proposition for you." I couldn't imagine what old Doc wanted.

"Young man, I'd like to propose that we trade bodies."

At my present stage of maturation, I can barely recall having a body anyone would barter for, but Doc Gardner was living out his final days. The glint in his eye betrayed his boyish orneriness. I laughed, politely declined his offer, and strutted on to my busy day. I probably stayed awake through all my classes, ate a couple of big meals, endured and enjoyed the rigors of baseball practice, rejoined my folks in the evening, and slept soundly as, well, as only a growing teenager does.

I did these things nearly unconsciously. I probably didn't even think of Dr. Gardner's little mind game for years thereafter. We all seem to live that way – sort of unconsciously – giving no mind to old man time shuffling toward us from beyond the curb.

Last Saturday evening the memory of that exchange with Doc Gardner returned to me. My wife and I had chosen the beautiful high grounds of Grandview Cemetery for our evening stroll.

This followed by only a few hours the news of the sudden loss of John F. Kennedy, Jr. That uncommon tragedy coupled with the hundreds of common tragedies represented by the gravestones we were passing reminded me of my mortality – of our mortality.

I spend a considerable portion of my professional life advising individuals on planning for passage of their property upon their deaths and assisting those people receiving assets of those who have died. In the tombstone twilight last Saturday evening, I pondered whether my work was indeed a little vain – futile, useless, without lasting result.

I don't actually believe that proper estate and financial planning is in vain. Wise people make proper preparation for the orderly passage of their property by executing wills, trusts, deeds, beneficiary designations, and other sensible instructions. True vanity is to live as if we are not really mortal.

Deaths of the famous and deaths of the common, the JFK, Jr.'s and the Dr. Gardner's, remind us to live while we have life.

In Chapter 12 of St. Luke's Gospel, Jesus spoke to this. A farmer who had a great crop year spent his energy planning bigger barns to secure his future. His life was demanded of him that very night.

Because he had stored things up only for himself, he was called a fool. Verse 15 sets forth the lesson: "...a man's life does not consist in the abundance of his possessions."

I recently learned that Dr. Gardner penned some poetry in his spare time. Some would call it doggerel, but I found some fun in the few of Doc's ditties I obtained.

Doc loved his horses and most of his verse follows an equine theme. The last stanza of one of his poems titled, "A Horseman's Prayer" summarizes well the point I am attempting to make about us humans. After describing the characteristics of the ideal horse, the mythical horse all horse lovers yearn to own, he concludes:

Such horses, I find, are hard to get,
Few people have owned such an animal yet,
But we who love horses will always keep trying
'Till Old Father Time swings his sythe (sic), and we're dying.'

Most keep trying to obtain possessions until death knocks.

When Doc Gardner was breathing his last, I'm sure he cared little about the ideal horse he never found and much about the fun he'd had with the common ones he did own. From what I know, JFK, Jr., lived his life not to add meaningless sums to the pile of assets his family already had or even to add meaningless fame and glory to the abundance already existing. He lived a civil, sensible, and useful life, enjoying the privileges life granted him, but not lording it over those around him.

So it should be when each of us at last, or maybe tonight, shuffles off into eternity. Whether we die young, middle, or old, the wise ones of us will have lived to stock barns besides our own.

All Heroes Should Act Like the Glenns

You never can tell whom you may meet in the grocery store. For some unknown reason, a few years ago I began shouldering most of our grocery shopping duties. I've grown rather to enjoy it.

And the people I see! Students I taught during my brief teaching career nearly forty years ago. At least they have changed in appearance more than I have. And clients, past and present (how embarrassing when I can't remember some of my current ones). And even family members. Weddings and funerals occur only intermittently, but, well, a guy's gotta eat every week.

But you'll never guess whom I not only saw, but met in a grocery store today! Today I met two, genuine, legitimate American heroes. Here's how it happened.

I was standing in the seafood section of Trader Joe's. While trying to discern between farm-raised and wild-caught, I spotted an elderly couple just behind me, hesitating ever so briefly before the cheese shelves. The distinguished looking, yet sportily dressed gentleman veered off from the little lady and headed for a rendezvous with the dairy department. The pleasant-looking, proper lady proceeded straight ahead in my direction. By the time she reached the pork chops (hormone free), I was able to confirm the identity of the heroes.

Colonel and former U. S. Senator John Glenn and his wife, Annie, were in the store. I felt like I had just met Ferdinand Magellan, the Spaniard who first circumnavigated the globe in a ship, at the gas station. Had it been a Seven Eleven, I would have begun my search for Elvis. I felt about like I had when I ran into Wilt Chamberlain in the concourse of the Fairgrounds Coliseum one night when I was still a kid and he was still a Harlem Globetrotter. He had the most interesting belt buckle.

Readers who are my contemporaries will have no trouble remembering that John Glenn was the hero of the free world in 1962 when he became the first American to orbit Earth in a spacecraft. I was in ninth grade when it happened. Then here I was, forty-seven years later, in the kosher chicken section pondering whether to interrupt the marketing mission of the couple who flew and prayed through one of the most famous aviation missions of human history.

I looked around for clues as to my appropriate course of conduct. How were the staff and the other patrons reacting to this startling development? The answer: they weren't. At first, I figured those folks were just too polite to consider interrupting the Glenns in their gastronomical gyrations. My next thought, a more valid one, no doubt, was that all these young folks did not recognize the heroes among us. This confirms the negative comments we have heard recently regarding the miserable state of the teaching of history in our schools. I bet these types would not have recognized Abraham Lincoln had he ambled in with an ax in his hand and a stovepipe top hat on his head.

Well, I just had to meet Mrs. Glenn, so I intercepted her as she reached the fruit stand. In a stammering way, I introduced myself and stated that I wanted to tell her that my wife and I greatly admired the devotion she and her husband had shown each other over the years. What a polite lady she was! She acknowledged my comment, but quickly turned the conversation toward me, my home territory, and my marital history. What a gracious person! What a class act!

As I tried to excuse myself, she insisted instead on herding me to the milk stand to meet a true American hero. I can only describe the experience as surreal. Senator Glenn, successor to the Wright Brothers, looked me squarely in the eye, firmly shook my hand, and chatted amiably for a moment about the blessings of a long marriage. He did not seem the least irritated that his enthusiastic wife had, for no good reason, interrupted his ruminating (no pun intended) about his dairy choices. And he couldn't have been courting votes. He's not running.

When my wife caught up with me a few minutes later at the checkout counter, I related to her my amazing experience. She then sought out the generous Glenns and received the same genial treatment.

So, what conclusions have I drawn from this unexpected pleasure? First, fame does not necessarily create arrogance. In fact, apparently, fame does not even excuse the famous one from doing his/her own grocery shopping. Not all heroes worship themselves.

Second, and more importantly, devoted love is beautiful and rare. Annie had told me that she and John had been married sixty-six years, having first met in second grade. In retrospect, I realize that Senator Glenn's patience with my interruption of his shopping expedition had nothing to do with me – it had everything to do with his enduring love and respect for his beloved Annie when she thrust upon him for, I am sure, yet another time an unknown and bothersome well-wisher like me.

I wish all heroes behaved like these two. I know meeting them inspired me. You just never can tell whom you may meet in the grocery store.

March 11, 2018

<u>Remembering Reverend Billy Graham</u>

I encountered Billy Graham personally, sort of, three times. The first two experiences occurred conventionally, i.e., as expected and just as hundreds of millions of other people had and would do over the years. I attended a session of each of his two crusades in Columbus, Ohio. I took in the first in 1964 at Jet Stadium as a teenager of 16 with a group from my church. By the time Rev. Graham hit Columbus for his second set of meetings in 1993 at the same stadium, by then renamed Cooper Stadium, I was a middle-aged man showing up with my wife, two adult children, and my mother-in-law.

These two evangelistic campaigns constituted less than one-half of one per cent of the 417 Graham and his associates conducted in 185 nations from 1947 to 2005, reaching over 200 million people...well, 199,999,999 seeing as how I attended twice. (NOTE: This piece will not be an account of how I walked the "sawdust trail" or the infield dirt or the artificial turf. I had done that at an earlier date at another place without Billy's invitation).

Our third meeting was a little less conventional, in a more intimate setting, actually just a tad beyond arm's length. On Saturday, August 28, 2010, wife Beth and I were participating in a three-day Bible seminar at the Billy Graham Training Center, aka The Cove, a beautiful little campus built into the side of the Blue Ridge Mountains just outside Asheville, North Carolina. Mr. Graham did not preach, teach, or lead at The Cove. Instead, his association merely invited other highly regarded preachers and teachers to conduct sessions at that facility. Incidentally, Graham's body recently first lay in repose in this serene spot before resting in the rotunda of our nation's Capitol and then finally near his burial place at his library at Charlotte, North Carolina.

We were gathered with the other 200 or so attendees in the cozy, tiered "classroom," listening to the evening presentation being delivered by the excellent teacher, Woodrow Kroll, when we noticed a rustling on stage right, just out of the view of the audience. Whispers. Furtive little movements. An air of excitement fluttered like escaped butterflies across the room. Then, we saw and we knew! Billy Graham himself had arrived unannounced. Emerging from the shadows, being pushed by his daughter, the greatest, most respected, most effective evangelist of the last hundred years cruised gently into the light of center stage, not more than 35 feet in front of us.

We, of course, were ecstatic. This bonus, all for the same price. Imagine for a moment the emotions of speaker Kroll, a Bible teacher presenting his lecture, who glances over and sees Billy Graham listening in the wings. That would be something like realizing that Julia Child is peering over my shoulder while I stand cooking a humble supper at my kitchen stove.

A little background would help now. The Cove had billed this conference as a "Senior Event." (Don't you dare ask!). Cliff Barrows, Billy's crusade song leader, then aged 87, was leading the weekend's proceedings. Apparently, someone had invited George Beverly Shea, Billy's crusade soloist, often described as America's beloved gospel singer, then aged 101, and Billy himself, America's pastor, then aged 91, to a little surprise gathering of the great triumvirate. Beth and I happily found ourselves as what is known in the law of contracts a "third party beneficiaries."

Within a few minutes, attendants placed two chairs on the platform, one on each side of Billy's. Cliff and Bev settled onto their perches. Microphones were given. Chatting began. We were privileged to eavesdrop, if you will, as these companions reminisced about the roads they had traversed together for nearly 60 years. These gentle giants of the evangelistic hall of fame, who had worked together tirelessly and without dispute to reach hundreds of millions of souls for Christ, now before our eyes and ears were reviewing and renewing their old enduring friendship.

They spent as much of their hour or more good naturedly "jabbing" each other as they relived the glory days. They spoke and acted in the manner that all old comrades do whether down at the coffee shop or around the plastic table at McDonald's. These old boys even broke into song here and there, always amiably highlighting Graham's inability to carry a tune in a collection plate. The tender love and respect flowing between these veterans of the spiritual wars was palpable. And it was quite touchingly beautiful.

The night was fleeting, just as were the lives of these aging lions of the faith. Clearly, these fellows had not had this opportunity for a long time. Just as obviously, they would probably never have this chance again. Billy's daughter intervened to tell him he really should be getting on home now. His energy level was flagging. Parkinson's is a terrible thing. In a flash of authority, Daddy firmly rejected her first overture, informing her that he was not ready yet. A little later, upon her second approach, he relented. The spirit was still willing, but the body had weakened.

We watched as the old gang broke up. Each rolled or hobbled into the night. Bev Shea's rich bass-baritone was to be silenced in 2013 at 104. Cliff Barrows' unbridled enthusiasm was finally to be curbed in 2016 at 95. William Franklin Graham, Jr. was to lay down his Bible for the final time on the evening of February 20, 2018 at 99 before meeting his Maker the following morning. All have flown away.

Rev. Graham was not a perfect human. In fact, his good behavior did not qualify him to enter heaven on that Wednesday morning. Only the grace of the Savior about whom Billy Graham spent his life testifying allowed him, or Bev, or Cliff, or you, or me to enter into God's eternal presence when we leave behind this vale of tears.

Our prime "take away" from witnessing that unusual Saturday night meeting: great people of God are humble people of God. That night, nearing the end of mortal life, the great minister, Billy Graham himself, never once referred to his successes. He could have reminded his colleagues of the number of converts he led to Jesus, of the number of presidents, popes, kings, and queens he counseled, of the number of headlines he appeared in, or of any other aspects of his star power. But neither he nor his mates performed any silly "end zone dances."

Rather, as befits their hero and Savior, Jesus Christ, their behavior illustrated their humility, their joy, and their contented condition in lives honestly consumed all out in the Lord's work.

What better benediction could any of us ask for our lives?

October 12, 2014

Aging Stays like Unwelcome Relative

More reminders of my aging I did not need; nevertheless, they appeared. This birthday morning both my digital bathroom scales and the exercise bike at the gym challenged me to confess my true age, to admit that the hourglass of life had turned again. Knowing that lying to those unyielding technological marvels would be futile, I bravely reset the screens from their shining "66" to the slightly less luminous "67."

Truth be told, plenty of other indicators of, shall we say euphemistically, my maturity level have visited me already. For example, for years now I have experienced a mirror problem. Repeatedly I have gazed into the looking glass and immediately wondered why I looked so tired. Now I fully recognize my true condition, and it is not fatigue. Tired goes away. What I have does not leave. In fact, aging puts down its roots and stays like an unwelcome relative. Without an invitation, the aging process takes up residence.

Other evidence of my later-life period exists. I recently retired from the practice of a profession I love and never expected to relinquish voluntarily. I surprised myself when I sold my homestead in my hometown village and moved into a condominium in the county seat. I used to joke about Old Arthur causing my little aches and pains. Lately, however, Mr. Arthritis has actually come to live in me under the name of Basal Thumb Osteoarthritis. And now, worst of all, cancer, the bane of all ages, recently flung one of its poison arrows at my beloved, so we are circling our wagons to defend against that enemy. Mother Nature and Old Man Time are conspiring against us, robbing us of our youth and vigor the way Bonnie and Clyde used to blow into town to loot the bank, without notice and without mercy.

Beyond these personal, internal indicia of attaining "over the hill" status, external evidences abound around us, too. A case in point serves to illustrate. We all know how cute young animals look. Well, I have noticed of late that all humans under 35 years of age remind me of puppies and kittens: fresh, bright, and lovable. Furthermore, Beth and I seem to be attracting new, young friends. Some occasionally come to our condo just to "hang out." [We have concluded that such is their term for a social visit with no particular boundaries or purpose. . .other than enjoying each other's company]. We'd like to think this phenomenon relates somehow to our utter irresistibility. Instead, I suspect the magnetism that brings folks to the site of a train wreck, a bridge demolition, or a building implosion deserves more of the credit. The young-uns seem fascinated that we old fogies can still function on any meaningful level.

Matters of public etiquette also present noticeable generational obstacles at this juncture. I once attempted to allow a young lady to precede me through the automatic entry doors of K-Mart. After all, in my day, we observed the now no doubt sexist habit of "ladies before gentlemen." This female would have none of it. She absolutely refused my gallant offer. Maybe she was relying upon the principle of deferring to the elderly. I'd do that too, but I'm having trouble finding souls more elderly than I who can still walk without assistance.

When dining out recently I respectfully stood when a female server initially approached our table. She reflexively assumed her Kung Fu self-defense stance, apparently believing I was preparing to attack her. At other times, I have doffed my cap in accordance with the old rule that a well-mannered man removes his hat inside a building. Other inhabitants seem to think I'm preparing to scratch my mostly bald head or swat an insect. Time passes. Habits change.

Maybe I'm just middle-aged. Bob Hope defined middle age as the age at which your age begins to show around your middle. I certainly qualify on that measure, but the only way I can truly say I am now middle-aged is if I can live to age 134. Forgive my pessimism. Maybe it is unfounded. Reference to life expectancy tables reveal that, on average, men who reach my present age may expect to live another 17 years or so. Trouble is, one can't know if he's average until he's gone.

Searching for an escape from this aging malaise, I sought Webster's definition of aging. The first definition of aging, while accurate, does not encourage: "to show the effects or the characteristics of increasing age." I prefer the second: "to acquire a desirable quality (as mellowness or ripeness) by standing undisturbed for some time." Now we're talking.

I'm not growing old. I'm just mellowing like a fine cheese. I'm just ripening like a select apple. I'll have to try that definition next time Beth approaches me for help in cleaning the condo: "Sorry, Honey, I'm sitting undisturbed while I mellow a little more. Try back in a couple of weeks."

So, I don't need more dour reminders that I've aged. I just need to remind myself that I am alive today and have the opportunities that come with that happy occurrence. Just as the Good Book discourages us by confirming that our days are numbered (Psalm 90:10), it also recommends that we should be glad on each day the Lord has made for us. (Psalm 118:24) Yes, that's the kind of reminder this old boy really needs.

May 3, 2015

Let Down Today, Lifted up Tomorrow

The sight of Pete Rose disappointed me. In the early spring of 1963, Coach Walsh had arranged for our little ragtag Kingston-Union High School baseball team to attend, with hundreds of other high schoolers, the annual instructional clinic put on by the Cincinnati Redlegs. All of us country boys, especially our first baseman, beheld in awe the scenes of that day. Gail admitted he had never been in a town bigger than Chillicothe in his 17 years. None of us had experienced big league life this close-up.

Crosley Field, the ballpark itself, was the first "star" we encountered. The hallowed ground warmed our imaginations as surely as a vision of heaven warms the heart of a true believer. Our virgin eyes had never viewed such pristine, vividly green grass anywhere, let alone on a ballfield. Ours in the alley back in Kingston sported a hardpan all-dirt infield and an outfield full of weeds. Since 1912 The Redlegs had been sailing in this creaky old ship, one of the smallest (capacity fewer than 30,000) and certainly one of the quirkiest. Yonder we spotted the odd terrace at the base of the left field wall. Babe Ruth had fallen on his face trying to negotiate that little knoll in 1935 during the twilight of his career. To my knowledge, he was not given a Breathalyzer test to determine if he was guilty of FWI (Fielding While Intoxicated). All of us baseball bumpkins were giddingly glimpsing baseball past. I didn't realize that I was about to glimpse also a big slice of baseball future.

We enthralled attendees first roosted en masse in the grandstand. Breakout sessions followed. We amateurs then gathered by playing position on the actual turf, natural turf that was, to receive instruction from a Redleg. Being a shortstop, I joined the herd of middle infielders, i.e., shortstops and second basemen. As we hustled out to second, we were all hoping that a well-known veteran would be our up-close and personal tutor: maybe Don Blasingame, who started nearly every game at second in 1962, or that slick-fielding Latin shortstop Leo Cardenas.

Instead, our dreams crashed when we met our teacher to be, a shortish, stocky, very young, not much older than our Gail, rookie with "14" on the back of his shirt. "Who is this guy?" I do not remember any of the tips he conveyed. He did not teach us to slide head-first or to sprint to first after obtaining a base on balls. And he certainly didn't reveal to us his plan to amass 4,256 hits over 24 seasons to become the all-time hits champ of the big leagues. I recall nothing but the letdown from failing to meet a genuine star.

Well, of course, the joke's on me. First impressions can mislead. Young Mr. Rose went on to become the National League rookie of the 1963 year and never looked back. He crafted a hall-of-fame career, but stumbled in his latter days, like Babe on the terrace, and has not yet entered the Promised Land at Cooperstown. I now sadly realize I should have saved the bubble gum card of that rookie who disappointed me so. Had I just known then what I have come to know now!

All this to say: present circumstances may seem disappointing, but we mustn't despair. Later, in retrospect, we may realize that blessings were being planted in what we perceived as unexciting, if not downright negative soil. Losses can teach lessons that lead to future victories. Storms can clear the skies and lead to beautiful days. Obstacles can build ability with which to avoid future hazards.

As with my minutes with Charlie Hustle, we may be disappointed in the present simply because we cannot know the future. What comes later though may just prove that our present is much better than we currently believe. Indeed, 'twas better to have been keenly disappointed at the sight of Peter Edward Rose in 1963 than to be recalling in 2015 the lukewarm memory of a Don Blasingame. One never knows how today's letdowns may become tomorrow's highlights.

V.   Politics

The old saying warns against inserting matters relating to politics or religion in polite conversation. Please pardon me. I have not entirely resisted the temptation to explore some of the political waters in our nation. While trying to avoid partisanship, I simply had to seize the low-hanging fruit provided by nine presidential election cycles to add my two cents' worth to the overflowing accounts of the wild and wacky political goings on of our era. After all, politics has become entertainment.

January 25, 1992

Puzzles: Altered Perception Sometimes Helps Solve Them

Perspective – point of view – modifies attitudes, perceptions and even abilities drastically.

Have you ever been gravely ill? Those who occupy sick beds tell us that hurdles which once loomed large in their lives dissolve when approaching the ultimate barrier – death. The patients' attitudes toward life's little everyday problems soften immediately.

Remember the sketch that appeared in our psychology texts in school? Viewed from one mind set, the lines on the page appeared to form a beautiful young girl. Seen from a different state of mind, they revealed an ugly old lady. The marks on the page did not change, only the perceptions of the viewer did.

Educators have conducted an experiment in which skill tests were administered to a group of students. Those scoring higher were told they were scoring lower and vice versa. The students' beliefs as to their abilities became self-fulfilling. Those with the poorer actual scores performed better on future tests than those who actually had tested higher. Seeing themselves in a new, albeit artificial light, the poorer students improved their perceptions and performance.

In our personal lives, we are often better able to solve a puzzle if we can back away from it somehow. While mowing the yard, the brain mysteriously engages to reveal the solution to a difficulty we have struggled with at work for three weeks. A separation from a spouse clarifies how we really do feel about that spouse. Just the right word for that poem leaps from subconscious to conscious during the middle of the night. While strolling the beach during vacation, a nasty knot in life is miraculously unraveled instantly.

Your writer's perspective has changed this week. Instead of sitting at the foot of Mt. Logan (Alt. 800 feet) with the waters of the Scioto to the west, he is languishing at the base of the Saddleback Mountain Range in Southern California (Alt. 8,000 feet) with the waves of the blue Pacific within his sight a few miles to the west. His good fortune in being able to enjoy this change in point of view allows him to put some personal items in proper perspective. It also allows him to view a larger issue with more clarity.

In a few days the New Hampshire primary election will initiate our next campaign for the choosing of one president, all of our representatives to the U. S. House, and one-third of our U. S. Senators. Does it matter?

One would think so. Problems abound. The budget is more unbalanced than Roseanne Barr and Pee Wee Herman on a teeter-totter. Violence is an epidemic, threatening to force us to return to the law of the Old West, i.e., protecting ourselves because the government is incapable of doing so.

We are beginning to gag on the waste of our own consumption. Fewer and fewer can afford our better and better health care services. Japanese captains pilot our economic ships while the only business that seems to prosper here is poverty.

Will the results in November matter? Probably not.

Our current leaders are followers. Rather than rallying the citizens to self-sacrifice, the politicians encourage more self-indulgence. They tell the media not to expect significant legislation during an election year. Those we have voted in cannot take a stand on any important issue for fear we shall not vote them in for another term of inaction.

And now, the point of this political science lesson! Is it not time that the vast majority of our national politicians, Republican and Democrat alike, be given the opportunity to change their perspective? Their attitudes, perceptions, and abilities may be improved only by a chance to see the nation's problems from our side of the Potomac.

In his inaugural address President Bush promised: in crucial things, unity – in important things, diversity – in all things, generosity.

Wouldn't it be great if, by changing the perspective of our elected officials, we could at least have in some things, sanity!

November 20, 1993

Nation's Hope Died with Kennedy

Three decades have taken me from a teenage boy, preoccupied with losing ball games and girlfriends, to a truly middle-aged man, focusing on losing my grown children, my energy, and my hair.

Three decades have taken our nation far enough to reflect somewhat objectively on the events and impact of the assassination of John F. Kennedy. Let me share one baby boomer's view.

Those who didn't experience the early 60s can understand intellectually the horror of a presidential assassination. They cannot, however, appreciate the depth of emotional despair they sense in us oldsters when we discuss those unforgettable hours in 1963.

My children have difficulty envisioning me as a teenager. After all, they never saw me in that condition. Similarly, they and their generation did not see or feel the adolescent-like vitality our country was experiencing during the early, and only, years of the Kennedy administration.

A reading of the cold historical facts does not generate much excitement. JFK did not succeed in passing much legislation. His actions in the Bay of Pigs debacle were not those of an expert. JFK probably marched our country the first few steps into what became the quicksand of the conflict in Vietnam. In retrospect, his personal life and behavior certainly do not inspire admiration or imitation.

So the young folks of today ask, "What's the big deal?" The big deal is hope: hope created, hope lost, hope yet to be restored.

When the secretary to the superintendent announced at the door of our typing class, just after lunch on Friday, Nov. 22, 1963, that the president had been shot, that part of my 16-year-old self which was still a child was suspended in mid-air. The child came crashing down irrevocably twenty minutes later when the death of a president was announced in study hall. I remember walking home from school and entering my empty home, feeling as though I had been robbed, but of what I was unsure.

I was midway through my second decade on earth. Maybe our country was a teenager in "nation-years" – a little more than midway through its second century of existence. The Revolutionary War constituted birth pangs. The Civil War represented sibling rivalry. The World Wars proved the nation had developed its muscles and could use them to good end. Upon the arrival of Kennedy's Camelot crew, the USA seemed poised to enter maturity – ready to acknowledge the civil rights of all its citizens and to work for the welfare of the whole world's inhabitants through programs such as the Peace Corps.

Then, the adrenaline drained from our nation's veins as the young President's blood drained from his. Only disease and poison seemed to remain in the body politic. More assassinations followed: Martin Luther King Jr. and brother Bobby. Vietnam was major surgery on the psyche of our citizens. Watergate symbolized the creeping illness of a nation that had not been honest with itself. The junk food diet of free drugs and free sex resulted in a severe case of domestic indigestion, to-wit: crime, illegitimacy, and general brokenness.

In healthy youth, hope reigns. The reality of life has not yet sapped the joy from the child. Until 11-22-63, our nation was young and full of hope. National hope seemed to have died with JFK. Hope! That must have been the intangible which I had felt was stolen from me that dreadful day.

In a way, our nation has languished since then. Some tangible progress has been made. We've been to the moon, perfected computers, and made giant strides in medicine. But hope and the accompanying lighter step has not yet been revived.

If we want a nation that is young again, we must restore hope to our citizens: hope that discrimination can be ended, hope that our children can have decent job opportunities, hope that the trend toward crime and violence can be reversed, hope that families can again become a viable unit of our society, and hope that the world can be made free and safe for all.

John F. Kennedy espoused these attractive ideals, ideals that excited many of us about the potential of America. Rededication of our government and ourselves to these ideals can instill hope and vigor in an America, which is too young to die.

January 17, 1996

Government Bashing is not as Much Fun as We Get Older

Maybe it's my age. I think I'm tiring of government-bashing. I've taken my turns. I've used this very column to bash and lash a few politicians.

And now I have my own personal reason to rail against the bureaucrats. I'm remodeling an old building for my future office. The process reminds me of the old song lyrics, "The knee bone's connected to the thigh bone." All I wanted to do was put up a few partitions, but I'm learning a new tune: "The job's connected to the general contractor. The general contractor's connected to the Ohio Department of Building Compliance. The Department's connected to the architect. The architect's connected to the electrical engineer. And the whole thing's connected to my pocketbook!"

No more abstract arguments needed! I have concrete (no pun intended) motivations. I should be at the top of my bureaucrat-busting form. Instead, I just cannot get interested. Have I gone soft on crime? Churchill would be ashamed of me. He said, "Do not criticize your government when out of the country. Never cease to do so when at home."

I should be on fire. The fuel is abundant. Government continues to horn into the lives of us little people. Years after the Reagan Revolution was to get the monkey of big government off our backs, we feel as powerless as Fay Wray in the fist of King Kong. In Washington, Congress and the President fiddle with the next temporary bill to fund our government while local government workers justifiably burn over the absence of paychecks. In Columbus, the city building inspector "condemned" an igloo David Nicklaus built in his own yard for his four year-old daughter. In McArthur, the shadow of the U. S. Constitution was enough to convince the locals to accede to the ACLUS's request that a cross be removed from the courthouse roof. Big Brother is here and, by the looks of those muscles, he's been working out on his Nautilus machine.

So, what's my problem? I should be sounding the alarms. Good lines should be jumping into my head . . . lines like:

1) If General Washington had needed a permit to cross the Delaware, we'd all be drinking tea each afternoon at 4 p.m., and

2) If our Constitution were interpreted earlier as it is now, a quarter would need to be the size of a medium pizza in order to have room for our motto: "in a) a higher power, or b) ourselves, or c) modified anarchy we trust."

Hypocrisy is not attractive. Maybe I've seen some in my mirror. I do not want to be one of the selfish people identified by the late Chief Justice Earl Warren. He said, "Many people consider the things which government does for them to be social progress, but they consider the things government does for others as socialism."

None of us complains about Big Brother when he defends our borders against foreign powers. We don't mind the government establishing and maintaining an interstate highway system which allows us to drive from here to the Atlantic Ocean with hardly a traffic signal to encounter. We aren't about to recommend that the bureaucrats get out of the law enforcement business. We know that as individuals we would be unable to defend our nation effectively, to establish roads over mountains, to maintain peace in our neighborhoods. We formed governments for the common good.

Too many of us have become Constitutional chameleons. Government should balance its budget, we say, but don't touch my Social Security check or my agricultural subsidy or my mortgage interest deductions. Government should protect me from criminals, but don't go protecting my child from my own ignorance in putting her under a 25,000 pound block of ice which is bound to melt. Government should keep my neighbor from putting in a junk yard, but don't slow down my project by making me comply with fire, safety, and handicapped codes. Government should protect my right to worship as I please, but don't stop me and my fellow believers from using our majority strength to force believers in other religious systems to view our symbols in "high" and official places.

Aging certainly has ways of changing things. My hair is vanishing. I can't eat cucumbers or drink caffeine without dire consequences. And now I'm losing my bent for critical thinking. I hope I don't lose it all.

A degree of skepticism, even cynicism, benefits a society. But as our American systems ages, I hope, along with that skepticism, we can develop a sense of fairness and consistency in our criticism of our own government.

October 7, 1998

Citizens are the Problem

I was hoping that it would go away. It hasn't.
I was hoping I could avoid writing about it. I can't.
I refer to our nation's troubles with our leader's troubles.

Commenting upon another's defects, especially moral defects, invites criticism of the commentator. "Holier than thou" status I desire not. "He who is without sin, let him cast the first stone."

I am a weak human, full of my own foibles, so I will attempt to avoid throwing stones. Observations, however, differ from judgments in the same way that marshmallows differ from stones. So allow me, please, just a few marshmallows.

Private has become public and political.
Politicians have exhibited human shortcomings from time's beginning. The startling thing today is for such intensely personal matters to be so unashamedly placed in the public eye.

We shouldn't be surprised.

Sex, violence, childbirth, and intestinal surgeries are now available for consumption by all who have a TV with a cable connection or a computer with Internet capacity.

A society without shame (or is it without pride?) ultimately adopts that shameless characteristic both publicly and corporately, as well as privately and individually. The adoption appears to be nearly complete in our country.

The leader is not the major problem; the citizens are.
Two-thirds of Americans just don't care about anything other than themselves. Apparently, we'd rather be governed by anybody as long as we have bread in our box than by worthy and exemplary leaders who require sacrifice and discipline from themselves and us.

Again, why be surprised? A survey cited by David F. Wells in his recent book, *Losing Our Virtue*, indicates that 74 percent of people asked said they would steal without hesitancy if given the chance to do so successfully. Seventy-five percent would lie to a friend.

What a standard! No wonder our accused leader seems genuinely surprised that his escapade and his lack of candor about it has ruffled so many feathers.

This crisis has disoriented many groups.

A few Democrats are calling for the head of their leader. Parents are forbidding their little ones from keeping up with current events through newspapers and news programs. Women and women's groups are forgiving conduct which they have uniformly condemned when performed by other men, men usually known as male, chauvinist pigs.

One year ago this past weekend, my son and I sat, stood, and knelt on the National Mall in Washington, D.C. with a million other men. Attending the Stand in the Gap event sponsored by Promise Keepers, we confessed our individual and national misdeeds and prayed to God for forgiveness, guidance, and blessing.

At the edge of our gathering, representatives of the National Organization for Women worried that we pigs were a threat to our nation and our families because of our supposed grandiose scheme to take over the government and repeal women's rights.

Now N.O.W. is ready to fight to protect our leader, who was too busy in the Oval Office to join our little group of "rebels" last October.

I'm confused that people can be so confused.

This, too, shall pass.

Thank goodness. Right now it's passing as a kidney stone does – slowly and painfully. Just think how good we'll feel when it's over.

We may even learn a few things from the ordeal. Maybe I should say we'll be firmly reminded of truths we already know.

"Your sins will find you out."

"No man is above the law."

"Actions speak louder than words."

In 1922, the French author Anatole France wrote: "Without lies humanity would perish of despair and boredom." Look at the bright side. Thanks to this long night of national turmoil, we are not near to death by boredom.

May God have mercy on our nation and on each of us. Clearly, we need it.

November 21, 2000

Taking the Higher Road

Sometimes we lose our way. Since Election Day, many feel the U. S. is wandering in the desert.

The Delongs of Green Township, Ross County, Ohio, had seen lots of clover, but no cloverleafs prior to their 1957 trip to Waukegan, Ill. Sister Ruth Ann had married a sailor stationed at Great Lakes Naval Training Base there. Dad must have had the crop safely in the barn. We loaded the old '51 Merc on a Saturday and headed for the Northwest Territory.

The road from here to Waukegan leads through Chicago. Carl Sandburg liked it better than we would. The night was late when we hit the city known as the "nation's butcher." Stockyards we would have been comfortable with. Freeways we weren't.

Somewhere at the edge of town, U. S. 33 turned into a freeway, the first we'd experienced. The Calumet Skyway invited us to hurtle over the city. We took off, but landed much too soon.

We took a little lane that terminated on the surface of mid-town Chicago late on that Saturday night. We had experienced our first exit ramp. We must have looked like the Beverly Hillbillies, or just plain old hillbillies, as we attempted to find a corresponding entrance ramp.

We were fish out of the farm pond. We were scared. Our hearts hadn't beaten so fast since the hog showing contest at the Ross County Fair.

Now, Dad and Mom, in the front seat of the Green Monster, were not normally exempt from the time-honored spousal travel banter.

"Are we lost?"

"No, I just don't know where we are."

"Well, ask for directions."

"No need – I'll just drive around awhile till I see something I recognize."

None of that this night! With the silver locks hammered down on the four doors of the tank-like Merc, with a minimum of talk, Dad and Mom quietly poked the grill around a few corners until The Way Out presented itself. With relief, but without fanfare, no horn-tooting, we reentered the "high" way and slid on through the night toward Waukegan.

On our way to the next four years, our nation has taken, unintentionally, an exit ramp. Our family has landed in unchartered territory. Nothing looks familiar. We were having such an exhilarating ride. Now, we are fish out of our constitutional pond.

Our eyes are glued to the guys up front fighting for the steering wheel. On the earlier part of the trip, we heard them nitpicking each other. The first would accuse the second of a lack of driving experience.

The second would fire back that the first had been helping drive eight years and hadn't really gone anywhere.

We kids in the backseat are hoping that those guys up front keep their heads about them and their tongues in their heads. We'd be happy for them to act like the parents rather than the kids.

Let's pray that both the drivers and the passengers on this national excursion settle down, and with eyes open and mouths shut, together find the entrance ramp to get back on the higher road to the future.

A Few Tips for Candidates from a Convention Viewer

Somehow I remember my first glimpse of a national political party convention. In the summer of 1956, as an 8-year-old boy in the back room of Uncle Harold's farmhouse, I saw on the flickering screen President Dwight Eisenhower peering out from the Republican National Convention.

I do not remember what he said (although he looked authoritative saying it). I do not remember what happened there. Only history tells me the party renominated him and he was reelected.

I have found nearly all such conventions have carried the same impact. The nation may remember who was there, but it does not remember what was said or done. Of course, the 1968 Democratic National Convention in Chicago provided the exception to the rule with its awful head-bashing and contentiousness.

The presidential campaigns formally begin on Labor Day, just following the conventions. With the nominations wrapped up by the primary voting months ago, the conventions now are just another stop on the non-stop campaign trail ending, we hope, on Election Day.

I would just like to address the contestants with a few pleas I suspect many share.

Just say you don't know.

The erudite Adlai Stevenson (or maybe it was Arthur Goldberg, lawyer-judge-U.N. ambassador) stated, "A politician is a statesman who approaches every question with an open mouth."

I really doubt even our extremely well-versed, well-advised, well-spoken candidates know the solution to every problem. I am not so insecure I need to swallow the illusion that our leaders must be omniscient. So just once along the perversely prolonged path to the polls, please, one of you, be brave enough to utter: "I have no idea how to fix that. We'll just have to work together and muddle through."

Just say you won't be able to do all you hope.

I would love to have a dollar for every time I've heard a candidate say, "If you elect (retain) me as President, I will (fill in this blank)."

Oh, come on, guys! We are electing the head of an executive branch, not a king or a dictator. You will do exactly what the 535 members of Congress, the nine justices of the Supreme Court and 293 million citizens allow you to do and nothing more.

So just once along the excessively elongated entry to the election, please, one of you, mutter, "I cannot by myself accomplish much of anything."

Just give the other guy a little respect.

I thought honor exists even among thieves. Are all the candidates so arrogant they cannot ever bring themselves to say something complimentary about their opponent? I am sure bashing is more fun, but I believe all of our candidates are good men who have the good of our country in mind and at heart.

So please, along the horrendously harsh highway to the harvest, one of you, generate the guts to say, "My worthy opponent, although differing from me on many important issues, is an honorable fellow whom, I believe, is doing his best to improve our country."

And, finally:

Just poke a little fun at yourself and your colleagues.

Why not? Everyone else in the country is.

Yes, I know, our nation is dealing with deadly serious issues. So was Winston Churchill. So was John F. Kennedy. So was Ronald Reagan. All of them seemed to be able to summon up a little good humor even in the midst of the darkness.

So, just once along this vexatiously vituperative voyage to the voting booth, please, one of you, if you can't bring yourself to prick the balloon of your personal pride, at least quote a source such as Will Rogers, who said things like, "The more you read about politics, you got to admit that each party is worse than the other."

Happy viewing!

November 2006

The Pendulum of Government Swings Again

Tick-tock . . . Tick-tock. The pendulum of Doc Lightner's massive black office clock positioned on the wall of the little waiting room of his simple G. P.'s office swung to and fro, to and fro, relentlessly marking the countdown of seconds until little Mrs. Lightner would appear at the interior door of the room and announce those dreaded words, "Dicky, it's your turn." As a lad in the 1950's awaiting the doom of receiving my smallpox vaccination or a penicillin shot, I prayed that somehow time would stand still. But time never did and never does. The pendulum always swings back.

An election cycle has just expired. Most of us are expressing our gratitude that time did not stop before that cycle's end. Being trapped in election season would be a pain of mythological proportion. The Greeks told of Sisyphus pushing a boulder up the mountain all day every day, only to awaken each morning to realize the stone had rolled back down to the bottom during the night. Suicide might be an attractive alternative to an eternity of junk mail, back-to-back TV ads, and mechanical phone calls from those so desperately seeking to serve us in government positions.

Not particularly profoundly, but accurately, John F. Kennedy in Profiles in Courage wrote, "We, the people, are the boss, and we will get the kind of political leadership, be it good or bad, that we demand and deserve." Judging by the recent national, state, and local election returns, we, the boss people, have had a change of heart. The political pendulum reached the limit of its arc on the right and has begun the inevitable swing back to the left. Citizens under a free government must come to expect this.

Look back. Hoover's inactivity yielded to FDR's active New Deal. Eisenhower followed with stability. Kennedy's New Frontier and Johnson's Great Society stirred things up again. Nixon acted up. Ford settled down. Carter confused. Reagan and Bush I reasserted conservatism. Clinton rode the political pendulum for eight years in the opposite direction. Bush II jerked it back. Tick-tock. Tick-tock. And so it goes.

Is anyone dizzy besides me? Does anyone have the feeling I had in Doc Lightner's office? Now that the rightward thrust has been reversed, I anticipate that we'll cling to the pendulum to the far side of left again. Can this pendulum be stopped?

One of the wisest persons I have known was not a president, not an educator, not a judge or lawyer, and not even a political pundit on CNN or Fox News. Fred Orr was a farmer, but a man full of wisdom. He reminded me repeatedly: "Any excess is a defect." Every time he applied that law of nature to a set of facts, he convinced me of the truth of the maxim. Too much, even of a good thing, becomes a bad thing.

Many, including your humble correspondent, yearn for a time between the extremes, a time for civil discussion, a time for mutual respect, a time for pulling together to reach a common good, a time for the elephant to lie down with the donkey. Yearn . . . yes. Expect . . . no. While brief interludes may appear during which civility and common sense prevail, partisanship and parochialism are safer bets. The pendulum swings. Time marches on.

Maybe that's not all bad. Had I been able to stop Doc Lightner's clock, I may have died of smallpox by now. If we could interrupt permanently the normal political cycle, the republic could be deprived of creative solutions to old and new threats to our nation. These swings may be a sort of inoculation against extremes.

My advice: "Chill." Whether you are exultant and expectant after your party's or candidate's victory or depressed and disgusted after defeat, remember: "This, too, shall pass." As King Solomon wrote in Ecclesiastes 3:1, "There is a time for everything, and a season for every activity under heaven." Time passes. The pendulum always swings back. Tick-tock. Tick-tock.

June 13, 2007

No Presidential Bid for this Columnist

The presidential election season comes earlier each cycle. Here I sit, on Memorial Day, 2007, with Election Day, 2008, only seventeen months away; and I have not yet decided whether to make a bid for the presidency.

Instead, on this day that we especially honor those men and women who have served militarily in the past and present, my mind wanders backward, not forward. I think of my wife's mother's only brother, Uncle Bud. He died a young man in the early 1940's from injuries he had received while fighting in WWII on the European front. Then I think of my Uncle Walter, a D-day veteran who is still with us at the age of 96 years. Bud and Walter and hundreds of thousands of others fought for the French, fought for the British, and fought for the homeland. They fought for those living here then and those of us living here now…in the glorious freedom their blood and sweat purchased.

From our distant perspective sixty-six years later, the decision to get in and stay in WWII seems to have been a no-brainer compared to the complexity of our present dilemma in Iraq. I have read enough history, however, to know that some in this country said in 1941 that we should fall back, protect our borders, and let the rest of the world protect itself against Hitler's war machine and Hirohito's forces. Had we listened, we might now be eating schnitzel and sushi exclusively.

Before forming a committee, raising campaign money, and entering the first "beauty contest" primary (probably a pre-school class poll at some prep school in Portland, Maine to be held after this summer's school picnic) I must decide what is right and required re Iraq: stay the course or stray from the course and get out?

I admit I'm having trouble deciding. Are any of you other potential candidates having the same trouble I am? I suspect so, but decide we must. Nearly all of us agree that the continually increasing death toll is continually decreasing our confidence that this course is succeeding. On the other hand, the potential courses laid out thus far by the declared candidates do not inspire much confidence either. Their suggestions remind me of the comments offered by the proverbial stubborn husband who is lost on the highway explaining to the wife and kids how he will be able to find his way back even when he doesn't have the foggiest notion of where he is. "Sure, Dad, Sure!"

My head tells me to agree with the "cut bait and run" crew. I'm the furthest thing from a military expert you can get, but common sense tells me if we pull out of Iraq before noon tomorrow, our national borders will not crumble by the end of next week (assuming, of course, they have not already crumbled). Many Iraqi citizens would be in a heap of hurt, but as to the immediate security of the good old U.S. of A., I am convinced that it wouldn't be endangered much in the short term.

My heart also tells me to agree with the "enough already" position. I ask myself, "Would I volunteer to die in this conflict?" That question isn't the appropriate one. I know that Uncle Sam would not want me even if I said yes. I'm so old I couldn't fight my way out of a one-ply garbage sack. I'd have trouble finding my way back to my bunk in the middle of the night even wearing infrared goggles. I think even my son and son-in-law are too old and unhealthy to qualify as soldiers. But the personal question as a litmus test is not entirely moot. I must ask myself this: "If this conflict were to drag on for another decade or so, would I be willing for the life of any of my four grandchildren to be sacrificed for the cause?" Now, you're getting my attention. While I grieve with the families who have lost their loved ones and while I thank these brave soldiers and all those who have fought for us before, I would really struggle to answer "yes" to that last question. I can understand why President Bush and, let's not forget, Congress inserted us into this conflict; but the advantage that hindsight now grants us makes me hesitant to pledge more American lives to wage what many believe is an unwinnable war, at least in the traditional sense of winning. The historical principles of wars between nations apparently do not apply to wars between ideologies.

Nevertheless, contrary to the messages from my head and my heart, my gut tells me to be careful, to watch out, to be extremely cautious about abandoning the struggle. I am in favor of government by rules and order. I am a believer in freedom and democracy. I do feel threatened by the self-avowed enemies of America. If I adopt the "get out" position, I have a duty to offer an alternative plan to protect the country I love and the principles I espouse. What's my alternative for assuring that order will eventually prevail in Iraq and environs? What's my plan for keeping terrorists away from our shores, from my grandkids' schools, from wife's car, and from my church's sanctuary? I don't have much of an answer. I perceive that many of you, gentle readers, and many of my fellow presidential candidates do not really have an effective answer either.

The '08 presidential candidate who can speak to conflicted minds such as mine will likely be granted the opportunity to apply her or his hand to the rudder of this ship of state.

So, after these reflections, I've made my decision. I'm not running. How about you?

November 8, 2007

Looking for a Hero this Election

These days I'm having trouble finding a hero. In the 1950's I found two: cowboy Hopalong Cassidy and Ohio State halfback Howard "Hopalong" Cassady. The first rode his white horse Topper in the movies and on television. He worked for good in the Wild West. The second wore a white helmet on his way to the Heisman. He worked for Woody in Ohio Stadium.

The lesser imitates the greater. I copied one Hoppy with my BB gun in the hayloft of our barn on Blackwater Road. I mimicked the moves of halfback Hop by sliding in the mud of our barnyard with a pigskin under my arm.

Time passes and the rocks of reality batter boyhood dreams. One day I learned that the Wild West had already been tamed. No one needed a Hopalong Dicky. Later I realized that my little public school did not have a football program. Woody wouldn't be needing Hopalong me who had never played in an actual game.

Nevertheless, we never outgrow our need for a hero. A year from now, our nation will elect its next hero or heroine, as the case may be, to lead our country. I've been looking for a Hopalong or a Hopalette to ride or run into view; but, alas, I fear none will be arriving.

My political American idol would possess character as a hallmark. Character trumps reputation. Character seeks what's right, not just what's expedient. Character, according to Mr. Webster, includes moral excellence and firmness.

My Election Day idol would strive to be noble. Just as H. Cassidy, who was known as the epitome of gallantry and fair play, this elected servant would labor primarily for the good of the whole and not for advancement of self. As H. Cassady, this one would recognize a boss, the 300 million Woody's who inhabit our nation. Nobility not by birth or notoriety, but by possessing outstanding qualities: intellect, honor, balance, openness, and selflessness – that's the public official I'm searching for, but not finding.

My elusive idol would endeavor to handle the admittedly impossible job of president with courage. The commander-in-chief of our armed forces must lead, not just send, in military ventures without regard for one's own political safety. As counselor-in-chief of our insufferably complaining and whining citizenry, a courageous president must be bold enough to insist that the nation move forward by acting as a unit and not as a loose collection of feuding factions.

Finally, a touch of humility adds an heroic air to even the most accomplished, talented, and powerful person. I do not recall either Hopalong bragging about his accomplishments or victories. Instead, each Hoppy allowed actions to speak. How refreshing! My American electoral idol would admit a little humility.

Now, I may be naïve, but I do not agree with the many who characterize the present field of presidential candidates as selfish, incompetent, know-nothing nincompoops. I believe most are actually dedicated Americans who have accomplished much and have exhibited a fair amount of the qualities I am seeking, to-wit: character, nobility, courage, and humility.

I fear the problem may not be in the stars, but in ourselves. Somehow in the past 50 years, we have authorized our stars, our entertainment, sports, and even political celebrities, to operate beyond the realm of everyday humans. We expect our entertainers to be spoiled brats and tolerate or even encourage behavior that would be unattractive in normal folks. We worship most the athletes who portray the bad boy, I'm bigger-than-the-team attitude. We promote the politician who brags best. Neither Hopalong would have gone along.

It boils down to this paradox: I want to vote for a candidate whose prime concern is not whether I will vote for him or her. I'm looking for a hero (-ine) who will not sacrifice personal character at the altar of public expectation. I'm scared not that no such hero exists, but that in our quest for celebrity, we will not permit any who do exist to be elected our supreme leader. Hoppy, Hoppy, come back!

July 6, 2008

Lighten Up Already

Darkness approaches. Wars, earthquakes, hurricanes, tsunamis, crime, violence, hatred, disease, pestilence, food shortages, and energy shortages abound. Enemies to the left of us. Enemies to the right of us. Can America as we know it survive? Can the world survive?

Let's go back a half century. Maybe we can find some light there. June, 1958. I'm a 10-year-old boy on the little farm outside Kingston that my dad rented from Doc Yaple. I lived in the glorious light.

School was out. Little League baseball was in, but without the pressure today's sports regimens force upon youthful participants. We didn't travel farther than the next township. We didn't have uniforms, but we did have fun.

Not all the games were organized either. The imaginary World Series was held in my own yard that summer. The Reds beat the Yankees in seven games on a grand slam homer with two out in the bottom of the ninth. I played the roles of all the players for both teams. Quite a spectacular series as I recall!

I rode lazily atop many a load of hay, five high and tie, and even up high on the old Allis-Chalmers wheat combine as Dad pulled it on S. R. 159 from one field to another. No driver blared on the horn in anger, only in salutation. I had the luxury of time to skip along our tributary of Blackwater Creek following the stick boats I had thrown in, time to tramp through the woods up behind Doc's cabin wondering what Indian or pioneer may have tread there before, and time to finish the day with Dad, maybe watching wrestling on channel 4, WLW-C, one of the three channels we received our little Philco, while downing a pint of Borden butter brickle ice cream straight from the rectangular cardboard carton.

The world was bright or, should I say, my world was bright. My youthful innocence coupled with my parents' care kept the shadows from reaching me. My folks didn't tell me how difficult it was to keep above water economically for our little family with no advantages. Yes, prices were low, but incomes were drastically less, too. I didn't recognize living with no indoor bathroom signaled near-poverty status. We had a washhouse and a Wheeling tub. We had a path and an outhouse. We didn't have health insurance, but we had Dr. Lightner a mile away. We didn't have a new car, but we had cheap gas for the old one. We didn't have investments, but we never missed our daily bread. Until I had more, I didn't realize I had had less.

I knew the Reds of the sports pages, but thankfully I didn't know the Reds (Communists) referred to in the headlines of the front pages. I didn't know that the Soviets had beaten us into space with their Sputnik and possessed a nuclear capability to put an immediate halt to my idyllic childhood.

Today darkness seems to have swallowed the light. Whether the foreboding news from the far corners of the globe or the sickening news of the bizarre behavior from the house down on the next corner, things look bleak. But, really, have the basics changed? As is often said, "The more things change, the more they stay the same." I suspect that the things that make the world go around keep hanging around, just in different forms. Robert Frost wrote, "Most of the change we think we see in life is due to truths being in and out of favor." Our view of issues changes, but the central issues of life in this world don't change much.

We baby boomers may have changed. We've lost much of our boom. Our famous "can do" attitude has faded with the arrival of our "can't do" bodies and brains. But these changes are not unique. They simply duplicate what all generations have endured or someday will.

The world's not stuck in 1958 or even in 2008. Time marches on. Crises come; crises go. Leaders come; leaders go. Much as some of us doubt it, our nation will find appropriate leaders to guide us through the current variety of crises: terrorism, immigration, energylessness, moral bankruptcy, and the rest.

Today, Democrats feel a McCain victory in November would signal "a third Bush term," bankrupting the county and resulting in a total loss of international respect for the USA. Republicans fear an Obama victory would amount to casting out into deep, uncharted waters that likely will result in the shipwreck of America and the sinking of our national fortunes. Deflating as it is to the egos of the partisans on both sides of the aisle, the fears of both are overstated if not just plain wrong. Our government, i.e., our people, survived to thrive after Republican Herbert Hoover's Great Depression, Democrat Carter's Great Malaise, and the missteps of all the rest of our well-meaning, but very human leaders. Likewise, we will survive the effects, intended or unintended, of the McCain years or the Obama years.

And, if the good Lord tarries, fifty years down the road in 2058, I'll guess that my now 11-year-old grandson Adam will be writing about how bright and great things were back in 2008.

Lighten up. Enjoy the sunshine.

August 8, 2009

Government Oversteps its Bounds

Last fall I was walking down the main business block (O. K. ... the only business block) of our little village on a crisp Saturday morning. I had cradled my basketball under my arm and was heading for Boggs Chevrolet to beg a little air to inflate my seldom-used sphere to bouncing standards. The grandsons were to arrive soon. I wanted to be ready.

The realization struck me that I could have been repeating a scene from nearly fifty years ago: same kid, same block, same Boggs Chevrolet, same purpose, . . . not the same hair though. Some things never change. Some do.

Well, something else has changed since that day last fall. It was the same old General Motors then; it's not your father's GM now. It appears that that GM will probably become the invisible GM in our little town in the near future. The old jingle of the old GM was nice: "See the USA in your Chevrolet." In our town, now it may become: "Good bye Chevrolet in the USA." The Chevy that used to be a good buy is fast heading for a good-bye.

Lest you think this is some kind of rant against the current administration and the current congress, let me state that I'm an equal opportunity grumbler and a realistic one at that. I understand that hard times sometimes dictate harsh actions. Much as I revere our personal freedoms, I begrudgingly submitted to President Bush's insistence that some had to be sacrificed (hopefully only temporarily) in order to forestall terrorism. Much as I respect and participate in our great capitalist economic system, I reluctantly stand aside as President Bush, President Obama, and their respective administrations and corresponding congresses have suspended the normal process of winning and losing in a free market in order to forestall a total collapse of the system.

I repeat the adverbs: begrudgingly and reluctantly. I understand the dangers of inaction in the face of threats to our national security. I don't claim enough information or expertise, however, to evaluate whether these cures are worse than the diseases. I do know that I do not want the personal and economic freedoms taken from me and my fellow citizens permanently.

Any excess is a defect. Correction brings pain. Excessive greed-personal, corporate, and national- has brought us down a notch. But let's not kid ourselves. Greed will be back. Human nature does not change. The Bible says the poor will always be with us. So, conversely, some less than poor will always be with us, too. Greed may be on vacation, but it hasn't died. It will come home again.

That's why I do not believe the government will be able to regulate greed. Oh, yes, the government does have an obligation to monitor the economic players to be sure the system can work without downright manipulation. But generally I'd rather have the shareholders acting through their CEO's making the decisions, not the government. None can resist the government.

Last year the USA pressured Bank of America to buy Merrill Lynch. Bank of America stock plunged. An irate shareholder was quoted as follows in her remarks aimed at Ken Lewis, CEO of Bank of America: "I find it incredible you didn't have the guts to stand up to the U.S. government."

Get real, lady. It's not a question of guts; it's a question of power. The U. S. government trumps any corporation, including GM, if we the people allow it.

I change, GM changes, the country changes, the world changes, but one thing won't change. People yearn for freedom. Note the current struggles in China and even in Iran. Protection is good and sometimes necessary, but freedom is better. I'm willing temporarily to sacrifice some convenience in order permanently to secure my personal freedoms. I am not willing permanently to sacrifice my freedoms for some temporary convenience.

In basketball parlance, "taking the air out of the ball" means a team in the lead stalls in order to protect that lead. I fear that our country has gone into a stall by taking the air out of the capitalistic ball at precisely the wrong moment. We weren't winning. Why stall when we're behind? Re-inflating the ball of capitalism will get us back in the game more surely, if not more quickly, than allowing Uncle Sam to rewrite the rules of the game.

July 11, 2010

Maybe Advice to Fix the Oil Spill will come from the Unexpected

"Hairdressers rule!" That's been my battle cry lately when faced with insoluble issues. Troubles plague this old world and all of us in it. When the physician runs out of pills, when the attorney runs out of advice (not likely!), when friends and family fall silent, and when Oprah no longer opines, who can help? You guessed it: your brotherly barber . . . your babbling beautician . . . your confessor cosmetologist . . . your humble hairdresser.

I've never had a handyman, a psychiatrist, or a personal trainer on retainer; but I did have Bob, my faithful barber. He included in the price of a plain old haircut plain old words of wisdom. Bob shared his list of building do's and don't's before I (i.e., my contractor) began building my house. He reminded me not to get so hung up on eating healthy that I forgot to eat happy. He always added perspective to my attitude with a pithy platitude when the pressures of my profession threatened to capsize me. "You pay your money; you take your chances." "You can't fight wind, water, and ignorance." Gems like that can cover a multitude of dilemmas.

Bob's retired now. I've moved on to Vicki. While I sometimes feel like Samson going under Delilah's clippers, I have found that female hairdressers have the same knack for cutting through not just hair, but also the haze in getting to the root of a situation. From gallbladders to grocery stores, from bargains to brownies, Vick's the go-to gal. She's got the answer or can get it.

Bob, Vicki, and, I'm convinced, all the hair doers in the world dispense more common sense every week than all the politicians, philosophers, and professionals in the universe in a decade. Not to say that these hair pros surpass others in raw intelligence. They just beat all the others in distributing insight, discernment, and judgment. They provide useful, practical information and advice.

I have often posited aloud: "Someday we may all wake up, look at each other, and find that nobody can fix anything anymore." The world may grind to a halt because everyone finally reaches my personal level of "practical incompetence." Although raised as a farm boy, apprenticed as a plumber's helper, and contained three summers in a paper mill, I have now over the long years climbed the educational and professional ladder to the point of near total inability to do anything of true practical value, i.e., fix anything that's broken. I can carry my whole tool set in my hip pocket. The neighbor kid with his Mattel tools could probably fix my tractor more proficiently than I. I know my grandkids, maybe even the 3-year old, could get my wayward computer on track faster than I. Intelligence and education, of which I have an average and an above average amount respectively, do not automatically result in fixing anything.

So, here's what I'm wondering (only partly tongue-in-cheek). The solution to the tragic Gulf oil rupture has eluded all experts to date. Presidents, prime ministers, and CEO's all have their proper places. We need led and inspired. The trouble: talk doesn't stop a leak. We need some plain old common sense applied to stop the leak, clean up the damage, and put in place protections to prevent future disasters. Could it be that the most effective way to find the wisdom to conclude this fiasco is to convene a group of barbers and beauty operators to give haircuts to our president, BP's top executives, Admiral Thad Allen of the Coast Guard (His shouldn't take long.), and the FEMA administrator. After listening patiently to all the troubles expressed and the failures confessed, I'm confident that the tonsorialists will point the way to success.

Please don't mistake my whimsical suggestion as an indication of any callousness to the very sobering, deep catastrophe and its awful effects. I would not want my home, my office, or my kid's dog coated with petroleum. I am only suggesting that we may be aiming too high if we expect the intelligentsia to solve this problem from the top down. I'd sooner think that the best prescription for the illness will bubble from the bottom up. Just as common haircutters often have the experience to analyze complex circumstances and offer simple yet helpful advice, the common folk of the sea and land should be consulted with respect to The Spill.

Proverbs 15:23 states: ". . . {h}ow good is a timely word." As is often the case, the good and timely word regarding The Spill may come from unexpected voices, the voices of experience. After all, as you now know, "Hairdressers rule!"

February 19, 2012

Things Seemed Simpler in 1956

I'm really only seventeen years old . . . if you calculate my age in leap years. Born in 1947, I cannot remember the leap years '48 or '52, but I have some memories of '56, when I was three leap years old.

Of course as a little leaguer I remember the highlight of 1956: Yankee hurler Don Larsen's perfect World Series game of October 8, 1956. I remember, too, carefree, sun-filled days on our rented farm. As an 8-year old I was too young to be expected to perform heavy farm duties. Aside from morning and evening chores, I set my own schedule: cowboys and Indians in the haymow, baseball solitaire in the barnyard (I could spend a full afternoon performing a 9-inning fantasy World Series game between the Reds and Yankees. I pitched, I batted, I fielded. And, of course, my Reds always won; treks through the woods alone; and excursions by the tributary of Blackwater Creek which ran through our farm. Or I could just sit atop Fox Hill, surveying the farm below, the Kingston water tower a mile to the east, and, in my imagination, the world beyond.

Never having heard of cholesterol, obesity, or body image, I ate, maybe for the last time, without thought and without guilt: sweet corn slathered with real butter and smothered in salt; all the Borden's ice cream I could contain right out of the rectangular cardboard container; and Carroll's potato chips, preferably a full 16 ounce bag (69 cents) at a sitting.

Oh, life was good and life was simple. The world did encroach a little that summer. Americans elect presidents in leap years. Again, I was too young to be expected to consume much of the political fodder offered up in leap years, but my earliest memory pertaining to leap year politics popped up amidst my other memories of that idyllic leap year summer.

TV, still a toddler technology, wasn't so pervasive as now. Even owning a TV set was not a given. Having one connected to an antenna on the roof properly positioned to allow reception of all three channels transmitted from Columbus, 4, 6, and 10, was a near miracle. My Uncle Harold, a swine farmer on the Famulener farm a couple miles east of Kingston, had his primitive Philco set with its massive 12 inch or 15 inch screen situated in his "back room," sort of a lean-to attached to the kitchen.

From that hazy screen one day that lazy summer I remember President Dwight David Eisenhower, the Republican nominee for November reelection, speaking to me from the lectern at the Republican National Convention. Of course, I had no idea or interest in what General Eisenhower may have been saying, but I remember being impressed. If the military savior and now the political leader of the free world had something to say and it was being broadcast to my Uncle Harold's back room, the message must have been momentous. I don't now remember the message, but I do remember the moment.

All this to say: I'm not sure we're making progress. I'm not sure I want to endure another leap year full of campaign shenanigans. I'm not sure I can take the political pounding I've already been and will be receiving from the presidential aspirants and the professional pundits for the remainder of this leap year. If I could jump over this leap year, I would be tempted to do it.

Things seemed simpler in 1956 - - in politics as well as down on the farm. Eisenhower seemed more of a statesman than I see on today's menu of day-to-day candidates of either party. (Of course, "I like Ike" fit on a lapel button better than "I'm adoring Santorum" or "I adulate Obama.") The thought of the coming onslaught of network and cable news overkill makes me yearn for Uncle Harold's old antenna system. Contemplating the thousands of articles and editorials with which my four daily newspapers will bombard me in the coming year forces me to consider asking if I can subscribe to just the sports, food, and comics sections. And then there's the Internet! Oh, my! Maybe the recent Wikipedia one-day strike could be extended web-wide for this whole year.

What could be a worse prospect? Well, coming back to the real, grown-up world of my seventeenth leap year, I will tell you. British statesman Winston Churchill, Ike's contemporary, once declared that democracy is the worst form of government . . . except all the others. What could be worse than our leap year election process fiasco we're all now enduring?

My three word answer: "Not having one." I reserve the right to think and speak cynically of our system; but I would dare not trade this leap year lunacy for the severe hopelessness experienced by those millions living under the convenient orderliness of dictatorship.

Eisenhower himself once said: "An intellectual is a man who takes more words than necessary to tell more than he knows." I guess I'd better shut up and just leave you with:

"Happy Leap Year!"

August 19, 2012

Well, Whad'ya Know!

The 2012 presidential campaign zoomed through my village of Kingston tonight. I guess the preferred route between the second capital of Ohio (Zanesville) and the first and third capital of Ohio (Chillicothe) proceeds not always through the fourth and current capital (Columbus) after all. Instead, it runs right down Zane's Trace from the National Road to the capital city of the old Northwest Territory.

Important folks have come through our town before. Zane's Trace constituted a sort of outer belt of the frontier days. Actually, inner belt may describe it better. In order to travel from the southern interior wilderness of the country to the new national capital city on the Potomac, travelers negotiated Mr. Zane's pike diagonally from Maysville, Kentucky to Zanesville and from there eastwardly on the National Road to the swamp known as Washington, D.C.

Senator Henry Clay of Kentucky, the Great Compromiser, voted one of the five greatest United States Senators in history, passed through more than once. He probably tipped a little Kentucky whiskey here. General Santa Anna, President of Mexico, also made his way through. I doubt he found a taco though. These and other luminaries of the mid-1800's no doubt stopped by Thomas Ing's tavern on their ways to somewhere. They came not because they wanted to be here, but because they had to go through here to get where they wanted to be.

Tonight, as I stood on the stoop of the building(circa 1835) at 1 N. Main Street in which I daily ply my practice, I watched the Romney bus, its accompanying entourage, and the dozen or so Ohio State Highway Patrol motorcycles and cruisers fly by, strobes flashing wildly. My mind flashed back to the times when Mr. Clay and Senor Santa Anna would have passed by this very general store structure in stagecoaches on a dirty, dusty trail. The smell of diesel fumes had replaced the odor of horse manure. I thought of how much our country had changed in those decades, but also about how it has endured. And I concluded, in some miraculous way, we country mice must still matter in some measure to the process and to those political processors who are pulling the government levers.

Chillicothe has received many powerful personalities over the many decades. We know from our wonderful local outdoor drama presentation that Tecumseh regularly visited Chalagawtha. In 1960, I know presidential candidate Lyndon Johnson stumped on behalf of John F. Kennedy on the courthouse steps because I played trumpet in our little Kingston-Union High School band on the occasion. And we know actual presidents have frequented the first capital often lately. I refer to Presidents Clinton, Bush, and Obama.

My point is this. We do have a wonderful system of government. We tend to become cynical and join in the chorus of those who sing the tune that our government and all who work in it are corrupt, power-hungry, and uncaring about the little guys and gals. In reality, let's give some credit where credit is due. Even though the millions of voters are concentrated in population centers elsewhere, to-wit: New York, Chicago, Los Angeles, Miami, and other metropolises, the electoral system encourages, nay, forces those who want to govern us all to pay some attention even to remote portions of Appalachia such as our fair territory.

Yes, the bus came through and stopped a moment for us. Just as in olden times, these political passengers have come not because they desired to be here with us, but because they knew they mightn't be able to get where they wanted to go, the swamp in Washington, without coming through here. The route to the White House runs by our little courthouse.

Whad'ya know!

February 12, 2016

"Establishment" Not as Bad as it Seems

Have you heard the latest curse word making the rounds? The word appeared regularly in the cataclysmic, countercultural, revolutionary 1960s, but its modern popularity threatens to exceed its initial fame and favor. In my adulthood, I fairly successfully have avoided the personal use of profanity. I have plenty of other weaknesses to make up for that small virtue. Please know, then, gentle reader, that my inclusion of the vile word that the seed of this column is strictly for educational purposes. Let's hope the editor of this family newspaper even will allow such an indecent set of letters to be published. Anyway, here goes. The newest dirty word in our culture (I just know you'll be blushing): "ESTABLISHMENT."

As we have observed in the current silly season of seemingly endless series of presidential candidates' debates, both Democratic and Republican, the surest and surliest insult one hopeful can unleash toward an opponent is the assertion: "You are an Establishment candidate." The recipient of such a verbal missile visibly wilts from the withering blow. One may as well shout that the scummy opponent is a leper, a prostitute, a pimp, a carrier of bubonic plague, or...or...or...maybe a Michigan fan. The wounded debater can usually manage only a weak retort such as, "Well, you were too before you weren't," or, "So is your mama," or, if responding to Governor Jeb, "So were you father and brother."

Please do not accuse your humble correspondent of attempting to feed his political orientation down your esophagus. Gee, I myself am continually disoriented politically. I merely want timidly to theorize that the allegation that a person is part of the Establishment need not, nay, should not, be a belittling comment.

The dictionary (if you young people don't know what that is, look it up on Wikipedia), informs that establishment means "a settled arrangement, a permanent organization, or an order of society." Call me a Neanderthal if you want, but I wonder what's so bad about any culture which rests upon a foundation laid over a period of generations by a consensus of reasonable adult citizens of our republic.

An establishment establishes, i.e., brings into being, sets up things, puts a firm basis. Our established government, working with an even through our established capitalistic businesses, has laid down our roads and bridges, has built our sewers and sanitary systems, and has developed and supported our police forces and fire stations These necessities sound suspiciously like achievements that people in the Establishment would applaud.

And aren't you glad…when you drive to work, when your toilet works, and when you sleep safe and sound in your home? Had these basics not been established, every highway would be a toll road, every stream a cesspool, and every public safety officer instead a private servant hired only by those who could afford the luxury of protection. The Establishment exists to further the common good. Enduring institutions properly situated and maintained serve to stabilize our society.

Now don't get me wrong. I recognize that too often the actual practice of the Establishment serving the common good is the exception rather than the rule. The Establishment regularly needs tweaked and occasionally overhauled. Government certainly governs imperfectly. As 20th Century humorist Will Rogers put it, "I don't make jokes—I just watch the government and report the facts." When established government becomes a joke, it needs a good cleaning. The baby should not, however, be thrown out with the bath water.

The truly profane epithet should be the opposite of "establishment lover." A more pertinent and pungent pejorative would be that long word which perennially challenges spelling contest participants: "disestablishmentarian," that is, one who opposes an established order. Those who hope to abolish the Establishment by condemning anyone who has been associated with it are revolutionaries, at best, and anarchists, at worst. Revolutions are sometimes necessary, even sometimes glorious, but only rarely successful in effecting basic, permanent change. Anarchy, a culture without a government, without an established order, is never safe or productive for the general populace, for the common good. Neither revolution nor anarchy appears yet on the nation's radar screen. A real irony does exist, however, bringing a somehow satisfying smile. Even if one of the disestablishmentarians is elected, he or she will awaken on January 21, 2017 as the supreme leader of, guess what, the Establishment.

"Throw the bums out" once in a while? Sure! Dismantle all of what the "bums," the voters' elected representatives, have been constructing and establishing since 1776? Not on your life! That would be a curse on our house and on all of our houses.

August 7, 2016

Either Way, the World - Our World - Will Go On

Decisions, decisions! Indecision hurts. Fence straddling takes energy. Can we get a decision here and move forward?

It's 1956. I'm nine years old. I'm standing in front of the glass-front candy counter of Jum Buchwalter's little, dark independent grocery store in the village of Kingston with a nickel burning a hole in the pocket of my J. C. Penney dungarees, husky style. The old reliable, scrumptious Snickers beckons. My five cents will cover it. On the other taste bud, I can opt for the $0.03 Klein bar, with its admittedly inferior chocolate, but have two pennies left to snatch both a jawbreaker and a hunk of Dubble Bubble. Quality or quantity? The eternal struggle! The conundrum of the ages!

Everyone struggles making decisions. Of course, Yogi Berra sought to simplify life with his advice: "When you come to a fork in the road, take it." Robert Frost wrote more realistically of the angst experienced when wondering if one has chosen the better path: "I took the one less traveled by, And that has made all the difference." Life is full of decisions presenting more serious matters with heavier consequences than a nickel treat. Keep my current, yet common job, or take the offer of a higher-flying one with a riskier future? Buy that plain house now or continue renting and save for the dream house later? Stay single or marry? Operate or medicate? Mature folks try to gather all the evidence, carefully consider it, and make a reasonable, responsible choice. Sometimes, however, the prudent way forward remains murky.

After months of preliminary blather, U.S. voters finally squarely face the quadrennial quandary, the general election. The primary election season exhibited a game-like atmosphere. Eventual nominee Trump played whack-a-mole with his Republican challengers. Ultimate nominee Clinton fought down Bernie in a kind of a king-of, whoops...queen-of-the-hill battle. Now, as the championship game begins, I rather envy those who vote a straight party ticket every election. They escape the magnified agony of indecision now being experienced by the vast ocean of "undecideds."

A choice between two pretty good things, e.g., my showdown at the Buchwalter candy counter, does not much disturb one's equilibrium. Either way, sweetness awaits. Unfortunately, many feel that the names now being printed on the November ballots will require choosing between two not-so-good options. Either way, bitterness awaits. That prospect has thrown these people and this nation off-kilter. Some might agree with a statement by the famous trial attorney Clarence Darrow: "When I was a boy, I was told that anybody could become President; I'm beginning to believe it."

Well, if you are among Great Unwashed, impaled on this fence of political indecision, don't look to this humble correspondent to rescue you. If asked, I shall not tell you how to vote. You are on your own.

I do offer you a little salve for your wound. Without minimizing the outsized problems and disasters our country and the whole world face, to-wit: terrorism, poverty, intolerance in all directions, among many others, I encourage the addition of at least a dash of optimism.

A trusted friend of mine recently reminded me that our government, with its wonderful three coequal branches of government, has endured 240 years, during some of which unreliable or even eccentric captains have been at the helm of the executive ship of state. The ship never sank. Additionally, I have recently recalled the words of my late, wise father-in law, uttered often in tender times: "This too shall pass." Finally and best, I rest in the promises of the Good Book, specifically the one in Lamentations 3:22-23: "Because of the Lord's great love, we are not consumed, for his compassions never fail. They are new every morning; great is your faithfulness."

We can't be sure how we shall feel when we awaken to the election results on the morning of November 9, 2016, but have a little faith. No matter the results, our government is not likely to collapse. Time will march onward. God will show mercy. You might even want to celebrate with a Snickers.

November 6, 2016

Those We Love Have the Most Impact

There on the portico of the Ross County Courthouse on September 29, 1960 stood U. S. Senator Lyndon Baines Johnson from Texas, the Democratic candidate for Vice President of the United States of America. There at the base of the concrete steps leading up to LBJ's proposed vice-bully pulpit sat I, a barely 13-year-old eighth grader from Kingston Junior High School. The senator was tooting his horn vigorously for the election of John Fitzgerald Kennedy, his party's presidential nominee. I was tooting my trumpet dutifully in our ragtag school band, just grateful for a few hours of escape from the prison of a school building.

History was passing before me, but I couldn't see past the music on my stand. At that point this country boy probably couldn't have distinguished Lyndon Johnson from Howard Johnson. At that time of my young life, I know very well I would have ingested one of famous restaurateur Howard's famous 28 flavors of ice cream more thoroughly than I did Lyndon's bloviations. (NOTE: Ohio's Warren G. Harding, who should have known, described "bloviation" as the art of speaking for as long as the occasion warrants, and saying nothing"). Of course, neither I nor any of the adult public gathered in our public square could have foreseen the wild, wooly decade which was to come and in which our bloviator would have a central role. JFK elected, then assassinated. LBJ succeeding to the presidency, being elected outright, initiating "The Great Society," and then declining to run for reelection as a consequence of the tragic involvement in Viet Nam.

The event over, the masses withdrawn, and the banners banished to the closet, LBJ boarded his wagon to continue his perpetual political pilgrimage to the larger world beyond our little First Capital. Our tooting having terminated, my mates and I piled back onto our little yellow bus, crawled the 10 miles back to Kingston, and resumed our inconsequential lives of farm chores and ball practice, of pinball and television.

Our nation now concludes the 14th quadrennial election cycle since that fateful 1960 campaign 56 years ago. What a ride this one has been! Whether we applaud or loathe the outcome, the candidates, both winner and losers, are getting back on their planes and heading down the runways to negotiate as best they can the unknown landscape our nation and our world will be encountering over the coming four years. And we citizens, sometimes not able to see beyond the end of our bank statements, will return to our quiet lives of desperation (See Henry David Thoreau), just trying to keep our heads above water.

I should have been more impressed with LBJ that day long ago. I didn't have enough sense or presence of mind to realize that I might have been in the presence of a prominent leader of the world. 10 or 20 years later, I would have paid more attention. Paradoxically, however, now at this juncture of my life, knocking on the door of 3 score and 10 years, I have come full circle. I have not lived life at a high social station. After all, I plied my profession in the same village where I learned to play the trumpet. I have never again come so close to one who would become POTUS. I have, however, had the chance to observe up close and interact a little with a few folks who sat in the chairs of authority in the fields of law, politics, and business, people who had achieved great worldly success and riches. Putting it as mildly, as politely, and as humbly as I can, let me just say that many famous folks, standing proudly at their marble monuments, have feet of clay, maybe even heads of clay.

I do not wish to depress you, my gentle reader. I admire those willing to lead, even though I do not always admire each leader's ability, attitude, or even motivations. Instead, I want to remind you that even those playing 2nd trumpet in the band, supporting the woman or man speaking up on the porch, count more toward the character and progress of a culture than do the few "porch dwelling" leaders.

As we citizens return to the routine chores and joys of our daily lives as Americans, whether delighted or dismayed by the 2016 election results, may we take heart in knowing that the manner in which we and our families and our neighbors play the instruments of our everyday lives may have greater impact on the world than the noisy words and actions of those who will soon climb the steps of that little white house on Pennsylvania Avenue, aka The People's House.

Don't Shoot Your Cousin

I shot my cousin. Well, I did, but let me explain. As a farm boy growing up brotherless in the mid-1950s, having company always excited me. Cousin Tim, my contemporary, appeared one day from his farm across the river. I grabbed my prized Daisy Red Ryder BB gun. (Yes, think Ralphie in the later-to-be-released classic movie). We set off across the fields on our adventure.

The pioneers of 1798 had scared off or eradicated all the bears and mountain lions of Green Township's frontier days, so all we could scare up was a bunny here and a birdie or two there. We probably stopped to plop a few rocks into Blackwater Creek. We may have pitched a couple of crusty cow patties at each other. Just good, clean fun. Possessing no electronic devices, we may have even spoken to each other during our safari.

As the expedition progressed, I noticed a weakness in my arsenal. With my naked eye, I observed the BB's emanating from the barrel of my trusty Red Ryder traveling just a few feet and falling harmlessly to the ground. Knowing I was not packing a cannon and although not especially familiar with the standards of firearm performance, even I recognized that I had become impotent.

Here's where human frailty and equipment malfunction intersect. Tim tramped a few feet ahead of me. I suppose I had seen too many cowboy shows on our little black-and-white Philco. The good guy always got to shoot the bad guy, but he was in the wrong place at my right time. Without malice aforethought, but only because I could, I pulled the trigger and plugged Tim in his backside.

I may have overestimated the level of my weapon's disability. Tim seemed to appreciate receiving less than I enjoyed sending. Even my own mother didn't seem to beam with parental pride when Tim reported our Roy Rogers moment. Can you imagine the Lone Ranger's mommy scolding him for a good day's work?

Tim forgave me when the stinging subsided. After all, Tim's no stranger to mischievousness. Mom's discipline must have scared me straight. I don't remember shooting anybody since.

This story contains a moral: "Don't pull the trigger just because you can." You may possess more firepower than you think. Regardless of your lack of harmful intent and your view that your act won't harm your target much, both you and your shootee may be bruised.

Our nation has more than seven months to tramp along the campaign trail until the November election. We expect that the actual combative electoral candidates and their staffs will be lobbing verbal boulders and slinging proverbial bull manure. Just as surely each of us at some point will be walking along or sitting with a sibling, a cousin, a co-worker, or genuine friend, or a mere acquaintance when we realize we have the perfect opportunity to fire a political projectile into the flesh of that unsuspecting fool who is ignorant enough to disagree with our perfect world view. Stop and recall Will Rogers' wisdom: "Never miss a good chance to shut up."

Please don't misunderstand. I do not propose that you take no active interest in the election. A well-informed citizenry serves as the bedrock of our republic. Stop, look, and listen to the candidates' ideas. Separate the wheat from the chaff. Be prepared to give a well-reasoned argument when asked for your opinion. After all, I like a debate...whoops, a discussion, as well as the next lawyer. I support free speech, even dumb free speech. Too often, however, our attitude matches the words of a character in an old James Whistler novel: "I am not arguing with you--I'm telling you!"

My advice: "Hold your fire!" Your zinger may carry more punch than you expected. You're not likely to change your target's opinion of anyone but you. I wanted to emulate Hopalong Cassidy. You may wish to imitate Rachel Maddow or Sean Hannity. We'd all lose fewer friends following St. Paul's counsel to his protégé, Timothy: "Refuse to get involved in inane discussions; they always end up in fights." 2 Tim. 2:23 (The Message)

Don't shoot your cousin!

VI.   Amusement

Readers enjoy a little humor to help them get through a column, but I learned early in my efforts that the writer must use attempts at levity judiciously and sparingly. Think of cooking with spices. The right one in the proper dish in the appropriate quantity adds pleasantly to the dining experience. Too much, however, and the dish is ruined. I was proud of my first wholly satirical column until I began receiving responses like, "Richard, I usually enjoy your writing and generally agree with your ideas, but I was greatly surprised that you think we should build condominiums on the face of Mount Logan and convert Adena Memorial into a an amusement park." If a writer must explain his joke, the joke's on the writer. Here are a few columns, which I hope brought or will bring a knowing smile or chuckle.

March 5, 1988

Progress: Modest Suggestions for Growth Would Lift City

A melancholy sight it is to observe that Chillicothe has not become a metropolitan area.

Chillicothe, 185 years ago, was the leading municipality of this area – capital city of Ohio, a commercial and industrial center, a hub.

On the brink of becoming the next New York or Boston or Philadelphia, Chillicothe failed to progress. Why? Maybe it was our inaccessibility to the political power centers of the East, or maybe our lack of easily navigable waterways or maybe our sparse agrarian population.

More likely, the character of our people prevented the world from thinking of us as cosmopolitans. Chillicothe had become a stable place. The transient was out; the permanent was in. Citizens knew their neighbors and cared about them. Values held were solid ones: hard work pays; family counts; God exists. This may sound admirable to utopians of the 1980s, but these were not the virtues upon which a great city could be built.

Much has occurred recently to erase the memory of those stagnant days. Chillicothe is again on the move toward urban living. As least 33 restaurants now exist on the strip of Bridge Street between Main Street and Hopetown. That same stretch has a dozen or so traffic signals. Traversing the strip can be a good way to spend the afternoon – the whole afternoon.

Chillicothe has no enclosed shopping mall, but does have its share of chain stores. Law enforcement officials recently reported that the crime rate for 1987 was up substantially. The Ohio EPA is threatening to close the city dump. Congestion, traffic, uniformity, crime, garbage – we are nearing our urban potential.

I now humbly propose a couple of my own ideas, which I hope will not be objectionable, on how to move into the 21st Century as a modern, urban area with all the advantages of the big city. My ideas concern two or our greatest community landmarks: Mount Logan and Adena. Of course, both landmarks are now owned by Ohio; but annexation will be assured when the state realizes the extra taxes, which will be generated by making these properties productive.

First, I propose that an ultra-modern village within a city be laid out on the face of Mount Logan. The development would include homes, apartments, condominiums and trendy shops. I strongly believe that heavy industry should be excluded from the project so as not to desecrate the beautiful mountain.

After its annexation to the city, the hill would need to be clear-cut of all timber. Some of the lumber derived could, however, be used to construct the supports for the various billboards advertising the new development on U. S. Route 23, 35 and 50. Of course, no billboards would be allowed in the development itself.

The roads and cul de sacs would be laid out. Street names would then be assigned. To honor the heritage of our Indian predecessors, I suggest names such as Tenskwatawa Trail, Blue Jacket Blvd., and Wasegoboah Way.

Proceeds from the sale of these lands could be used to install utility services to the development. The garbage disposal problem might be solved by a device recently tried by our urban cousin, New York City. A large barge could be stationed on the Scioto River at the base of Mount Logan Village.

The garbage of the area could be fed through a series of chutes emanating from the mountain. The full barge could be cut loose to drift down the Scioto, Ohio or Mississippi until a taker is found. After all, one city's garbage is another city's treasure.

To top off this project, large while letters spelling CHILLICOTHE should be placed upon the highest ridge of Mount Logan, a la HOLLYWOOD.

Some may say this is a short-sighted project and that a landmark such as Mount Logan should not be squandered even to promote growth. Nonsense! We have many more hills in the county. In fact, the beauty of the plan is that the scheme is expandable. After Mount Logan, we can develop Mount Ives, Bald Knob, and the other mountains of the Mount Logan Range to and including the beloved Sugarloaf.

Second, I propose a change at Adena State Memorial. One bar to attracting growth to our area is said to be the lack of an amusement theme park here. We drive to Kings Island, Cedar Point, Disney World and the rest. Let's establish Adena Amusement World and attract the throngs here.

The centerpiece of that park would remain Worthington's mansion, but the house would be modified to resemble Cinderella Castle. Inside, restaurants and shops would be installed. Other attractions would carry names designed to memorialize the famous residents and guests of old Adena: Tecumseh's Turbo-charged Tunnel Ride; Santa Anna's Revenge (as super roller coaster); Harrison's Hideout (a super spook house); and Tom's Tower (a space needle with a perfect view of the newly developed Mount Logan Range).

Use of those names will preserve the memory of our gallant forbears while the park itself creates the additional revenues needed to reach and maintain urbandom. These two suggestions are, I admit, not without fault. I shall leave it to others to perfect the execution of these plans. I am sure that many more suggestions will be forthcoming on using our natural assets to aid expansion. A word of warning is in order though.

Some nitpicking naturalists and panicky preservationists may fret about damaging our reputation as a living museum of Ohio history. I can only remind this community of its responsibility to future generations to open the new frontier of Southern Ohio urban living. I hope the leaders of the community will swiftly consider these proposals.

January 15, 1994

Life Too Short to Obey so many Rules

The post-new year's resolution period presses with all its weight (no pun intended) upon us. A fortnight after the folly of stating our annual intentions for improvement, we are desperately looking for loopholes.

The no-smoke promisors already sit in the smoking section just to absorb every bit of secondary smoke they can. The determined dieters by now believe that potato chips are health food so long as no dip is used. Those who covenanted to exercise daily have taken to counting getting out of bed as exercise. The only pull-ups they still do are at the fast-food drive-through window.

I'm all for self-improvement. Deprivation does build character. But this sunless season coupled with the self-imposed discipline of resolutions can make for some long, dreary days. Life is too short for this. As Mark Twain joked about a friend who was attempting to deprive himself of a loved habit: "Giving it up may not make him live longer, but it'll sure make his life seem longer."

So, for this one column, no ruminations on law or politics. No advice for leaders or complaints on our culture. Instead, attempting to provide some relief from our dismal march toward spring, I direct your attention to a little book written in 1991 by H. Jackson Brown entitled "Life's Little Instruction Book." The book collects 511 suggestions for a happy and rewarding life. Some relate to our health, some to our relationships and others just to everyday living. Allow me to share some of his recommendations to you followed by my own editorial comments.

No. 41: Brown says, "Don't postpone joy." I say, "That's right. Go ahead and break those resolutions early in the year, so you can get back to your joyful habits as soon as possible."

No. 56: Never mention being on a diet. Hope that your friends think you actually prefer celery and water every day for lunch.

No. 52: Avoid overexposure to the sun. Continue to live here in Ross County for the rest of your life.

No. 166: Avoid negative people. Invite all the people you are not avoiding to meet for a convention of totally positive people to be held in the nearest telephone booth.

No. 330: Rekindle old friendships. No, don't torch your ex-roommate's house.

No. 240: Drink eight glasses of water every day. At work, always try to get the office nearest the restroom.

No. 209: Observe the speed limit. And, after observing it, actually obey it sometimes.

No. 112: Never argue with police officers and address them as "officer." Mr. Clinton, if stopped by an Arkansas state trooper, be extremely polite and courteous.

No. 377: Carry jumper cables in your car. Always carry a bag of miniature Snickers bars in your car.

No. 200: Learn to show cheerfulness even when you don't feel like it. Be sincere, whether you mean it or not.

No. 303: Never go to bed with dirty dishes in the sink. Besides being crowded, it makes the sheets awfully squishy.

No. 225: Never tell anyone they look tired or depressed. And, I suppose, never tell anyone they look as if they've just been run over by a Kenworth.

No. 73: Never forget your anniversary. Always remember to send a card to your ex-spouse.

No. 74: Eat prunes. And, again, I say, get that office by the restroom and always carry a bottle of Kaopectate in your car.

No. 199: Park at the back of the lot at shopping centers. The walk is good exercise.
Always carry a loaded six-shooter when going shopping. And never forget to reload before making the return trip to the car.

No. 200: Don't watch violent TV shows. Convert all your TV sets into nice planters.

No. 83: In business and in family relationships remember that the most important thing is trust. And remember that the second most important thing is an iron clad contract with plenty of collateral.

No. 246: Wave at children on school buses. Plead not guilty at your arraignment for soliciting minors.

No. 91: Avoid sarcastic remarks. Sure! As if big shot Mr. Brown never says anything nasty to anybody. Right!

No. 85: Never encourage anyone to become a lawyer. I wonder who reviewed his $1,000,000.00 contract with his publisher. He can't really mean this.

No. 69: Be original. Sorry, I can't think of anything that's not already been said on this one.

No. 480: Take a kid to the zoo. Unless you receive a really good offer to purchase, take the kid back home with you.

No. 151: Get acquainted with a good lawyer, accountant and plumber. Ah, Ha! I knew it!

No. 192, 193, 194: Drink low fat milk. Use less salt. Eat less red meat. And remember, after those delicious prunes and sparkling water, the world is waiting. Get going in 1994!

October 9, 1999

Creative Thinking can Solve Bridge Street Traffic Problem

Crisis consumes us. Solution eludes us. Chillicothe, indeed all of south central Ohio, faces a challenge beyond all those faced before in its glorious history. Dealing with Tecumseh and the Indian nations now looks easy. Operating as the capital city of the Northwest Territory and then of the state of Ohio now appears as a piece of cake. Handling the influx of tens of thousands of World War I doughboys at Camp Sherman a pre-school exercise in retrospect.

Today, we face a truly monumental task. We must resolve a crisis threatening our very way of life. To fail in unthinkable. We must marshal all our fortitude, all our grit, all our resources to conquer the most intractable conundrum ever faced West of the Alleghenies. Yes, you guessed it: the traffic on Bridge Street.

The officials of Chillicothe city government have fearlessly tackled the problem by prescribing lane changes and traffic signal modifications. Farsighted and creative as these may be, I humbly suggest that we all brainstorm together to see if some "non-invasive" panaceas might be implemented which would offer unexpectedly quick relief.

We must reject no idea – no matter how simple or silly it appears upon first review.

I suppose they snickered at the fellow who first suggested indoor plumbing, but how relieved we all are now that the man had vision.

So, here goes. And don't you dare laugh.

A co-worker suggests that driving on our hallowed neon strip be regulated by alphabetical assignment. Names beginning with letters A through K may drive on Monday, L through Z on Tuesday, and so on. This should cut traffic in half while doubling applications for name changes at Probate Court.

I recommend moving Shawnee Lanes northward to, perhaps, the edge of Circleville. This would thin traffic on Bridge greatly since all those young folks cruising the strip and turning around at Shawnee's parking lot would be driving a half hour out and a half hour back to make the Shawnee loop. The rest of us would have room to spare on the six-lane serpent.

Or, how about this one?

Recognizing that different groups use the road at different times, we could prohibit their use at those very times. For example, from 7 a.m. to 1 p.m. no senior citizens allowed. From 11 a.m. until dark, Baby Boomers are prohibited. From dusk until 1 a.m., teens are banned. Some might prefer a more direct approach. Just declare that engineering nightmare a toll road. That ought to slow the flow. After all, how many people take the West Virginia Turnpike just to get a taco and video? Yeah! Taco Turnpike!

Could we win by making a bad thing worse – intentionally? Reduce the traffic to one lane each way. The congestion would escalate to the point that most of us would find an alternate route – maybe Possum Hollow or Lower Twin Road. If your goal is to decrease the car count, that just might do it.

Now I'm warming up. I envision other solutions.

Let's put sideboards on it and flood it. We were once a great canal town; we could be again. Little Venice! Only boats could navigate that thoroughfare. How many people do you know who own boats? How many who own cars? Get it? This could be our waters over troubled Bridge.

Another remedy is relatively rough, but effective nonetheless. After all, good manners are what put us in this fix. In high school, we often played "commando" basketball. No rules of conduct existed. No violations could be called. No dribbling necessary. Tackling allowed. Just get the ball in the hoop. So, declare Bridge Street a "commando" traffic zone. No traffic rules. No tickets. Just get there however you can. Drive your muscle car. Rename the way Demolition Drive. At least, this would deter the Lexus and Mercedes crowd from preening up Boulevard Bridge.

If Commando Row insults your sensibilities, I have a more refined prescription. Establish and enforce a strict drivers' dress code. Suits and ties for the gentlemen. Dresses and skirts for the ladies. That oughta clear 'em out like nothing yet proposed.

Well, I hope you're getting the idea. Your community needs you now as never before. If you love the American way, if you care about commerce, if you want your grandchildren to have the chance one day (I mean – in one day or less) to drive from Shawnee Square to Hopetown, then I know you'll flood this newspaper with your own great plans to get us out of this jam.

As we move into the next millennium, let's make our forefathers, foremothers, and I guess forechildren proud of us.

Off-the-Track – Some Creative Solutions for Chillicothe's Caboose Controversy

The First Capital faces another crisis. Wars and pestilence, booms and busts, depression and recessions have buffeted the brave souls of the Scioto Valley. Now another dilemma threatens our placid metropolis – What shall we do with the cabooses (or is it cabeese)?

THE PROBLEM

Our convention bureau acquired and prominently placed two genuine B & O cabeese (or is the plural still "caboose," e.g. one deer, two deer?) at the head of Yoctangee Park.

After refitting the cabooses, the bureau used them for office space and for tourist information distribution points.

The cabooses (maybe we could call them "trailers," as they once literally were) appear to have outlived their usefulness . . . again. Some propose their sale and removal. Others say, "Stay."

A brave writer to the editor of this journal, which, by the way, has been running longer than the railroads, suggested that we convert the cabooses into mini-hotels, not just the Red Roof Inn, but the Red Roof and Red Walls Inn.

That writer invited others to suggest solutions. This writer is taking up the challenge.

POSSIBLE SOLUTIONS:

Thrill Ride (Caboose on the Loose). Cut the cabooses loose from their moorings. Drag them over to the elevated intersection of Water, Paint, and Riverside streets, charge a buck a head and pack them with thrill seekers. Then, push them north until they careen down the hill into the park.

Advantages 1) revenue producing; 2) allows younger generation to see the trains run. Disadvantages: 1) dragging the cabooses back up the hill; 2) the cabooses' clatter may scare the fish in the park pond. (The shocks on those cabooses are nothing about which to brag.) And, oh yes, if we really do want to get rid of the armory at the base of the hill, this should do it in about seven well-laced runs.

Trolley Caboose (Main Street Mainliner). Let's put tires on those babies, add a couple Kenworth engines, give them to Chillicothe Transit System, and use them as buses. San Francisco has its trolley cars. I'd put one of our Big Reds up against one of their flimsy jokes any day. I'll bet no one would cut off our caboose bus in traffic.

Restaurant (The Red Goose Caboose). Everybody loves to eat – especially in unique surroundings. Realism sells. The menu could include dinners out of a black metal lunch box – just like the authentic railroad workers used to carry. Maybe we could add a few cinders to the soup to add to the "true-to railroad life" flavor.

Gus Macker Headquarters (The Little Red Bunker). Already situated in the center of the area where Ross County's greatest tourist attraction is staged, the Gus Macker 3-on-3 basketball extravaganza, these impregnable bastions from the railroad's heyday could become the refuge for the Gus-busters (quad-referees) who are being pursued by the angry mobs of losing players, parents, and fans – Where sportsmanship fails, the steel caboose prevails.

World's Only Submarine Train (1/2 of a League under the Lake) or (The Red Lagoon) or (parting of the Red Pond) or (A Caboose Runs Through It). First, lay a track on the bottom of Yoctangee Park Lake. Then, charge a buck a head and run those suckers right through it.

Advantages: 1) revenue producing; 2) allows younger generation to see the trains run; 3) satisfies the scuba types; and 4) may be combined with the thrill ride option mentioned above.

Disadvantages: 1) may slightly inconvenience the participants in the annual fishing derby.

Traffic Stopper (Pain of the Train). Remember those good old days when two out of three trips anywhere were interrupted by waiting in your car at the tracks for a slow train to clear? Those days can return. Choose our busiest thoroughfare, place the two cabooses at a spot perpendicular to the street. Then, every 18 minutes shove those red beauties onto the highway, completely shutting off the flow. Not only would this give us more opportunities to contemplate the golden age of railroads, we could also have extra time to fix our hair, talk on our cell phones, gobble more greasy, cold fries, and brush up on our swearing.

Whole Train (Rails to Trails). The caboose was once added to the train. Let's bring a whole train back and add it to the caboose. Build a complete train track around the perimeter of the park, and run a regular schedule. Go down Riverside, up the floodwall, back along Yoctangee Parkway, and then triumphantly east up Water Street. At that point, we will have restored the full glory of the 19th century to our forward – looking 21st century town. Maybe we could even rebuild the Canal. We're really getting nowhere . . . er, somewhere, now, huh?

These thoughts constitute only a humble beginning. The pump (house?) having been primed, I am sure other, more creative suggestions to solve the great caboose conundrum will be forthcoming. I predict that the positive response will be so overwhelming that the city and the Chamber of Commerce will want to buy more cabeese to station at all strategic locations in the First Capital.

Only then will we have earned the motto, "First Capital of Ohio – Last Capital of What's Left Behind."

July 27, 2002

Carlisle

Soon someone new will own the Carlisle Building. Even foreclosure actions do not last forever. When that time comes, we must be ready - - ready to resolve this Carlisle Building conundrum. "What's to be done?" We've heard that refrain now for the past four years as we pass by the burned out shell of the once Grand Dame situated on the prime lot of Chillicothe real estate at Paint and Main, the Broad and High, the Hollywood and Vine, the Times Square of South-Central Ohio.

"But how?" you say. Easy. Do it the all-American way. Hold a contest. Have all who care to share submit their brilliant ideas. The winning entrant will receive a great prize – maybe, for example, a full week's free stay in whatever eventually rests on the sacred corner.

I'll be disqualified since I originated the contest idea, but allow me to submit a few modest proposals, just to get your creative juices flowing. (Oh, yes. The non-local or uninformed local reader needs to know that the Carlisle Building, a four-story building erected in 1885 at the intersection of the primary streets in our county seat, the former capital of Ohio and seat of government of the Northwest Territory, was rendered useless by arson in April, 2003 and has stood largely untouched since).

Before casting my pearls, I humbly confess that my batting average for community development ideas is zero. I'm the guy who suggested (tongue-in-cheek) that we turn the Adena mansion into an amusement park, North Bridge Street into a canal, and the hill at Yoctangee Park into a caboose-on-the-loose thrill ride. All rejected! I get no respect! Not one to let past failures stop me, I submit the following entries to prime the Carlisle contest pump:

8th Wonder of the World – An international contest recently appointed the new 7 Wonders of the World. If 7 are good, why not 8? The only drawback: the Roman Colosseum, another dilapidated building of which you may have heard, made the list already. Two old wonders of that ilk may be one too many to honor.

Grain elevator – We'll call it Carlisle CORNer Elevator. (Get it? May be a bit too corny?) With the ethanol boom, we need all the corn storage space we can get. And talk about bringing more traffic downtown! Paint and Main will not have seen that many farmers since Saturday night in 1951. I'm sure you've all been missing Central Elevator, formerly at Paint and Water, since its dismantling a few years ago. Once again, the pigeons will be flying. Drawback: the railroad will need to be rerouted to run by the Carlisle. We'll need a motto. You have heard of rails-to-trails. How about trains-for-grains. Positive: we could then have a Times Square-type news ticker with the current corn prices being continuously posted.

School of construction – An architect/lawyer friend of mine suggests that we open classes right away. What better place to observe close-up the building techniques of the past century? Aspiring contractors could stand in one place and see a literal cross section of the history of electrical, plumbing, plaster, HVAC, roofing, and other building techniques. When the practicals start, the students might together actually make the old flagship sea worthy again . . . and pay tuition to do it!

I've got lots more creative ideas. Not all of these have been fleshed out yet, but here are some quick hitters. I'm sure the new owner and our city, county, and business leaders can contemplate, collaborate, choose, and carry out the best option submitted by you.

Purgatory museum – Kentucky's Creation Museum has drawn 100,000 visitors in its first two months. We could be next. Theological doctrines sell. I understand that purgatory is a place or condition of temporary suffering or misery. The Carlisle perfectly represents purgatory – that place between usefulness and uselessness. Nothing needs done. Just let it sit and let those who come ponder its mystical meaning.

Drive-in theater – Not enough room on the corner for this, you say? Balderdash! Nobody goes to drive-in movies anymore, anyhow, so there will be plenty of room for this enterprise.

Permanent flea market – Strong point: probably lots of fleas are already residing there.

Year-round fun house – Advantage: no renovation will be needed. Just leave the building "as is" and charge people to walk through. Without any investment, we will get people downtown. Note: be sure the budget includes an ironclad release of liability signed by all participants. Lots of folks might fall because…'er, I mean for this idea.

Prairie grass – If we really want to restore the corner to the way it looked when Nathaniel Massie first came over the hill, why not go all the way? Plant it, let it grow to 12 feet, and put up a plaque. Now that's restoration.

Enough already. I don't want to hog all the good ideas. I'm sure you readers want to get in on the contest now that you've been prompted.

Send your cards, letters, and emails. No idea is too preposterous (obviously) to be considered. Just remember, though, we want to get this contest going quickly so we can end this seemingly interminable wait to see what will rise from the ashes of the Carlisle. In keeping with this desire and with the history of this redevelopment project, I suggest the deadline for contest entries should be August 15, 2025. So, don't delay!

July 12, 2007

Seasoned Citizens, This One's for You

How about a turn for us oldies, er, I mean us mature folks? With Lori Graves having kicked off the fun by initiating a column in these pages informing us locals of some neat things to do and see in our very own mini-metropolis and with Kelsey Throne following up with a column devoted to family-friendly events, I thought it high time to highlight some potential attractions for the senior set. So, here goes.

---Prunes on the Pike

Our upper crust neighbors up north in and around the Fourth Capital no doubt spend numerous nights each year at wine-tasting events. I doubt we could match their grape fests, but why not head out Huntington Pike every so often for a prune-tasting party! I am sure Hirsch's Fruit Farm could rustle up some prime, powerful, purple fruits for us to enjoy. Some logistics will need to be worked out. Mid-evening, Sheriff Lavender may want to convert the pike into two lanes of one way traffic back to town to accommodate the stampede of prune-filled patrons hurrying to get back to the comfort of their thrones…whoops, I mean homes.

---Sundown Film Festival

Our beautifully restored Majestic Theater would be the perfect venue for a continuous 24-hour showing of some vintage footage only us old-timers could appreciate. Nominations would be taken, but only from those golden agers already receiving Medicare. Me? I could go for all Andy Griffith reruns, but some of my colleagues might not be up to such excitement with, you know, pacemakers and all. Maybe the travelogues of Lowell Thomas would be more their speed.

---Lawrence of Sugarloaf

The hard-working and creative members of the Scioto Society have been working diligently to add supplemental uses for the fabulous amphitheater in which the drama *Tecumseh!* has been performed for forty years. I and 1300 other fans thoroughly enjoyed a concert recently presented there by the American icon, Dr. Ralph Stanley, and his Clinch Mountain Boys. I suggest that now we invite another icon, Lawrence Welk and his Polka Mountain Orchestra, to perform there. Oh, sure, I am aware that a rumor exists declaring that Larry died a number of years ago; but remember Elvis. If Elvis is in the house, Lawrence can be on the mountain. I can just imagine the joy in the feet of the old-timers when Mr. Welk raises his baton. "Tank you, tank you, tank you, and keep a song in your heart."

---Gut Buster Tournament

The expansive parking lot of Ohio University- Chillicothe, home to the annual Gus Macker three-on-three basketball tournament, will again take on the air of excitement of top-level athletic competition when the Gut Buster two-on-two shuffleboard tournament comes to town. Who needs a cruise ship or Sun City Senior Center when we've got all that blacktop?

---Bike (o.k., Trike) Races

Some of you baby boomers and beyond may be able to just remember the bicycle races staged (by the local Jaycee's?) at old Herrnstein Field. Well, let's bring 'em back, but this time for seniors only. The "bikes" would be limited to the adult three-wheelers. Grocery baskets would be allowed as optional equipment.

---Denture Adventure

Dentists and dental clinics have proliferated around town lately. Look for one on every corner and behind every restaurant and bowling alley. Why not arrange for a sort of progressive examination? The participants would go, rapid-fire, from one facility to the next, to the next. At each, a quick exam would produce a dental diagnosis. The first senior patient found to have at least one permanent tooth left in his or her head would win a very small tube of toothpaste.

When I was a kid, back on the farm, I remember on long, lazy summer days, being bored silly, asking my mom, over and over, "What can I do?" Well, you Chillicothe oldies but goodies need wonder no longer. Get your orthopedic shoes on while I get my tongue out of my cheek. We're off to a world of fun, right here in our backyard.

What's Quacking

Old Chillicothe has garnered the attention of the world in many ways over the years. As Mr. Eckert has so masterfully revealed, Tecumseh roamed the hills and rivers of Chalagwatha. The pioneers plunked down the capitol for the Northwest Territory where Paint and Main would later cross. People all over have associated Chillicothe with Mead's Paper, Mead's smokestack, and Mead's smell. As an electoral bellewether, the First Capital has attracted Presidential wannabes and gottabes for decades. But, the most recent attraction takes the cake or maybe the goose pate. I am astonished that the ancient metropolis has become goosetown.

I refer, of course, to the recently exposed Great Goosecapade. Authorities have accused three suspects of luring a goose from Yoctangee Park Lake with a trail of bread crumbs, netting the creature, pitching it into the back of their car, and then attempting a getaway. This crouton caper has captured at least statewide notice in the news and social media. Our local chamber of commerce must be proud as a mother hen, but the merganser mystery raises some interesting issues and questions.

Did the accused actually commit this dirty crime? Was it actually a crime? What defenses are available? Maybe it's just a little misunderstanding.

- Possibly the goose just waddled into the auto on her own. Do geese catch spring fever? Maybe she wanted a joy ride. Maybe she was fighting for gender equality, so a male goose hitched a ride, and figured what's good for the gander gender ought to be good for the gentler goosette. Maybe the goose was looking for fame in the bright lights of show business, e.g., an audition for American Waddle, or the new comedic series, which may be necessitated by C. Sheen's departure, Three Men and a Goose. She'd be a shoo-in for America's Funniest Home Videos. I doubt, however, she'd volunteer for any of the food channel programs.

Could the alleged thieves have thought that Yoctangee Park had become the new site for the farmers market and that the New Year was being kicked off with a free goose promotion?

In these days of higher gasoline costs, everyone is looking for an alternative fuel. Couldn't it be that these folks were merely trying to harness a new form of manure power to give their internal combustion engine a little goose, er . . . I mean boost? Can't blame a person for that!

I wonder if the goose had been following too closely and ended in the boot of the auto when it failed to maintain assured clear distance. I'll bet the driver got some goose bumps when he saw a goose on his bumper.

The defendants may want to plead not guilty on the basis that they were performing a public service, a rescue mission to the save the goose from the abuse associated with living homeless in the park in a brutal Ohio winter and, thus, saving the public from swishing around in goose doo all summer. That defense probably stinks.

Maybe the goose was simply seeking proper medical attention, having found only quacks at the lake.   .

I'm sure some readers may hiss at this column. Some may suggest I keep my beak out of city business. Others may believe I've scored a goose egg this time and that the only direction my writing is going is down, that this effort may be my swan song.

Well, think what you will about this writer; but rest assured. Chillicothe, the gem of south central Ohio, has reassumed its rightful place at the top of the "what's happening now" heap! Let's revel in it!

VII.   Family/Personal

These writings were never intended to focus on my life. How boring that would be! However, I soon discovered that some columns that struck the most vibrant chord with readers were the ones centering on the most common human experiences: advice to a child, the birth of a grandchild, graduation times. I attempted to use reports of my personal experiences to make general points applicable to the human experience.

February 20, 1991

To my Son...Pray for Solace, Justice, Peace, and Healing

Dear Doug,

Son, this is a letter I'd rather not write. On this still winter night, as I sit safely in my den and as you and your mother sleep soundly upstairs, my pen agitates. A few people we know, and hundreds of thousands we don't, reside in the dusty, sweaty palm of danger and discomfort half a world away. They defend right—or at least that which a vast majority of nations defines as right. They are waging war on our behalf.

We have discussed many concepts in your 17 ½ years. We started with basics: good vs. evil ("Bad Boy!"); manners ("No burps at the table, please!"); property ownership ("Mine!"); crime and punishment ("You hit your sister?"); and the birds and the bees (I'm glad that one is over).

Lately, as your body and mine have grown, we've stretched to address more abstract notions: God, the universe, politics. But now, because that war is brought in our name as Americans, and because many of the soldiers are the same age as your sister at college and the age, which you'll be soon, we must take up war.

I'm sorry to spring this on you suddenly. This war, as most violent acts, hit without warning even with months of preparations. I, and the enemy, failed to absorb the reality that deadly conflict was so near. I was not prepared and did not prepare you to see war live and in color in our living room.

Quickly now, a disclaimer. I know not of war. I have read. I have watched. I have listened. But I have been spared the experience. You must visit with your great uncle Walter, who braved the shores of Normandy 29 years to the day before you were born, to capture the sensation of battle. You need to talk with some Viet Nam veterans at the local American Legion post to get a sense of men who fought with glory and honor in a war which history judged to be inglorious and dishonorable. You must stroll the grounds and halls of the local VA Medical Center to grasp the seriousness of conflict and the permanence of its result. Only these heroes deserve to be heard first.

One other group speaks strongly concerning war—without uttering a word. You have visited Arlington National Cemetery. You heard the solemn pronouncements murmuring from that ocean of simple white crosses. Those messages from those whom time left behind are timeless:

"Some things are worth dying for."

"The cost of war is most dear."
"Count the cost before entering in."
"Some are sacrificed for the good of all."
"Be vigilant, so that our deaths are not in vain."

These haunting voices do not compel our nation to rush to battle over every disagreement. To the contrary, they urge caution. They urge grave consideration of decisions, which will result in more grave markers. In the end, though, these voices remind us to be resolute to preserve that which is good.

Son, you may rightly be confused by this letter. I appear to be justifying this lethal conflict. Yet, at times, you have no doubt seen a bit of the pacifist in me over the years. I've not taught you to fight. I've tried to impress upon you that bullying is not the way to get along—that defusing violence is preferred to stimulating violence. I've chosen a profession that attempts an ordering, nonviolent resolution of humanity's problems.

I still admonish you to adopt these principles, all the while recognizing a basic truth. Human nature tends to employ force, tends to be selfish, and tends to survive by being fittest. Whether Adam's curse or biology's bane, this truth is undeniable. Until all humankind discards this tendency, the majority who want to abandon it must, paradoxically, use selective force against those stubborn, strong few who will not surrender this primitive stance.

Finally, son, the toughest issue. In your young life, you have demonstrated a keen interest in God and the things of God. You may wonder where God stands now. As is evidenced by Saddam Hussein, nothing is more dangerous than one who believes that God is on his side and only his side. Without definitive evidence, placing God in one camp is hazardous. God has a plan for humankind, but we continue to thwart it. God may not be taking sides, but merely anguishing in that His children solve differences by brutality and bloodshed.

How, then, can you pray if you can't pray the patently chauvinistic prayer—"Help our side win?" Instead, pray for safety of soldiers. Pray for solace for moms, dads, spouses, and children of soldiers. Pray for clear heads for leaders, pray for justice. Pray for peace. Pray for healing.

And, son, when this war ends, as it will, pray and work to see that children in all nations, including ours, can go to sleep each night with the same peace that we do here and now.

Good night.

Love, Dad

February 1, 1997

Wishes for a New Baby

Welcome, Adam.

Adam Richard Dauber! What a fine, solid name! You can carry that name proudly throughout your life. I know God loves that name. Of all the names in the universe, He chose that one for the first man He created. It must be His favorite.

And that middle name! Wow! What an honor for your grandpa!

Your name may seem inconsequential to you when you grow older. Remember, though, it is of utmost value. "A good name is more desirable than great riches; to be esteemed as better than silver or gold." Proverbs 22:1.

You didn't get to choose your own name, but some day you'll get to decide whether to honor it and protect it or devalue it by choices you make. I pray that you'll honor your parents and your creator by protecting your good name – your reputation for being a person of integrity.

I can't decide if you are ahead of schedule or behind. You were not scheduled to arrive in this old world until March 11, 1997. You must be a curious fellow. You caused your mom so many aches and pains that the doctors decided, for your sake and Mommy's, on Dec. 30, 1996, that you could see this world 10 weeks early.

In the past three days, you've had your first real bath, (in a plastic bowl made to accommodate a medium-sized grapefruit half), drunk from a bottle successfully and mesmerized your grandpa and grandma as they each held you for the first time. These things usually happen before babies are 4 weeks old, but, then again, they have happened to you six weeks before you were scheduled to be here. Being your grandfather, I've decided that you are performing at a rate of six weeks ahead of schedule. You're not a preemie; you're a premium child.

I have no plans for you, Adam. Your life is not mine to plan. But your grandma and I do have plenty of dreams for you. And these dreams can apply to all of the other babies being born about now – your generation.

I dream that you and they will have good health. You are getting early first-hand experience with the health care delivery system. You are a miracle baby. You may also be a million dollar baby in a very practical sense. Maybe you and your little friends can grow up to figure out how we can assure all our citizens from the crib to the rocking chair this wonderful health care without bankrupting the country.

I dream that you and they will be people who receive love and also give love. I know your parents pretty well, so I am confident you'll grow up in a stable home with love and attention showered upon you daily. Given the way things are going right now in our country that may make you rarer than a cloth diaper. Maybe you and your buddies can grow up and create a nation in which adults don't just say they love their children, but one in which adults make genuine commitments to provide loving, secure and stable environments for all children.

I dream that you and they will be happy people. That doesn't mean I expect you to have a smile at all times. Life is tough. Vicissitudes occur. (Maybe your dad will explain the slang version of this when you're watching a video called *Forrest Gump* someday.) And I don't want you to be able to avoid all troubles. I don't want you to get everything you want. (Although I'll probably appear to my friends as intending otherwise.) As I often told your mom and Uncle Douglas just after I'd said "No," "Deprivation builds character." Maybe you and your fellow babies will grow up to find the joy in sharing.

Adam Richard, I dream that you and they will grow. You've already gone from that initial 2 pounds, 11.8 ounces to your current hefty 3 pounds, 6 ounces. But I'm dreaming that you'll grow to be "bigger" even than your dad or granddad in a broader sense. You and your generation need to help the rest of us grow beyond our current limitations. Our nation is still trying to grow into the shoes our founding fathers made for us. We're still not feeding everyone, still not treating all without prejudice, still not nurturing the best in all our citizens. Maybe you and your mates can help America fully mature.

My boy, I'm looking forward to growing old as you grow up. My generation is called the "baby boomers." It will be going to seed just as you and your generation are sprouting. The cycles of life have been laid out wonderfully by the God who created both you and me – the baby and the boomer. As old plants wither and sift down into the earth, a rich and fertile soil is produced from which the young plants spring and prosper.

Adam, you and your generation are a promising seed. I pray that I and mine will provide suitable fertilizer.

I love you.

Grandpa Delong

May 12, 1999

A Grandpa's Wishes

The day – April 7, 1999.
The time – 11:49 a.m., E.D.T.
The event – your birth.

I'm glad you're here, Jonathan Robert Dauber. I want all the grandchildren I can get. Two may not be a full quiver, (refer to Psalm 127 when you learn to read), but you and your brother Adam make me a blessed grandfather.

The world will remember April 1999 for the conflict in Kosovo/Serbia – an external foreign war. Our nation will remember April 1999 for the school kids killed in Colorado – an internal domestic war. I'll remember it for you.

As I anticipate your future, I wonder what external and internal wars you and your nursery mates will need to fight in Century 21.

I pray the external wars will cease. May Carl Sandburg's tongue-in-cheek prophecy be fulfilled: "Sometime they'll give a war and nobody will come." May you never need to risk your precious blood for the safety of your parents, wife, children, or neighbors.

I also pray, though, that you will believe in something strongly enough to risk your life for it if necessary. Life's not worth living without belief in something worth dying for, a cause bigger than yourself: family, country, truth, honor.

I'd be happy if that thing were the same thing that your folks live for: God. Your daddy is a man of the cloth. Your mommy's his partner. That's why you're a P.K., i.e., preacher's kid. You're not a child of the cloth though. I know that a cloth diaper will never pat your posterior. So you're another type of P.K., too: a Pampers kid.

Even though, and maybe especially because, you are a P.K., you will face some internal wars.

In a few years, you and your teenage buddies will be straining to be born into personal maturity much as you squeezed through the birth canal last month. The labor pains to pass from childhood to adulthood seem to be increasing.

Grandpas are supposed to be wise, but I can't tell you what possessed those Colorado teens to murder their classmates, their teacher, and themselves. I can only tell you what can possess you not to lose your internal wars the way they did.

My boy, stay connected to the God who has just sent you here. I'm grateful you will be raised as part of His family. I pray that you will one day confirm that such is your real family and elect to stay in it forever.

And, Jonathan, never forsake the family into which you have been born. Because they love you, your parents will boss you around for the next couple of decades. Forgive them for it; nay, love them for it. The Duke of Windsor once facetiously remarked: "The thing that impresses me most about America is the way parents obey their children." Rejoice that you won't carry the awful burden of making all of your own decisions before you can be ready.

Adam will probably make you his punching bag for a few of your early years. Survive it. Sibling rivalry begets brotherly love.

I am hoping to watch you grow. I may even get the chance to assist in some small way to alleviate some of those unavoidable growing pains. If all goes according to nature's way, however, you'll live fifty years or so after I depart. So here's some advice you can keep for those days.

Your Old Testament namesake was both a brave, bold warrior for his nation and a warm, devoted friend to David. Follow his example.

Strive, young Jonathan, to develop a strong body and a strong mind so that you will be equipped to withstand the external trials and temptations that will come against you. Moreover, develop your character so that you can be kind and gentle as you devote yourself to the welfare of your family and friends.

Yes, I am glad you have come. On the eve of the next millennium, many peddle fear; dangers without, dangers within. Yet I see your birth as a gleaming sign of hope. You and your new kind inspire me and my old kind to remember the promise of spring, the promise of the future, the promise of new life.

I love you.
Grandpa Delong

September 19, 2004

Grandpa Welcomes Little One with Hope for a Better World

Joshua Douglas Delong, you have sprouted. Welcome to the field of life. Love will fertilize you.

Your daddy and mommy, your grandma and I, and all the many other members of your family have an unlimited supply awaiting application to you. May you grow tall and true.

Your late Great-Grandpa Wayne used to tell me about standing in the cornfield on a hot summer's night listening to the corn grow. That sound must have given a hope for harvest to Dad and his family. Numerous dangers lurked to dim that hope though. No one could control the weather. Heat, hail and drought didn't ask permission to visit a farm. Disease attacked without warning. For example, smut (the old type), a leaf-blackening soot, could rob yield as a thief in the night. Dad and the other farmers incessantly worked to stamp out a dreaded threat – Johnson grass.

They focused their attention, labors and eventually their herbicide sprayers on that creeping, crop-killing stuff. Some weeds threaten you and your generation, too, Josh. Some are as old as the day after creation. Weather is ferocious and unpredictable. Hurricane Charley ripped through Florida the same week you were born. He destroyed some crops. Disease persists. We root out some of the menacing old diseases, smallpox and polio; but new ones, AIDS and Alzheimer's, spring up to choke out the crops again. Other weeds are so new we haven't begun to learn to cope with them, terrorism most prominent among them.

Sometimes major threats fade quickly. People forget the primary bane of a previous generation. I haven't heard Johnson grass mentioned for years. (Thanks, Monsanto, for Round-up.)

Polio went from public enemy No. 1 to one of a large number of diseases prevented by a simple immunization. (Thanks, Drs. Salk and Sabin, for your research.) Communism failed like a day lily in a coal mine after a 90-year trial run. (Thanks, Ronnie, et al., for your persistence.)

Today we must explain Johnson grass, polio and communism to young people; they've not experienced them. Joshua, I hope by the time you're a teenager adults will need to explain terrorism to you as an historic relic.

I may not be around then to lend perspective to you, but from my perch now I can see a span of about 200 years. When I talk to my 92-year-old mother, I rewind to 1912, her year of birth, a time before we eradicated Johnson grass and polio. When I see you in your crib, I fast forward to 2112, a year you may well live to see. By the time you leave this old earth, I pray you and your generation will have conquered some of humankind's more enduring weeds: war, hunger, hatred, greed . . .

I wonder, "What kind of crop will your life yield?" I am confident you will produce an excellent crop. After all, your name, Joshua, means "the Lord gives victory." The Bible tells us your earliest namesake reported to Moses the Israelites could take the Promised Land, the land where the crops grew tall, only if they would be bold enough to claim it. I can see in your bright eyes that you're going to reach for progress and solutions.

For now, though, you're a field lying fallow. For the next few years, you can only receive. You will be dependent. Your folks will pour formula and love, applesauce and discipline, into you, preparing you little by little to become independent. Independence, maybe too much of it, will come naturally to you in your tumultuous teenage days. Then, in your adult years, you will achieve maturity, marked by interdependence. You'll depend on others for some things, but they'll depend on you, too. That's when the harvest begins.

A country preacher once visited a farmer who never had much time for church matters. Intending to plug his employer, the preacher complimented the farmer saying, "You and the Lord are growing a great field of corn there." The farmer, with an independent streak, responded, "You should have seen that field last year when the Lord had it all to Himself."

You, young man, cannot handle life by yourself right now. I trust you'll never think you can. You will, however, eventually need to take responsibility for your maturity. I pray the Lord's blessing upon you today and always, but advise you that true blessing will be yours only if you one day take responsibility for working with your God and your fellow creatures to stamp out life's weeds and to make a life worth living.

You and your fellow neo-natal kids are the world's newest crop. All of us farmers, we world-weary adults, look forward to watching you grow. We put out harvest hope for a better world in you and your little co-sprouts.

Grandpa loves you, Joshua. Go and grow. I'll be listening.

2006

My Grandson's Got a Problem

My grandson's got a problem.

Jonathan, seven, bright, happy, and well-adjusted, loves scooters, baseball, people, and God. He's into super heroes and high-tech, hand-held computer games his gramps cannot even activate. And he's awfully handsome.

Jonathan's got a lot going for him, but Jonathan's got a problem.

The problem is not behavioral. Jonathan rarely misbehaves. It's not emotional. His highs are not manic, and lows not depressive. It's not mental. Prospects are good that won't be a "child left behind."

Actually Jonathan is a special child, a one-in-a-million child. Jonathan is unique in that Jonathan doesn't eat. Rather, Jonathan cannot eat. You read me correctly; Jonathan cannot digest food. Since his system cannot convert food into absorbable form for use by his body, he dare not ingest any food. Many of us live to eat. Jonathan lives only by not eating.

Jonathan lives with eosinophilic esophagitis (EE) and eosinophilic gastroenteritis (EG). Eosinophils (leucocytes or other granulocytes with cytoplasmic inclusions readily stained by eosin), herein called "meanies," exist in the white blood cells of all humans. When the meanie count is normal, no problem. A difficulty does exist, however, when the meanie count is hundreds of times greater than normal. You see, meanies hate protein the way Superman hates kryptonite. They cannot tolerate protein. When protein appears in Jonathan's esophagus or stomach, the meanies send it back up the digestive chute, i.e. Jonathan "vomits his guts out." No admittance! Do not pass go; do not grow. In fact, do not survive. Oh, and in case you didn't know, all food contains protein. So, to simplify, but not overly so, food poisons Jonathan.

Wow! That is a problem you say. No, I haven't revealed Jonathan's problem yet. Abbott Labs, God bless 'em, has developed a liquid chemical formula called Elecare. This heaven-sent, but devilish-tasting, liquid can be ingested by the eosinophilic patient either by mouth or by tube feeding. Because this elemental elixir is broken down past the protein level in the lab, the meanies do not object. Nutrition arrives to the cells. Victory! Jonathan can survive and even thrive by obtaining and taking this stuff. [Note: This disease is much more complicated than I can relate here. Very little research has been completed regarding this mysterious disease. Go to apfed.org for more details].

So, what's the problem? T he problem is Jonathan's parent's health insurance company. Elecare, usually available only by prescription, cannot be found at your local Dairy Queen or in the dairy aisle of your local grocery. Even if it could, most couldn't afford it except as an occasional treat. (I have tasted a bit of it; it's not a treat to the taste buds). An amount sufficient to sustain a growing Jonathan now costs $40.00 per day... $15,000.00 per year. And the bigger they grow, the harder they fill. The teenage growth spurt may double the demand. Raising a kid on T-bone steaks would be cheaper.

"But, what's to worry," you say. "Submit the bills to the insurer. Sure you'll have some deductibles and co-pays, but that won't bankrupt you." Herein lies the problem.

The majority of eosinophilic children cannot stand or are unable to drink the smelly Elecare. The only way for this Elecare for their belly care can be received is by pump via a feeding tube. The insurance industry generally covers the cost if the formula is introduced in this matter. If the patient actually drinks the stuff, as does Jonathan, the company often denies coverage on the theory that their policy excludes nutrition. I've never seen a prescription for pizza.

Jonathan's parents, or their employers, pay hefty premiums for health insurance coverage to a conglomerate, which last year earned profit of $3,300,000,000.00 (that's three billion three hundred million dollars) and has assets exceeding $35,000,000,000.00. In 2005, it paid its CEO $8,000,000.00 in salary before bonus and perks. Additionally, this company, which cannot afford to classify Elecare as medicine, has given to the one CEO stock options now worth $1,6000,000,000.00 (Yes, that's one billion, six hundred million dollars).

Ohio supposedly regulates this company and the insurance industry. Those few children, and some adults, who have so many meanies that they cannot eat food must survive by ingesting a horrible liquid available only by prescription (sounds suspiciously like medicine to me). The health insurance company, which, by the way, spends untold hundreds of millions of dollars to treat the various lifestyle diseases we silly humans "volunteer" for by our stupid eating, smoking, drugging, working, and other elective habits, will not and are not forced by the Ohio Legislature to provide payment for this prescription liquid that keeps Jonathan alive. I have to wonder how this company would spent its money differently if it were not regulated by the government!

My grandson does have a problem. So does our health care insurance industry. So may you if your government continues to allow insurance company executives, rather than your physicians, to decide what constitutes a medicine.

Keep Jonathan's problems in mind the next time you get a chance to vote on any proposition or candidate promising to improve your health insurance by allowing the government to determine the medicine you need. You may be the next one who ends up with a problem.

New Life

You chose a beautiful day to arrive, my little lady, Lydia Renee Delong. February 2, 2007 dawned cold as a popsicle. The day deposited a little layer of pure white to cover the barren branches and leaden landscape of our Ohio winter: a perfect preface to your birth at 4:22 p.m. We in this tired world need a renewal. You have provided that fresh start.

Young lady, you and your nursery mates around the globe give a fresh start physically. The race run by the human race wears down the racers. Can't you see the differences between those of you who just heard the starter's pistol and those of us in view of the finish line? My 1947 skin looks like a dehydrated crocodile; your 2007 skin approximates pure cream. My well-used voice is losing its strength; your strong first cries carried above the din of the eight excited observers in the birthing room, through its closed door, and down the hall where your other grandfather and I awaited your debut. (You may want to consider opera or auctioneering as vocational possibilities). I'm at the point in life where I'm trying to decrease my eating; you are preparing now to drink and eat your way to toddlerhood and beyond. Your predecessors are downshifting physically; you are gearing up for the race ahead.

Sweet girl, as a female you also give a new beginning to our family gender-wise. In the past ten years, three cousins have preceded you into our clan—all boys, including big brother Joshua. Granted, they are grand boys, but life begs for a little balance. Some pundits tell us that the coming presidential campaign will be one in which the women predominate. I can see and accept that coming, so don't accuse me of being sexist or chauvinistic. I'm not pigeonholing you. Our family has no glass ceiling. I know you'll be beautiful in beaded gowns or in blue jeans. I care not whether you pilot a family or a rocket ship. I know, though, that male and female complement, if not always compliment, each other and that our family and the human family profit by the presence of both sexes. I can't wait to see what you teach me and the other boys in our family.

Pretty little one, I'm hoping you and your generation give my baby boomer generation a fresh and humble start socially. We need it. Yes, the B. B.'s promised a fresh start, too; and we have been making progress in many areas, including, for example, technology and health care. But we've not been able to bridge the communication gap between peoples and nations or often within our own families and neighborhoods even with the best computer systems. We've not been able, for the most part, to achieve better lives, just somewhat longer lives, even with the terrific medical advances that have come. We all need a fresh start socially. We place our hope for a better world in the hands of you and your fellow neophytes.

Most importantly, young un, we who are outgoing are looking to you who are incoming to give your family and your world a fresh start spiritually. Your daddy and mommy had something to do with it (When you're entering adolescence, ask for an explanation from them, not from Grandpa and Grandma), but your family believes that God actually knit you together in your mother's womb. (When you're old enough to read, read Psalm 139:13). And your family believes that God has a great plan already laid out for you (Jeremiah 29:11). But we also know that you will get to choose the road you wish to take. We pray that you, like your namesake in the Book of Acts, will choose the straight road that will lead to true happiness, deep satisfaction, and real security in your future and that your example will lead those around you to pursue the same path.

Honey, I heard a story about a grandpa who was rocking his three-year-old granddaughter. She looked up at her grizzled old granddad and asked, "Who made you?" The old man answered, "Why, God did." She followed up, "Who made me?" Grandpa answered, "God made you, too." After a moment's reflection, the little girl concluded, "I think He's doing a better job lately, don't you?"

Lovely Lydia, when I look within myself and when I look around me at the shape this planet's in, I'm happy I can look down at the fresh wonder and pure potential of you and believe that God's doing a better job lately. Although I won't live to see it all, I'm grateful I've seen this fresh start in you and pray that it will be followed by a carefree childhood and a long, productive, satisfying life that will reflect the foundation of a loving family, will reveal an investment in the lives of the people in the world around you, and will honor the God who made you.

I love you.

Grandpa Delong

February 11, 2010

We Need to Live Lives of Value

Uncle Walter turns 99 this month. Has he been successful in his life? By the world's standards, he may not have succeeded greatly. He has neither amassed a fortune nor achieved fame. But Uncle Walter has not aspired to meet the world's standards. Instead, he has taken Albert Einstein's advice: "Try not to become a man of success but rather try to become a man of value." Uncle Walter has achieved a life of value by rendering solid service to others during his 99/100th of a century, to-wit:

Family: As the firstborn to Remus and Jessie, his mostly sharecropper parents, Walter quickly became and long remained a dutiful son. Knowing his parents relied upon his assistance, he learned to work hard an early age; and he offered support to his folks until their dying days. He devoted himself to his beloved wife Marguerite and together they raised three great children. His grandchildren and great-grandchildren adore him still. He and his second wife Lillian have spent the last couple of "golden" decades happily enjoying each other and contributing to the well-being of their respective families.

Community: While working hard to scratch out a living from the farm, Walter never forgot his duty to his fellow citizens. He spent uncountable hours in meetings as a member of the local school board. He was a valuable and active member of the far-sighted hospital board which created the Adena Regional Health System campus. Walter believed and acted upon the scripturally inspired motto that to whom much is given, much is expected.

Country: I am proud to be related to Uncle Walter. He was proud to be related to Uncle Sam. When the call came in the early 1940's, Walter never wavered. He left his livelihood behind and stepped out to risk his life. You have read about and watched movies about D-Day, June 6, 1944. If you want to hear about that horrific, but inspiring day from a first-hand witness, Walter's your man (and one of the last.) He and his comrades exhibited a courage rarely seen among men down through the history of this planet as they landed amid bombs bursting in air and on the sands of Omaha Beach that bloody day. But you'll need to ask - - he won't volunteer to tell you. He's too modest. One of our evening cable commentators presently has a feature in his program in which he chooses a patriot of the day. Most of the choices pale in comparison to the type of patriot Walter defined for the world that day. While that was Walter's finest service to his country, he continued thereafter to serve well too, both as a volunteer in various governmental agricultural agency positions and as an employed civil servant, having been a rural postal carrier for many years.

God: Walter has always been actively devoted to his Lord. He always has attended and, even to this day, continues to attend worship services regularly. He has served in many capacities in his church and outside of his church that further the cause of heaven on earth. He has remained actively concerned about God matters and about all of God's people. Clearly, his service to family, community, and country grew from his dedication to God.

Bottom line: Walter has exhibited the mature person's qualities of loyalty, industry, devotion, courage, constancy, reliability, humility, and good humor. Just as important are the characteristics Walter has not exhibited: selfishness, pettiness, spitefulness, bitterness, and arrogance. In living his quiet life of devotion to the things that really count, Walter exemplifies his heroic generation, the one that Tom Brokaw has famously termed the Greatest Generation.

Uncle Walter's not giving up yet either. He's still active and witty. I recently asked him what he would like for his birthday this year. He said: "You don't have what I want." When I persisted, he said, "Ten more years." Always looking forward, that Uncle Walter.

Walter and his generation won't be here forever. Relatively soon the torch will be passed. Walter's standard of service challenges our family and, in a broader sense, our national family. The USA turns 234 this 4th of July. Our country has amassed a solid record of service to its citizens and to the world at large. Our predecessors, from the Founding Fathers, through the World War II veterans and even throughout the six decades since, have laid a strong foundation. When asked just after passage of the Declaration of Independence whether we had a monarchy or a republic, Benjamin Franklin stated: "A republic, sir, if you can keep it." Walter and those like him, people of value, have done their part to keep it. Can we?

I'm not wise enough to give specific guidance as to what political path our nation should follow in order to move America's torch safely forward. I do submit, though, that national security and progress will continue only if we continue individually and collectively to exhibit the values which Uncle Walter, one genuine American hero, and his heroic generation have humbly exhibited: service to family, community, country, and God.

Happy Birthday, Uncle Walter Hartsock! And thanks!

May 28, 2016

Grandson's Graduation Cause for Celebration

Good job, Adam! When your grandpa first addressed you in this column on February 1, 1997, you were 5 weeks old, weighed just over 3 lbs., and were barely clinging to life. Since your very premature birth, you had gained 10 oz., an amount I can gain in 5 minutes with my evening snacks. That's not exactly a rocket start, but with the help of your family, your doctors, and your God, you have resolutely progressed. You have reached a significant plateau: high school graduation. Congratulations!

You negotiated a rocky path. Realistically observing your disadvantaged beginning, we who loved you didn't give you much more chance of surviving than a snowball in Belize. After you did survive major surgery at 4 months and 4 pounds and again, after you came through a second surgical ripping of your thorax before age 3, we gratefully celebrated your continued existence, but figured you would never be able to accomplish much in this competitive world. We concluded that your chronic digestive, respiratory, neurological, speech, tactile, and other development delays as a preschooler would preclude you ever participating in "regular" classes in conventional schools.

Boy, have you proved us wrong! As a consequence of your parents' faithful dedication to your care and of your determination to overcome obstacles and complete your assigned tasks, hour-by-hour, day-by-day, year-by-year, you have succeeded beyond the wildest expectations of all who knew of your inauspicious initiation.

You have amassed a wonderful academic record, graduating with honors at your "regular" public school. You proficiently play guitar, drums, and keyboard (not concurrently, of course). You compose songs. You have an insatiable desire to follow rules, a happy circumstance for your lawyer grandfather to contemplate. You are polite and mannerly beyond nearly anyone of your generation or, for that matter, any other generation. You serve others, both near and as far as Belize, that tropical country where the snowballs melt.

Above all, you set your mind on things above all this world offers. You love God and prove it by your speech and actions. You talk and walk the way of Jesus, whether on the way to a foreign country or to the grocery store. Nothing could make your old grandfolks happier.

In that first letter to you, I listed some dreams your granny and I had for not just you, but for your whole generation, now known as Millennials. Let's check the progress you and your blossoming colleagues are making toward those goals.

Good Health: We give thanks that the health care system has worked ultimately to deliver you, a critically ill preemie, and your cohorts to young adulthood with great physical prospects. Regardless of all the blather about the deficiencies of our system, it has improved during your two decades and delivers excellent care for those of all ages, premature through superannuated. First Dream: substantially accomplished.

Receiving and Giving Love: You personally have been a winner in this dream department, but I sadly must offer that you and those like you are the exception rather than the rule. You and a few have been happily situated in families and communities that had no hesitancy in surrounding you with affection and safety, all the while affording you the opportunity to reciprocate. Unfortunately, for far too many families and neighborhoods, loving and protecting children continues to be hit and mostly miss. Too many parents love themselves more than the babies they create. Too many institutions, be they families, schools, churches, or towns, refuse to recognize that their youth are not mere inconveniences, but the actual future. Second Dream: selectively accomplished.

Happiness: Gran and I are grateful that you seem happy, Adam. Your handsome smile fills our hearts. Better yet is the contentment we see in you. Sad to say, we don't perceive that same settled sense of joy in living in many of your fellow young travelers. We don't confuse your contentedness with complacency. You exhibit plenty of ambition, the will to accomplish and to make your life worthwhile. We trust that your cronies will break out of any mold which holds them back from enjoying the gift of life. Third Dream: somewhat accomplished.

Growth and Maturation: You and your schoolmates are certainly realizing this dream. In each of your 19 years, you have grown physically, mentally, intellectually, socially, emotionally, and spiritually. You may not have grown taller than your grandfather, but I and all who know you must look up to you. You have reached a wonderfully fine stature...for a person of any age. Good character beats mere height any day. We are counting on the character of your generation to lead our nation to bigger, better things. After all, think of it. Gran and I can't even operate our smart devices without nearly daily tutorials from you and people your age. Fourth Dream: accomplished

My boy, in our culture high school graduation signifies passage into adulthood. Dependence fades; independence flourishes. In your case, Mama's strict house rules will give way to dorm rules. Papa's lectures and demands will vanish in favor of the professors' lectures and expectations. The tether is being severed or, at least, loosened.

Independence is exhilarating, but fearsome, too. With independence comes responsibility, first for oneself, then for others. That can create a real sense of loneliness. Thus, interdependence might be the best ultimate goal.

Adam Richard, I am privileged to have had the opportunity to grow old while you have been growing up. Retired and aging, my fellow Baby Boomers and I are going to seed just as you and your Millennials are blooming. We are all, though, interdependent. As you and yours continue to grow into strong, mature plants ready to produce flowers and fruits to beautify and feed the world around you, I pray that you can depend on me and mine for any help we can still give.

Young man, may the Lord bless you and keep you.

I love you.

Grandpa Delong

June 4, 2017

Grandson's Graduation Letter

I confess. I don't remember a thing my high school commencement speaker said. Routinely though, such speakers state that the graduates are not so much completing a big process (schooling) as they are beginning a bigger one (life). In a way, that diminishes the accomplishments of the students. Celebration of attaining a diploma merits praise.

Jonathan Robert Dauber, when you soon walk the stage of your high school to claim your sheepskin, this grandpa wants nothing to dull the shine of your achievement. Your graduation matters. You can be proud.

You have had to negotiate an abnormally rocky path. Born in April 1999, you personally, and the world in general, too, have endured some tough times in the past 18 years. Just before your arrival, the Columbine, Colorado school massacre occurred. Before your first birthday, the earth held its breath as the calendar page flipped to 2000. None of the predicted Y2K disasters appeared, but as you neared 2.5 years of age, the 9/11 attacks changed the world. Nothing's really been the same since. I am saddened that you and your generation have had this darkness cast over what should have been the sunny, carefree years of your youth.

Yes, Jonathan, the world outside you has faced grave difficulties, but you have coped with a more immediate problem inside you. Let me describe you to those who may be reading this letter over your shoulder.

[Jonathan's a bright and usually happy young guy. He's well adjusted. He loves people, and he loves God, having served both, locally on his church worship music team and globally on mission trips to Central America. Like his contemporaries, he's into social media in a big way. He loves the NBA and soaks up all things Hollywood, even publishing on the Net his own rather sophisticated movie reviews. And he's awfully handsome. (He must favor his parents and grandma in the looks department). But, as I said, Jonathan's got a problem.

The problem's not behavioral. Jonathan rarely misbehaves. When he does, he repents quickly and thoroughly. Nor is the problem emotional. He may suffer the ups and downs of a normal teen; but the highs are not manic, and the lows are not depressive. The problem's definitely not mental. He's an honor student. Finally, the problem's not lack of motivation or talent. He has run with his school cross-country team and has sung the male lead in his large, talented high school chorus.

I can accurately state that Jonathan's problem makes him nearly a "one in a million" kind of person. Seven painful months after Jonathan's birth, pediatric gastroenterologists diagnosed him with eosinophilic esophagitis (EE) and eosinophilic gastroenteritis (EG). Space considerations and the ignorance of your humble correspondent do not allow full explanations of these very rare conditions. Suffice it to say that they create nearly constant severe pain, intestinal "distress," both through the northern and southern routes, and sometimes even premature death. No known cure exists. The only treatment available, believe it or not, was to stop Jonathan from eating or even coming into the near presence of all food.

As you might guess, this complicated life considerably for Jonathan and his family. For more than a decade, Jonathan survived by drinking chemicals mixed into a liquid formula called Elecare. This heaven-sent, but devilish-tasting, elixir, along with the excellent care of Dr. Phil Putnam at Cincinnati Children's Hospital and, of course, his devoted parents, allowed Jonathan to live. Whether by passage through puberty or by God's miraculous intervention, a few years ago Jonathan gradually was able to ingest a few foods without ill effects. He still relies on Elecare to assure that he gets proper, balanced nutrition.]

Jonathan, you surely didn't complain, whine, or bellyache much about this randomly assigned malady. Only once did I hear you question, "Why did I have to be born like this?" We couldn't answer. We only could cry...with you.

Jon boy, remember when you were finally freed from the burden of being isolated at your own individual "safe table" in your school cafeteria? We all thought you would immediately celebrate. Instead, you expressed that you felt that you may be losing your special identity. You quivered a little when you said, "But that's who I am!"

No, son. That's not who you were. EE didn't and never will define you. You have not been the boy with EE. You are instead the young man who has bravely lived with and overcome EE. You are the toughest guy I have ever known. You are not a snowflake. You will not need a "safe space" when you reach the college campus. You have faced down adversity.

Author Elizabeth Brown Pryor recently wrote, "The pride of being something more than you were expected to be is part and parcel of the American dream." Jonathan, you have become all and more of what we hoped you would become. When you walk off that stage with diploma in hand, hold your head high. Yes, future mountains await, but today celebrate past challenges met. We are celebrating with you.

Young man, may the Lord bless you and keep you.

I love you.
Grandpa Delong

VIII.   Holidays/Spiritual

Holidays, whether secular, patriotic, or spiritual in nature, provide times to look back to remember the old days, to focus on what's meaningful about the present celebration, and to take a breath and contemplate tomorrow and the future. As I suspect is often the case with professional writers and teachers, too, the one who intends to inform and instruct others gains more from the process than the receivers do. I am positive that the contemplation and process of preparing these offerings impacted me much more than they did my readers.

December 15, 1990

Christmas: Despite Commercialism, it's a Season to Enjoy

It's that time of year. 'Tis the season to be jolly; it's time for mistletoe and holly. It's also time for the annual altercation between the secular and the sacred. Crèche on the courthouse lawn or not? Santa at the Sunday school party or not? WWJT. What would Jesus think? To arrive at that answer, let's first examine not what is the reason for the season, but what are definitely not the reasons Baby Jesus showed up in Bethlehem on that silent night two millennia ago.

Jesus was not born in a courtroom to be our lawyer. Now, He would be a fine attorney. He would have a full understanding of how the system works. He is, after all, omniscient, all knowing. He would be loyal to His client. Once He enters a relationship, He never backs out of it. He would always be truthful, since He is truth. He would never work a fraud on the court. In fact, He is our Great Advocate (Job 16:19). He is my counselor, and I personally am relying on Him to plead my final case. But, He was not born simply to be our advocate. After all, He will one day be our judge (2 Timothy 4:1).

Jesus was not born in a rotunda to be our politician. Yes, He was a proven vote getter. Remember the palms in the streets and the "Hosannas" in the air. And what a fiercely devoted inner circle of advisors He assembled, a talented cabinet, aka the disciples. He could certainly draft laws. He came, in fact, to fulfill the law. (Matthew 5:17) The prophet Isaiah even tells us that the government will be upon His shoulders. He is the foundation of all human institutions, including government; but at the same time, He is beyond them. So, He advised His advisors to let Caesar, the government, do its thing without interference from Him and His. He was to be about matters beyond politics and earthly governments. He is less concerned about His place in the public park and more concerned about His place in the private heart. Clearly, He was not born to assume a political role.

Jesus was not born on a soundstage to be a performer. Oh, He knew how to attract and satisfy a crowd. He spoke like no one else ever did or has since. He held audiences spellbound more than once. Then, He fed the throngs with but two fish and five loaves. His Nielsen ratings would have been unsurpassed. But, He did not seek the spotlight. In the end, He was not born just to entertain. When His listeners got past what He did to discover Who He was, they switched channels. He was willing to pray for the crowds, but unwilling to play to the crowds. No, He was not born to perform.

Neither was Jesus born in a studio to be a commentator, a forerunner of O'Reilly. He's watching out for us, all right. And the spin definitely stops with Him. He does ask all the tough questions. The difference is: He answers them, too. He is the answer. He's just not nearly abrasive enough for the anchor's job. He was not born to screech.

Certainly, Jesus was not born in a mall to be a merchant. Jesus wasn't materially minded enough to make it in merchandising. He didn't shout, "Get." He shouted, "Give." He pedaled treasures in Heaven while eschewing treasures here on earth. He displayed one of His few flashes of anger when the marketers entered the temple. He drove them out. (John 2:15) If Jesus operated the mall, the shoppers would be gone. Jesus was not born to chair the Chamber of Commerce.

If Jesus didn't intend to engage the world in these ways we moderns invite Him to, then what was His plan? What was His reason for showing up for the initial Christmas season? As the lyric of a contemporary Christian song goes, "What a strange way to save the world?" No one caught on to the plan very quickly. Joseph was skeptical and needed an angel to convince him. Mary was amazed, but she shouldered her assigned duty/privilege. The only light resembling a spotlight was the star over Bethlehem. The humble shepherds were the first people to recognize Him. Some still don't. How strange it all was and is!

The world did not then, and we do not now, need another lawyer, politician, performer, commentator, or merchant. The world is and has always been full of them, and they can give us no more than temporary relief. We needed God not just to look down at us, but to come down with us. Looked at that way, it begins to make wonderful sense.

Jesus, Emmanuel, was born in a stable to be our Savior. Celebrate it. Merry Christmas!

July 4, 1996

Be Thankful for Freedom

As we go about celebrating the 220th anniversary of our nation's independence, I have come upon a letter, written by F. N. R. Redfern, an attorney who had practiced in Adelphi, on Dec. 15, 1942, to one of that village's young men, Pvt. J. A. Mahoney, who was serving far from the village during World War II. I have not served in our armed forces, but I have eternal respect and gratitude for those brave men and women who have. As a token of my appreciation and that of all citizens who are continuing to enjoy the fruits assured us by the service of veterans, dead and living, I offer the following:

December 12, 1942

My Dear Dick:

It is with pleasure I write you a few lines telling you that your mother is well and attending to business as usual, and that there is nothing startling or strange to report to you. I am glad you are now in a warmer climate. The Carolinas are great states. My father's people migrated from North Carolina to Ohio about the year 1807.

Now, Dick, remember you are from the old Buckeye State, a proud member of the grand Old U.S.A., and you are one of the vast throng that are fighting for the grand heritage left us by our forefathers, a government of the people, for the people, and by the people, Glorious old Democracy. Freedom. The grandest country on earth is not putting it too strong. So get your mind settled on doing anything and everything that you can to help with the war.

Be brave, be true, be firm and honest, as I know you will be, and when the strife is over, and you stand in silence and see Old Glory floating in the breeze, untarnished, unscathed, and still standing as a symbol of a free nation, then how proud you will be that you went forth in your young manhood to defend her.

In this great country of ours we regard no man for his royal birth but we do regard him for his moral worth.

The boy born in a log cabin has the same right and opportunity as the boy born in a mansion. It is up to the boy, and if we are patriotic, and submit to discipline, and obey our supervisors in office and never shirk a duty, then, it is, that confidence and respect will be reposed in you by your officers and great honor for you is in the offing.

So, in conclusion, my dear boy, will say, be brave, patriotic and strong . . .Remember Pearl Harbor, my boy, and give the scoundrels all you have got.

With a prayer for your safety and with kindest regards and best wishes, I am very truly yours.

F. N. R. Redfern

Mr. Redfern died in 1954. Dick Mahoney died on April 2, 1996.

Let us resolve that we will continue to be grateful in a way as genuine as Mr. Redfern's to all those who have served or are serving as did Mr. Mahoney.

December 24, 1997

Power of Message is Awe

"How could he stand it?"

That's what I thought as I slogged with my stubby eight-year-old legs through the cow manure carrying hay from the barn to the cattle feeder.

How could Dad stand to be out in the bitter cold as dusk gathered around us and snow blew like frozen darts on Christmas Eve in the mid-1950s? I was dressed like Admiral Byrd heading for the pole – heavy coat, woolen cap pulled down far over my ears, flannel shirt and gloves so thick I could barely grasp the hay. Inside it all, I still felt like a popsicle in a deep freezer.

I could not comprehend how Dad could be out in that weather all day, driving that Farmall H back and forth, back and forth, and not even put down the ear tabs on his cap. The word "wimp" had not yet found its way into Webster's, but I know now that I felt like one then.

And I can now find a word to describe what I felt toward my father that Christmas Eve: "awe."

Strange what the mind chooses to remember, isn't it? I've experienced 50 great Christmas Eves. I remember many vividly.

Santa somehow appeared at our door when I was about five-years-old and gave me a little wind-up motorcycle which ran round and round on a cable. Spending my first Christmas Eve with my girlfriend Beth (still my girlfriend and now my wife, too) and her family, away from my own family, was a departure point.

Using the characters of our nativity set, I dramatized the Christmas story each Christmas Eve to Amy and Douglas during all the years that they were growing up. Christmas Eve 1996 found me at the hospital bedside of my daughter, watching her fight a delicate battle to bring her son to life while clinging to her own.

Nevertheless, that cold Christmas Eve of my childhood still bubbles to the top when I put my mind to Christmas Eve cogitations.

The joy of anticipation often exceeds the pleasure of experience. The anticipation of what was to come in the next 12 hours must be the glue that fixed that moment so firmly in my little brain on that frigid evening 42 years or so ago.

As I shivered, I anticipated with my senses the warmth soon to envelope me as I reached my pole – the inside of our humble home, the tenant house. I knew how the streams of hot air shooting from the fuel oil stove standing against the wall of the dining room would melt the ice from my eyebrows and would turn my frozen red cheeks into rosy, toasty ones. The black chunks of coal burning in the living room fireplace would restore my feet to feeling.

I knew that my frozen nose would soon know the pleasing aromas of Mom's kitchen. Fast food hadn't found our farm yet. I had not yet smelled pizza or pita bread. The expected entrée was pot roast or Swiss steak or even common rivels. (If you don't know that one, ask your grandma). Add the scent of some fresh baked rolls. The prospect of that glorious supper overcame the bleak stench of the present circumstances.

No visions of sugar plums danced in my head, but the falling of dark raised my expectations of the gifts to be mine at the next dawn. Today's children might refer to their Christmas bounty as loot, but that has the wrong ring to it for those times. Loot connotes excessive or large-scale. I had no delusions of grandeur. A basketball would satisfy me. If some clothes or candy accompanied that, fine; but I really just needed the ball. I was sure it would arrive by morning.

We slammed and secured the barn doors and headed for the house. The best hours of the year lay just ahead. Mom and my sisters were inside the door leading from the back porch to the kitchen. Supper would lead to a warm bed in a cold room. Sleep would lead to the magic morning. Lunch with the Delong dozens would follow at Grandma Delong's. Supper and gifts and foolishness at Grandma Hartsock's would finish the perfect day.

I know now what I didn't know then. The greatest anticipation was that of being with people who loved me and wanted to be with me. That's the awesome power of the Christmas message, too.

Prophets foretold and the angel confirmed that baby Jesus would be called Immanuel, i.e., God with us. How could Dad forego ear tabs? How could the great God of all, forego his divinity to become human? Why did adults want to be with me? Why did He want to be with us?

Reflecting upon my barnyard decades ago reminds me of the stable in Bethlehem centuries ago and fills me with anticipation of the One who is coming tonight.

May 6, 1998

All of Kingston Prayed

One ironclad law of the universe states: "School children will jump at any reason to escape class." I nearly broke that law one autumn day in 1959.

Nancy was a friend of our family. My senior by two years, she was too old to be a love interest, but close enough to my age to be within my range of interest. She was like a third big sister to me.

Unless you are the patient, open-heart surgery sounds today as simple as hangnail removal. In that day, however, open-heart surgery on a "young-un" was cutting edge (no pun intended) stuff. My "big sis" was to be a pioneer.

Little Kingston and environs were sobered by the thought of one of its young daughters having her chest cut open to remove her hardened heart lining. The event so touched the community that it undertook extraordinary measures.

One of those measures threatened the aforementioned law of the universe. Local churches opened their doors all day on Nov. 10, 1959, Nancy's surgery date. The Kingston-Union Board of Education decreed that any student wishing to join in the concert of prayer would be excused from school for an appropriate duration.

For once, I wished I did not have an excuse to leave class. One of my own friends lay in distress. My blue slip resulted only from her misfortune. I am sure I left school for a while on the prayer mission. I did not violate the law of the universe.

The outpouring of prayer for little Nancy was not the first time I had seen or participated in prayer. It was the first time I had seen a community express collectively the belief that prayer could make a difference.

No doubt other forms of help had been given to Nancy and her family. I'm sure food was taken, cards were sent, calls were made and help was given with the farm chores and with the care of her siblings. But on this day when the doctors were opening the body to attack the hardened heart with scalpels, prayer was all that was left. In the mind of our community, only God could save Nancy now.

I recount this incident now because this Thursday many in our county will choose to participate in the National Day of Prayer.

Some, including this humble writer, believe that the heart of America has now been hardened. I'm not generally pessimistic, but being simply realistic reveals the sad truth. The crime level is high and the types of crime are hideous: witness the rash of senseless mayhem by juveniles. The morals of all, including our leaders, appears to be declining. Respect for others and their interests (formerly called manners) has nearly disappeared.

Our nation has tried other forms of help to remove this hardening of the heart. We've tried the New Deal and the New Frontier. We've instituted a Great Society and launched a sexual revolution. We've tried to return to a morning in America and entered a new Contract with America. All of these have proved to be mere bandages for the hemorrhage.

Maybe it's time to recognize another law of the universe: "We reap what we have sown-individually and as a nation."

Humans always look for ways to sidestep the laws of God, but ignoring God's rules does not mean that the rules no longer exist.

Thursday provides us all as a community and a nation the opportunity to express collectively our belief that prayer can make a difference for our country and ourselves. Don't mess with the law of the universe by missing this opportunity to ask God to change the universe.

Oh, yes! Nancy survived and thrived. And she believes prayer made the crucial difference.

December 14, 1999

Big Gifts Come in Small Packages

Cecil, our hired hand, lived in the shanty.

The two room shack that Dad's farming helper called home squatted next to the chicken house. No thought existed that the chicken operation would pollute Cecil's water supply. The shanty had no running water or any other amenities save the roof, a floor, and walls.

Cecil and my family shared the restroom facility. It stood midway between the shanty and the plain tenant house in which my sharecropping dad, my mom, my two sisters, and I resided. The one rule of toilet etiquette required knocking before entering. We needed no flush rule. One cannot flush a gravity-driven one-seater.

The century and I were still young enough that we didn't realize a poverty line existed. Cecil lived below that later-to-be-drawn line, and the Delongs didn't live to far above it.

Cecil dined at our table most evenings. No poverty existed there. Farm families, especially ones with a cook like my mother, ate well and heartily.

Come Saturday night, though, Cecil's spot was empty. Saturday evening Cecil traveled to town. He walked the mile to the Village of Kingston before dark. He returned long after.

I can only guess what places Cecil visited. The Town House served beverages in glass bottles; so did Gus's. Surely Cecil would have craved and deserved some relaxation and companionship after a long week spent in the fields by day and in the dark shanty by night.

Each Sunday morning did produce evidence of one establishment Cecil had visited. Without fail, when I tiptoed out onto the cool back porch in my flannel pajamas on Sunday morning, I spied and seized the small brown paper poke. Cecil had deposited it there in the wee hours as he migrated from the taverns to his shanty.

The contents of the bag proved that he had visited the penny candy counter at Jim Buchwalter's store prior to making his other evening rounds. He had spent a nickel or a dime of his paltry pay to satisfy little Dicky's sweet tooth. He must have squeezed that out of his entertainment budget.

He could not have given to me from his plenty. He gave from his scarcest asset.

Christmas Day culminates what our culture calls the "season of giving." Might we better name it the "season of giving . . . ourselves headaches?" Average people save all year (Christmas Club accounts) or pay all next year (credit card accounts) to buy gifts they cannot comfortably afford for people who really need very little and, the truth be told, many of whom they like very little, all with the expectation that they will receive reciprocal gifts of approximately equal value from the recipients.

In effect, we are buying ourselves gifts that we'd rather not extend ourselves to have.

Cecil knew I could not reciprocate. I doubt that I ever gave him anything. He was making a pure gift, a gift I could not earn. The gift was precious because it came not from the giver's abundance, but from his scarcity.

Maybe we could capture the genuine spirit of this season if we adopted Cecil's plan of giving. Determine what's scarce in our lives, then give some of it away.

Most of us in our hurried society groan constantly about our lack of time. A gift of spending more of our time with spouse, child, relative, friend, or even that needy stranger down the street would constitute a gift of our most precious commodity.

Others of us carry the burden of life so earnestly that smiles have become our scarcest commodity. We cannot show joy; life's just too serious. The gift of more smiles and laughter would be a precious gift to both the receiver and the giver.

Some of us guard our affections the way the army protects Fort Knox. Unlike gold, however, love is an inexhaustibly, self-renewing treasure. Instead of hoarding affection, give it away in large bundles this and every season.

Come to think of it, this season exists to celebrate just a precious gift – the perfect gift. The God who created and owns everything gave the thing He had only one of, a part of Himself. His only begotten son, to us.

The Christ child was born in a shanty to parents of little standing.

Thanks to Cecil and to God for their precious gifts.

November 2001

Be Thankful for America's Bounty

I must have been eight or nine years old. With no sibling within 6 years of my age, I spent lots of time randomly roaming our family's little farmstead, developing my imagination.

The haymow became the Alamo. I became Davy Crockett defending it. Blackwater Creek turned into the mighty Mississippi. I turned into Huckleberry Finn adventuring down it. The leech bed full of fresh, fist-sized boulders changed into a pile of baseballs beside the pitcher's mound at spring training. I changed into Bob Feller, firing another strike.

One day I chucked one of those stony chunks at a woodpecker sitting atop a mature apple tree. Always before, the pitch went wide, the bird fluttered upwardly, and I ambled on in my reverie. This time I was surprised; and the bird, I suppose, was shocked, (if shock can be felt before death instantly arrives).

I had harbored no ill will toward woodpeckers. Who would have "thunk" that I could hit that bird square in the chest from that distance? But I did! "Strike three – you're out!"

The "thunk" of that stone slapping that bird in the chest still haunts me a bit today.

Improbable events make lasting impressions.

The improbable events of September 11 hit us much the same unexpected manner with some of the same results. No, the U. S. eagle was not killed by the terrorists' missiles, but a measure of our innocence has died. "Who would have 'thunk' it?" reverberates in our collective minds. We have mobilized. We shall prevail, I am sure; but the improbability of it all has stunned us.

How, then, can we approach Thanksgiving Day this year? How can we express thankfulness so soon after thousands of our innocent citizens have been slaughtered? How can we enjoy turkey and trimmings when thousands of our best are still in harm's way? How can we appreciate the bounteous meal of American greatness topped with our individual blessings when our taste buds are numb?

The darkest nights produce the brightest stars.

In America's darkest days, Abraham Lincoln shone. President Lincoln originated a national Thanksgiving Day by his decree in 1863. In reviewing some of his thoughts, maybe we can engender an appropriate spirit of gratefulness even in this strange season.

"I intend no modification of my oft' expressed personal wish that all men everywhere could be free!"

So, be thankful that we are free and live in a free country.

"The ballot is stronger than the bullet."

So, fly your flag proudly, shout your allegiance clearly, sing your anthem stirringly; but don't forget to vote next election. Be thankful for the right to determine the course of your country.

"It is rather for us to be here dedicated to the great task remaining before us . . . that we here highly resolve that the dead shall not have died in vain, that this nation, under God, shall have a new birth of freedom; and that government of the people, by the people, and for the people, shall not perish from the earth."

So, be thankful for the hope of the future.

"The only assurance of our nation's safety is to lay our foundation in morality and religion!"

So, be thankful to have been reminded that the only sure foundation is not in mortar, but in morals, not in tanks, but in truth.

And lastly, let me offer a quote from the book that Lincoln was often found reading during his days of depression.

"Therefore, since we are receiving a kingdom that cannot be shaken, let us be thankful, and so worship God acceptably with reverence and awe" (Hebrews 12:28).

The darkness produced by the rock of September 11 is birthing a brilliant dawn.

Happy Thanksgiving, after all.

November 11, 2002

A Gesture of Honor is Well Worth the Effort

As the funeral procession continued its 10-mile crawl across the prairie to the hilltop cemetery, soon-to-be the resting place for our beloved father, the action of the farmer in the field next to the road grabbed and gratified us mourners. He shut down his tractor. He waited, motionless and silent, while we passed. His thoughtful manner of honoring the dead gave a blessing to the living.

When this newspaper invited its readers to offer writings to commemorate the one-year anniversary of September 11, I remembered this funeral image and attempted to create a column around it. I failed. To me, all statements, including my own, at that time seemed to be clichés. Any comments made seemed inadequate compared to the enormity of the loss and the dramatic nature of the shift in world perspective caused by the terrorist attacks of that day.

Now, Veterans Day approaches. I cannot let it pass without notice. We as a nation should not either. We need to "shut down our tractors" long enough to honor the dead, the soldiers who fell in battle or have since died, and to honor the living, those who have served and are serving us in the armed forces.

During the period from the Vietnam War through September 11, the concept of "armed force" did not receive much respect in our country. The use of force just didn't seem, didn't seem . . . well, polite or something. For America to apply force didn't seem fair. It didn't seem mature for big, old, untouchable, impregnable, weren't we?

Distrust of power has a fine tradition. We founded our nation in response to King George's attempts at remote control of us by exercise of his thronely power from England. Over and over in our history we have resisted the tyranny of the merely powerful. I suppose a number of generals with chests full of medals have had direct access to the most raw power in our country, but we have never been ruled by generals. Our commander-in-chief has always been a man in a gray suit sitting behind a desk working with 535 or so legislators down the street.

As Britisher Robert Mark commented; "You cannot control a free society by force."

So, we have had this double-mindedness about armed force and those men and women we have placed in position to build and use it. We seem to want them to have it, but we're not sure we want them to use it. In his "Measure for Measure," Shakespeare wrote, "O! It is excellent to have a giant's strength, but it is tyrannous to use it like a giant."

Now maybe we're getting somewhere. Be strong, but don't be a bully. Maintain strength, but use it only in a principled manner for just causes. Of course, defining just cause is the trick. One person's justice is another person's travesty.

Our country now debates what force, if any, to use against Saddam. Would such use be principled and for just cause? I cannot pretend to know. I am not privy to information that would allow me to decide. I trust our elected representatives to figure it out and let me know.

The practical-minded Teddy Roosevelt probably had it about right: "Do not hit at all if it can be avoided, but never hit softly." September 11 initiated a national funeral procession. We may not have reached the resting place yet. But just as the farmer's attitude and actions toward the dead blessed the living, we should strive to conduct ourselves individually and collectively in a manner which blesses the surviving and current members of our armed forces while memorializing those valiant members who died fighting for our freedoms.

Today, I plan to stop my tractor long enough to thank a veteran. Won't you?

December 17, 2002

Look for the Real Face of Christmas

Trees and trimmings, gifts and greeting cards, snowflakes and stores abound this and all yuletides, but those things have never revealed Christmas to me. I have seen Christmas only in faces.

I've no Christmas memory which predates my first views of Santa. In the early '50s only one Santa existed. He chose to reveal himself only from the Columbus, Ohio studios of WBNS-TV, Channel 10. Well, I guess he also found time to drop by the Lazarus department store for limited engagements with those of us little ones who needed to get up-close and personal. But he was the real Santa, the only Santa, the genuine article.

I could tell by looking in his face. Yes, his belly shook like a bowl full of jelly, but so did the bellies of most of the men who attended my family's annual reunion. Yes, he had big, black boots, but so did my dad when he was working in the manure in our cattle lot.

Santa's face distinguished him. That face, with the red cheeks and the twinkling eyes, gave him away. His face just shone . . . more brightly even than the nose of that Rudolph the flying deer fellow. Others might have doubts, but not yours truly. I could spot the real face of Christmas: Santa's.

A year or two later, Santa began showing up at our church after our Sunday school Christmas program. Certainly, we were all glad to see him, but I studied that face. Little doubts began attaching themselves to my believer's brain.

The condition of his suit had surely suffered since I'd seen him in Columbus. His tummy didn't shake like jelly; it rather quaked like pillows.

And the face . . . something had changed. When Santa's face headed north, his beard often started south. And, hey, the color of his eyebrows no longer matched the color of his beard. In fact, his face put me in the mind of our local undertaker; a member of our church. Where was Loring, anyway? He faithfully supported church activities, but he always missed this event!

Time passed, and other faces superseded Santa's. Some obscured the shine of Christmas; others restored the luster of the season.

I recall the hopeless, blank looks on the faces of family members to whose poverty-stricken (and smelly) homes my father and other school board members delivered baskets of food and supplies during the Christmas season.

Only now do I realize fully why Dad took a young lad such as I along to witness adults perform an adult job. He wanted me to lock my eyes with the hollow eyes of other kids who had less than I - much less.

On those Christmases, I saw desperation in their faces and compassion in his.

More recently and more often I see desperation and emptiness in the faces of the floods of shoppers and retail clerks who shepherd them.

The obligatory gift-giving doesn't engender the kind of shine I saw in Santa's face. He really did seem pleased to be giving things away, even though he must have known that we tiny tots would not be able to reciprocate. In giving, Santa received back only the gift of our joy.

Memories of my family members' faces from Christmases past shine so clearly that I need sunglasses. Our scrapbook contains a shot of our smooth-faced son, Doug, then aged 4 years or so, on the phone, eyes bursting with excitement, telling Grandma that he had just seen Santa - - the real one, of course.

My mind also retains the looks of my wife's wrinkly-faced Grandma Grace giving out presents of homemade crafts and foods she had spent the whole year preparing for her loved ones. I remember the recipients' faces, too.

But one face epitomizes Christmas. It brings the season alive. Like Santa's, this face was in one place, but is in every place too. Like Dad, this face recognizes sorrow and reaches out with compassion to those feeling desperation. Like the clerks, this face looks upon the flocks and offers guidance and assistance.

If you can pause even momentarily and look away from the dark distractions of today, you can just see through the crack in the stable door this bright and eternally shining face beaming at you from the straw-framed baby in the manger.

December 13, 2003

Jesus and Santa Claus Shouldn't Be Enemies

It's that time of year. 'Tis the season to be jolly; it's time for mistletoe and holly. It's also time for the annual altercation between the secular and the sacred. Creche on the courthouse lawn or not? Santa at the Sunday school party or not? WWJT. What would Jesus think? To arrive at that answer, let's first examine not what is the reason for the season, but what are definitely not the reasons Baby Jesus showed up in Bethlehem on that silent night two millennia ago.

Jesus was not born in a courtroom to be our lawyer. Now, He would be a fine attorney. He would have a full understanding of how the system works. He is, after all, omniscient, all knowing. He would be loyal to His client. Once He enters a relationship, He never backs out of it. He would always be truthful, since He is truth. He would never work a fraud on the court. In fact, He is our Great Advocate (Job 16:19). He is my counselor, and I personally am relying on Him to plead my final case. But, He was not born simply to be our advocate. After all, He will one day be our judge (2 Timothy 4:1).

Jesus was not born in a rotunda to be our politician. Yes, He was a proven vote getter. Remember the palms in the streets and the "Hosannas" in the air. And what a fiercely devoted inner circle of advisors He assembled, a talented cabinet, aka the disciples. He could certainly draft laws. He came, in fact, to fulfill the law (Matthew 5:17). The prophet Isaiah even tells us that the government will be upon His shoulders. He is the foundation of all human institutions, including government; but at the same time, He is beyond them. So, He advised His advisors to let Caesar, the government, do its thing without interference from Him and His. He was to be about matters beyond politics and earthly governments. He is less concerned about His place in the public park and more concerned about His place in the private heart. Clearly, He was not born to assume a political role.

Jesus was not born on a soundstage to be a performer. Oh, He knew how to attract and satisfy a crowd. He spoke like no one else ever did or has since. He held audiences spellbound more than once. Then, He fed the throngs with but two fish and five loaves. His Nielsen ratings would have been unsurpassed. But, He did not seek the spotlight. In the end, He was not born just to entertain. When His listeners got past what He did to discover Who He was, they switched channels. He was willing to pray for the crowds, but unwilling to play to the crowds. No, He was not born to perform.

Neither was Jesus born in a studio to be a commentator, a forerunner of O'Reilly. He's watching out for us, all right. And the spin definitely stops with Him. He does ask all the tough questions. The difference is: He answers them, too. He is the answer. He's just not nearly abrasive enough for the anchor's job. He was not born to screech.

Certainly, Jesus was not born in a mall to be a merchant. Jesus wasn't materially minded enough to make it in merchandising. He didn't shout, "Get." He shouted, "Give." He pedaled treasures in Heaven while eschewing treasures here on earth. He displayed one of His few flashes of anger when the marketers entered the temple. He drove them out (John 2:15). If Jesus operated the mall, the shoppers would be gone. Jesus was not born to chair the Chamber of Commerce.

If Jesus didn't intend to engage the world in these ways we moderns invite Him to, then what was His plan? What was His reason for showing up for the initial Christmas season? As the lyric of a contemporary Christian song goes, "What a strange way to save the world?" No one caught on to the plan very quickly. Joseph was skeptical and needed an angel to convince him. Mary was amazed, but she shouldered her assigned duty/privilege. The only light resembling a spotlight was the star over Bethlehem. The humble shepherds were the first people to recognize Him. Some still don't. How strange it all was and is!

The world did not then, and we do not now, need another lawyer, politician, performer, commentator, or merchant. The world is and has always been full of them, and they can give us no more than temporary relief. We needed God not just to look down at us, but to come down with us. Looked at that way, it begins to make wonderful sense.

Jesus, Emmanuel, was born in a stable to be our Savior. Celebrate it. Merry Christmas!

December 2004

What's a Person to Believe about Holidays?

Last Saturday's newspaper declared: "Religion is the reason for the reason."

Sunday my pastor said: "Christmas is not about religion."

This struck me as a role reversal: the secular reporting the sacred and the ecclesiastical denying it!

So, what's a person to believe?

December marches forward, as relentlessly as the toy soldiers in "The Nutcracker," bearing down on the 25th. Besides attending to all the ceremonies and preparations for the big day, now we must solve a dilemma. Why are we celebrating the Christmas season, really?

As a child I celebrated for one reason, and that was not religious. "Gimme-mas" would have been a good name for the day as I practiced it.

As an adolescent and young adult, I added a measure of religion, but not necessarily God, to the formula. I had come relatively early to seek the things of heaven above, or at least along with, the things of Earth. I certainly knew and believed the story of the Christ child. I paid obeisance to it at Christmastime by participating in its presentation to my community by my church. But the 25th itself? Get real! I still wondered more about what my girlfriend/fiancée`/wife would find to surprise me with under the tree than about the Star of Wonder.

Then along came my own children. As a parent, I removed my Christmas focus from myself, but I just shifted it to my kids. I do not mean for a moment my wife and I neglected our religious duties with our offspring. We made sure our young-uns served their time as giggling shepherds or tilted-halo angels in the Sunday school Christmas dramas. We even sang happy birthday to Jesus on Christmas morning before descending the stairs to our gifts, set knee-deep by Santa around the tree. But, the intensity of the celebration of the gifts from Santa outweighed that of the gift from God.

Not until my offspring sprung to adulthood and my materials had nearly caught up with my material desires did I actually begin giving "the real meaning of Christmas" more than just lip service. With the kids gone, December provided more opportunity for prayer, meditation, rest and reflection. The result: a better connection with the God about whom the season is. Finally, maybe religion had gotten on the scoreboard.

Now grandchildren have come along. One may conclude the only humans who act sillier than children are those children's grandparents. We grandparents often begin doing to and for our grandkids the same things we did to and for our own kids, but in spades.

These days comes more lap time with the little ones: talking, hugging, playing games and reading books, including Luke 2. And the grandkids' Christmas pageants look different through these older eyes. I hadn't noticed so much of the eternal watching my kids' performances.

So, shall we conclude the newspaper was right? Is religion the reason for the season? Well, not exactly, no.

Still, surprisingly, the pastor is right: "Christmas is not about religion." He is right because religion is merely a system of beliefs about God. We do not worship religion.

A religion was not born and laid in a manger. A religion did not grow up and give His life on the cross to save from their sins those who would place their faith in Him.

A religion does not give us the assurance of eternal life with God. A person does. His name is Jesus.

Have a meaningful Christmas.

December 16, 2005

Santa's Boss Will Help Us Out

Dear Santa,

I know you are very busy this time of year, but I'm hoping you have time to read my letter. I'm a few thousand years old (at least), and I live in the very big apartment just below yours at the North Pole.

I've been a good little planet this year. Well, I've been a fairly good planet this year. Oh, all right! I haven't been so good, but I could have been worse. Don't ask me how, but I know I could have been.

I haven't asked for much lately. I've kind of thought I could take care of myself without bothering you; but, as I look around, I see that I haven't done a very good job. I have a pretty long wish list, but I'll put just the most important ones in this letter.

It's been said: "You can't fight wind, water, and ignorance." So, I guess I should admit to you that I didn't behave so well in the wind and water department this year. Most years I'm satisfied simply to enjoy the stiff breezes always coming out of Washington D. C., but this year I couldn't seem to shake a nasty hurricane habit. After I saw the results of my orneriness, I was sorry; hence, my first wish: Could you send lots of help and comfort to all those hurt by my escapades?

And maybe you could bring me some of those boring educational toys under my tree this year. You would think as I've grown older I would learn to overcome some of the ignorance problems I've had for so long; but, Santa, I still need tutoring with the following:

Hunger – Even though I grow more and more food (on less and less ground each year, I might add) I can't seem to get the stuff to the right people at the right time. I see millions starving, many to death, each year. I'm so frustrated. I really hate it when I see those little kids hungry and malnourished just because the adults who live on me are too proud or selfish or lazy to handle my harvest properly. So, my second wish: Could you send some neat computer program, and maybe loan me an elf to run it that would provide a food distribution apparatus to satisfy this need?

Disease – Here's another of my old bugaboos. Every few years, my people and I conquer one of the terrible curses that have been around forever; then, out of nowhere another pops up to take its place. We finish off polio; up jumps AIDS. We eradicate smallpox; here comes bird flu or some other silly plague. Truth be told, although those affluent Americans who require so much of your attention and resources hardly realize it, many of the diseases they think are history still kill millions yearly around the world, many of whom, again, are children. You haven't heard much about malaria and tuberculosis in the developed countries lately, but those diseases are still big killers around my equator. A Mr. Gates, who, excuse me Mr. Santa, seems to have more money than you, is trying to put a dent in this problem; but it's not enough. My third wish: If you can't give me some magic potion to use to cure all these diseases, could you at least send a vial of eye drops to each household to open its occupants' eyes to this problem?

War – Now, I have to be really careful on this one this year. It's gotten to be a touchy issue around some of my parts. I've been broken out with this war rash ever since I began, or, I should say, ever since people have inhabited me. Now, don't get me wrong. I agree that some things are worth fighting for. It's just that I'd love to go a few years without the awful itch that comes with this war rash. My fourth request: Could you deliver ointment that could be spread over me to quell the tendency people have to harm each other?

St. Nick, I could ask for lots of other things; but frankly, and I hope you won't be offended, I'm starting to wonder whether you can really deliver anyhow. Maybe you should just stick with the dolls, balls, and bicycles. After all, my people and I have been begging for peace on me and goodwill toward men for what seems like eons; but with precious few exceptions, you really haven't delivered.

Santa, maybe I'm unfair to you. I've placed unrealistic expectations on you. You're in the business of meeting the material desires of me and my inhabitants. You've become (ahem) legendary at that, but the list I've given you includes seemingly eternal problems, some stemming from the very nature of people. I shouldn't expect you to deliver miracles.

No, I've been looking the wrong direction. Instead of focusing North on one to meet my physical needs, I'd be ahead to look East to the One born as a helpless baby in a stinky stable, but Who grew to master wind, walk on water, and offer comfort to the afflicted.

I'm sorry I bothered you, Mr. Santa. When I look back at this year, and every previous year, and at the help I really need, I realize that you're just not built to respond to my requests. You could do me one favor, however. Could you forward this letter to your boss and mine in the colossal apartment above yours? I have faith that He'll know how to respond.

Merry Christmas, Santa, and take a break.

Happy birthday, Jesus, and help us all.

Thanks,
Earth

December 13, 2006

Holy Birth

Better get ready...for the nearly inevitable post-holiday letdown. Excepting Mr. Scrooge and his kind, most folks suffer some degree of downward attitude adjustment in the days following the season of celebration. One need not be a psychologist to figure out why: first, the anticipation; next, the actual experience; thereafter, the void.

Often anticipation of an event actually equals or even beats the experience. How delicious looking forward to that coming vacation a day or two before it arrives. Thoughts of a great meal and even the aroma from the kitchen prior to sitting at the table give more pleasure than the actual tasting. (Remember, Beth, our first roast as ignorant newlyweds? It smelled great in the oven, but we should have known even in 1968 that 50 cents would buy us not a standing rib roast, but only a meatless soup bone.) Looking forward to gathering on or before Christmas with friends and family generally brings pleasure, notwithstanding memories of less-than-perfect Christmas pasts. Hope springs eternal. We always think this time will be better.

Participating in the celebrations of the season does bring rewards. Most of the gatherings are not the unmitigated disasters depicted in the movies. Hugging the necks of beloved kin, watching the enthusiasm of the young-uns, and catching up on the status of family and friends invigorates the soul. Having an extra day or two away from the job, without burning any vacation days leads to numerous pleasures: taking a nap without guilt; propping up the feet and watching a couple of games or movies without eye or mind on the clock; curling up under a blanket with a favorite book or magazine; sleeping in a little; eating a little more than usual; or just vegging out. Celebrating actively or even passively delivers pleasure.

Count on it though—depression will knock at the door of the house emptied of the tree, the tinsel, and the times. The company has left, but memories of their stinging comments or rude behavior lingers. The gifts have broken or vanished, but the credit card balances persist, sometimes even grow. The feasts have ended, but the pounds report in every morning on those scales. The notes of "Up on the Housetop" have given way to those of "Down in the Valley."

Chasing away the gloom may require changing one's perspective. Look forward to the next possibilities rather than the current void. A successful drama, on the stage or on the page, contains certain segments in certain order. The setting divulges who's who and who's where. Early on, a conflict or trouble appears. The bulk of the story fleshes out the difficulty. Then, the climax showcases the most intense action. The conflict comes to a head. This, however, does not end the piece. Finally comes the denouement (day-new-'mah), the working out of the final outcome of the complex sequence of events. The denouement is not depressing. It is instead satisfying.

Maybe post-holiday depression could be lessened by viewing Christmas and the days that surround it not as the climax, but as the mere setting for the coming year. In fact, such would match well with the sacred view of Jesus' birth.

The Savior's birth was not the climax of God's dealing with us. The coming of Immanuel just provided the setting for what was to come and is still coming. The baby Jesus grew and his earthly days contained much trouble, discomfort, and conflict. Easter provided the climax with His crucifixion and resurrection. Now all of history, including our personal history, involves the working out of our complex lives in relation to God.

Christmas Day can be wonderful, celebrating both the coming of the kin and the coming of the King. But as Yogi Berra famously said, "It ain't over 'til it's over." The way to avoid the January blahs is to avoid looking back as if the end of that day signified the postponing until next December of our quest to maintain and even improve our relationships with our loved ones and with the One who loves us. Christmas and the euphoria that accompanies it "ain't over."

Merry Christmas and, in the new year, avoid the letdown by looking forward and looking upward.

November 26, 2009

Cornstalks Remind Me of Source of our Bounty

For some it's the sight and smell of that golden, roasted turkey. For others, the day off with football on TV. And for still others, it's the family all gathering in one spot. For me, it's corn stalks.

Maybe my childhood farm experiences caused it. Maybe my rural location fires it. Whatever the basis, in recent years the sight of the forlorn fodder, the corn stalks left behind by the powerful harvesting behemoths of the local farmers, prompts me to remember that the last Thursday of November is coming soon and that I need to be giving thanks.

I'm not sure I know why. One would think that a view of a bulging grain bin, an overflowing bank account, or a replete refrigerator would stimulate the vibes of gratefulness. Beholding the limp lampstands that once held high shining yellow ears of grain should depress the viewer. But, at least for me, the empty stalks bent low remind me of the bounty which has flowed. The stalks bestow a certain comfort somehow.

An old 19th century hymn, "Come Ye Thankful People Come," contains a line: "First the blade and then the ear, then the full corn shall appear." The acres of barren stalks evidence to me that the full corn has appeared and then disappeared in the harvest. The Lord has caused the growth for yet another year, and the farmer has brought in the sheaves. Only the silliest, most arrogant farmer would claim that he or she made the grain grow from seed to blade to stalk to ear. Plant --yes. Fertilize--yes. Water--if an irrigation system has been installed--yes. Eradicate threatening weeds and disease--yes. But make it grow--no!

I guess the humble stalks remind me of the Source of our bounty. At the end of the day, at the end of the season, at the end of the year, at the end of our lives, only the most brazen, blowhards among us would dare put forth that whatever meager harvest we have reaped in life has been due solely to our initiative, our talents, our winsome ways.

That aforementioned hymn contains another line: "Lord of harvest, grant that we, wholesome grain and pure may be." That's my prayer as I see the stalks, once so essential, but now so dispensable and useless. I pray that as I pass through my personal autumn and head into winter ahead, I will have yielded an acceptable crop and that I will be thanking the One who made it happen. And, thus, my recommendation for you, gentle reader. As you survey your field of gray stalks at this time of year and at this time of life, resolve to remember your harvest that has been made possible by the growth of the stalks of your life and express your gratitude to the One who has blessed that harvest.

Have a humble and a happy Thanksgiving.

December 25, 2011

Try Looking at Life through another Lens

'Tis the season . . . . Q. What season? A. To be jolly! Hold on a bit, there. Is it? Jolly seems hard to come by sometimes.

Perspective makes all the difference though doesn't it? The vantage point from which we look at things often determines what we see. So it may have been with 2010.

In your humble correspondent's case, I certainly could not have guessed I'd spend so much time at funerals this year. My mom died in January after 97 years of life. Although she lived the full cycle of earthly life, sadly, many other loved ones left their loved ones prematurely: young friends, Sammy, 10, and Sydney, 13, in August; my soul buddy, Jerry, 59, in mid-November; and my wife's sister-in-law's grand nephew, Drew, 3 ½ from a heart attack on Thanksgiving Day. Each left a witness of a life well lived, but each left an unfillable vacancy on this earth. A season to mourn our mortality? Could be, but jolly?

The world's economy seems to be bumping along rather badly in most places. Unemployment still abounds. The real estate market still smells like Rudolph's manure. The guesses of the economists who are supposedly engineering our economy run off track as often as not. A season to lose faith in our system? Could be.

Maybe 'tis a season to regret the ugliness we see in the world: wars, rumors of war, threats of nuclear havoc, information leaks revealing unbecoming machinations by whole governments. This appears to be a season of waning confidence in the abilities and even intentions of our leaders. Not a jolly prospect.

Let's not leave out the common man and woman. Maybe it's just my age, but are we not ready to lament together the deplorable condition of humankind's character? The list of flaws never falls: lies, cheats, thefts, violent acts, murders. Sounds like the first five minutes of the evening news, doesn't it? It appears we are in the never-ending season of depravity.

But, maybe we should change our viewpoint, change the lens through which we are viewing this cultural carnage. The writer of the biblical book of Ecclesiastes wrote, "You learn more at a funeral than at a feast." Sounds morbid, but it needn't be so. Maybe we need to consider what we can learn by viewing things differently. All of our lives in this old world are full of downs and ups and likely will remain so. Only if we see our lives from the appropriate perspective can we avoid a crushing pessimism or a silly optimism.

In this season of the year as in all seasons of our lives, we should try looking at all of life through the lens of Jesus. We Christians believe He was born to die. That tends to temper the celebration of His coming. Yet, only through His death could we be reconciled to God. In this holy season, I pray you and I will see through and beyond the circumstances of the past year and the obstructions of the present to the glorious future that the coming of the Christ child promises.

November 28, 2013

The Hungry Need the Help of those with Full Bellies

I never saw anything remotely resembling an empty kitchen table at my childhood home. Raised until age thirteen on a small rented farm, I may have been existing at or near the federally defined poverty line, which had not yet been delineated in the 1950's; but I didn't know it when mealtime arrived. Food, good food, mostly grown or raised right there by Dad and presently prepared from scratch by Mom, appeared regularly and deliciously at our simple table. The ingredients and preparation may have been plain, but the resulting aromas and tastes were complex and satisfying. Yummy in the tummy!

I don't remember seeing in those very early years any other skimpily adorned tables either. Of course, most of our family's kin and friends lived the farm life, too; but even my visits to friends' abodes in Kingston, the village which was our township seat, and beyond to some city slicker friends' homes in Chillicothe, the county seat, revealed no lack of vittles. I'll never forget the Saturday French fries at Widow Irene Brooks' table or the never-ending pies and popcorn served by Betty Raymond Davis to the hordes of us local kids who continually paraded through her open door.

Reality eventually intruded. I remember just before Christmas one year as a grade schooler accompanying my school board member dad to a stinking (fact, not judgment) home not that far from mine to deliver boxes of donated food. That experience got me to thinking. Maybe some of the kids in my class with holes in their shirts, shoes, and pants also had holes in their food chains. Maybe they had empty places in their stomachs that I had never experienced.

As I've matured, or at least aged, I've learned of the widespread existence of hunger in the world. At church, I've seen the films and heard the missionaries' reports of starving babies, of children spending their days sifting through garbage dumps to find scraps to sustain themselves, and of mothers begging for the aid workers just to take their newborns back to the U.S.A. where they knew, at least, their beloved babies would find food and life.

And I've learned that one needn't look so far to discover hunger. The Gazette recently published the shocking statistic that more than twenty-five thousand residents of our little Ross County avail themselves of government food stamps. I vacillate between disgust and grief upon receiving such information. I protest that so many citizens rely upon the government to feed themselves and their families properly, but then I despair that our government is so ineffective that jobs may not exist for those who do desire to work and that our policies have created disincentives for many to work at all. Finally, though, I dwell sympathetically on the innocent children who, for whatever reasons, personal, cultural, or governmental, are feeling those empty places in their stomachs. For them, no yummy in the tummy, no jelly in the belly, but instead just an empty rut in the gut.

So, you may fairly ask, "What are you doing about it, Delong?" I could attempt a defense. I have worked hard and fed myself and my family; but, then again, I have had the opportunities of an education, a good job, and excellent health. I've contributed to local, state, national, and international programs, through both religious and secular sources, to feed the hungry. I have even kept my eyes open for and occasionally contributed directly to those acquaintances and neighbors around me who have been without their necessary daily bread.

But I have also made the same excuses others make: "Why should I sacrifice so that others, too lazy to work, can eat? Let the government handle it. Let the church handle it. Let the do-gooders handle it."

These rationalizations sound convincing at first. Even the writers of the gospels report that Jesus himself said: "The poor you will always have with you. . ." (Luke 14:7). As is often the case, however, we mislead when we use a biblical passage out of context to prove our point. No one can read the whole New Testament and argue honestly that Jesus didn't care about poor and hungry people. He fed those over and over and in every way.

Consequently. . . here I am. Here we are. Thanksgiving Day and the accompanying feasts approach. Some of the biggest challenges of the season for many of us will be how to get all of the groceries we purchase into our automobiles' trunks, how to get all the food we want to cook into our ovens, and how to fit all of the turkey and trimmings onto our tables. I trust that this year before digging in I and all of us who have plenty will stop for a moment and thank God for His provisions. I also suggest that we all begin looking around us for the near-empty kitchen tables. Many are willing to help stock these tables: the Salvation Army, the Good Samaritan Network, the Mid-Ohio Food Bank, your church, and others; but they need our help. Responding to an ache in our hearts to help out can relieve the awful ache of hunger in the stomachs of some of our neighbors, near and far.

Happy giving and Happy Thanksgiving!

December 25, 2013

Falling Away from the Manger

The old barn held center stage in the barnyard and in my young life. The gray, pocked, wood-sided, rickety building served as my primary playground during my early years. As the only man-child in my family, I played alone most days in and around that barren barn. A dangling rope invited me to conduct a pretend circus. A basket on the wall inspired me to create my own Ross County high school basketball tournament. Kingston always won. I fantasized my way through many of those hours with the now known to be politically incorrect game of cowboys and Indians. For drama's sake, I had to play the parts of both adversaries, but I must admit that, at the end of the day, my WASP cowboys always prevailed. I also spent much unstructured time just wandering the structure. I especially remember the large bags of 2, 4-D stored in the back of the barn. Some modern-day scientists would tell me that my contact with this deadly herbicide should have led to my untimely death years ago. I can report to you that I have survived.

An abandoned horse stall in the old place also interested me. Dad did raise livestock on our farm, but only hogs got to reside in our B & S, i.e., barn and slop. The beef cattle did not overnight there. Molly, the only horse I recall, and that merely from photographs, had died before my barn-roaming days began. Thus, the elevated feeding trough I discovered in the forsaken stall did not really resonate with me. As part of my forced labor on the farm, I regularly poured feed for the hogs into the ground level troughs and stashed hay into the upright wooden cattle feeders, but I had never filled the manger. I established no personal relationship with it. The lively scent of hog dung and cow piles followed me to the house each evening, but the empty equine enclosure and its purposeless manger became a forgotten detour in the memory of my childhood.

As an urban dweller living in a mostly non-agrarian America, the only manger I see or hear about these days materializes about this time every year. An empty manger awaiting the baby Jesus appears in thousands of nativity scenes, in and out of churches, all over our nation and the world. We hear or sing strains of "Away in a Manger" all during Advent. Then, we place the Christ child in the manger at the last hour on Christmas Eve. Soon thereafter, the whole apparatus, the manger and the straw, the baby and the bathwater, so to speak, vanishes for another year. That manger, too, fades into empty meaningless in most of our memories. Too often, we establish no personal relationship with it or its inhabitant.

Theologians tell us that God the Father sent Christ as a helpless child, born in lowly estate, purposely. His method was mindful; it demonstrated God's desire to be with us, Emmanuel, in a real way. Christ came and lived in the world, a world full of humble and humiliating circumstances: poisonous substances and stinking situations. Yet, He brought and still brings at this Christmas the message that through Him, God and humankind can reconcile.

I am sure at the end of some of the epic battles I staged in the old barn, I, with the tail of my coonskin cap flapping in the breeze, would shout in memory of Davy Crockett, "Remember the Alamo." As we now approach the close of this Christmas season and get back to and on with the mundane matters of this world, may we shout in honor of the baby who grew into the God-man, who offers to save us yet today, "Remember the manger."

May 24, 2014

Reflect, but Don't Forget to Look Ahead

Ta, Ta, Tah!

On a warm, humid Decoration Day (aka Memorial Day) morning in the late 1950s, your humble correspondent, then a mere schoolboy, stood with trumpet in hand on the dewy grass of Mount Pleasant Cemetery abutting our little rented farmstead. Apparently, the qualified upper class trumpeters in our school band had better excuses, so the duty fell to me to play Taps.

I now recognize the job was not a duty, but an honor, an opportunity.

Ta, Ta, Tah!

The honoring soldiers gathered to memorialize their late comrades. Some honored had fought. Some had fallen on dewy, distant fields and sandy, foreign shores during World War I, World War II, or the Korean Conflict. I knew little about military life, the sufferings endured, the sacrifices made. My dad and his people farmed. The nation had allowed him to stay behind in overalls and work shoes to produce while neighbors departed in uniforms and spit-shone shoes.

I knew Uncle Walter had served on D-Day, but I could not have recited the significance of that day. I vaguely remembered riding to Columbus with the family to deliver Uncle Jack to a train at Union Station. Uncle Sam wanted Uncle Jack in Alaska during the Korean Conflict, but I could not have explained how the USA related to either Korea. Those heroes for whom I was feebly tooting the notes of Taps knew the details of military life and strife. Their faces showed it. This solemn memorialized, but did not celebrate.

Ta, Ta, Tah; Ta, Ta, Tah; Ta, Ta, Taah!

These men, standing on and lying under this sacred ground, their brothers and sisters in arms from cross the nation, had known, had faced, and had vanquished the enemy. We children of these types recently named them "The Greatest Generation," and for good reason. They recognized challenges hurled at them by the enemy. Then, at great risk and sacrifice, they engaged and overcame. By shouldering their duty, they delivered great opportunity to us "Baby Boomer Generation."

Similarly, the brave soldiers who later answered the calls to prosecute our nation's actions in Viet Nam, Kuwait, Iraq, Afghanistan, and other spots in a troubled world exercised identical bravery, unselfishness, loyalty, and love. They deserved the same accolades received by that great generation. Unfortunately, we let them down. The outcomes of their battles could not be so easily categorized as victories. That should not have diminished our expression of gratitude for what these finest Americans did. I and the rest of us need to take every opportunity to thank and honor them.

Ta, Ta, Taah; Ta, Ta, Taaah!

I recently read a definition of old age: the time when one looks backward more than one looks forward. I qualify more each day. I wonder if America qualifies, too. One reason for such retrospective living is we perceive, individually and nationally, that things were simpler "back then." As a child, looking forward to the next Little League game was easier than now, as a senior, anticipating the next body part to fall apart or the next loved one to leave us. Nationally, although the sacrifices were great, fighting a vicious—but known—enemy then had advantages over today's external challenges to our nation's future. More than a decade after declaring our War on Terrorism, we still cannot always identify and focus on the enemy (or enemies), let alone declare victory.

Nationally, internal challenges persist, too. In fact, cartoon character Pogo may have been right: "We have seen the enemy, and he is us." I did not see ambivalence in the eyes of those old soldiers who listened to my weak trumpeting. They were resolute. They were unified. I fear that we, as a nation, portray to ourselves and to those around the world the quality of vacillation, not resolve; confusion, not purpose; dissension, not unity; permissiveness, not discipline.

Ta, Ta, Taaaaaaaah!

The playing of Taps signifies the ending of the soldier's day and, sometimes, the end of a soldier's life. But Reveille follows every Taps. It's time to wake up. It's time to get up. It's time to move forward. As St. Paul declared in Philippians 3:13b-14: "Forgetting what is behind and straining toward what is ahead, I press on toward the goal to win the prize for which God has called me heavenward in Christ Jesus."

On Memorial Day, we have a sacred duty to reflect thankfully on the past sacrifices made and on the present service being rendered by our dedicated service men and women. We also have an obligation to recognize and overcome the challenges of America present, so we can deliver to the next generation a nation just awakening to its greatest potential.

December 25, 2014

<u>Remember, Christmas is the Beginning</u>

Better get ready. . .for the nearly inevitable post-holiday letdown. Excepting Mr. Scrooge and his kind, most folks suffer some degree of downward attitude adjustment in the days following the season of celebration. One need not be a psychologist to figure out why: first, the anticipation; next, the actual experience; thereafter, the void.

Often anticipation of an event actually equals or even beats the experience. How delicious looking forward to that coming vacation a day or two before it arrives. Thoughts of a great meal and even the aroma from the kitchen prior to sitting at the table give more pleasure than the actual tasting. (Remember, Beth, our first roast as ignorant newlyweds? It smelled great in the oven, but we should have known even in 1968 that 50 cents would buy us not a standing rib roast, but only a meatless soup bone.) Looking forward to gathering on or before Christmas with friends and family generally brings pleasure, notwithstanding memories of less-than-perfect Christmas pasts. Hope springs eternal. We always think this time will be better.

Participating in the celebrations of the season does bring rewards. Most of the gatherings are not the unmitigated disasters depicted in the movies. Hugging the necks of beloved kin, watching the enthusiasm of the young-uns, and catching up on the status of family and friends invigorates the soul. Having an extra day or two away from the job, without burning any vacation days, leads to numerous pleasures: taking a nap without guilt; propping up the feet and watching a couple of games or movies without eye or mind on the clock; curling up under a blanket with a favorite book or magazine; sleeping in a little; eating a little more than usual; or just vegging out. Celebrating actively or even passively delivers pleasure.

Count on it though—depression will knock at the door of the house emptied of the tree, the tinsel, and the times. The company has left, but memories of their stinging comments or rude behavior lingers. The gifts have broken or vanished, but the credit card balances persist, sometimes even grow. The feasts have ended, but the pounds report in every morning on those scales. The notes of "Up on the Housetop" have given way to those of "Down in the Valley."

Chasing away the gloom may require changing one's perspective. Look forward to the next possibilities rather than the current void. A successful drama, on the stage or on the page, contains certain segments in certain order. The setting divulges who's who and who's where. Early on, a conflict or trouble appears. The bulk of the story fleshes out the difficulty. Then, the climax showcases the most intense action. The conflict comes to a head. This, however, does not end the piece. Finally comes the denouement (day-new-'mah), the working out of the final outcome of the complex sequence of events. The denouement is not depressing. It is instead satisfying.

Maybe post-holiday depression could be lessened by viewing Christmas and the days that surround it not as the climax, but as the mere setting for the coming year. In fact, such would match well with the sacred view of Jesus' birth.

The Savior's birth was not the climax of God's dealing with us. The coming of Immanuel just provided the setting for what was to come and is still coming. The baby Jesus grew and his earthly days contained much trouble, discomfort, and conflict. Easter provided the climax with His crucifixion and resurrection. Now all of history, including our personal history, involves the working out of our complex lives in relation to God.

Christmas Day can be wonderful, celebrating both the coming of the kin and the coming of the King. But, as Yogi Berra famously said, "It ain't over 'til it's over." The way to avoid the January blahs is to avoid looking back as if the end of that day signified the postponing until next December of our quest to maintain and even improve our relationships with our loved ones and with the One who loves us. Christmas and the euphoria that accompanies it "ain't over."

Merry Christmas and, in the new year, avoid the letdown by looking forward and looking upward.

April 5, 2015

You need not be Perfect to Impress God

Aunt Pat thought all the eggs had been hard-boiled. Little three-year-old Dicky didn't know hard-boiled from soft-boiled from no-boiled... until the no-boiled cracked, leaking its yellow yolk into and through the jacket pocket of his new, blue, short- panted Easter suit. I learned that day that clothes appropriate for Easter Sunday church may not be fitting for the afternoon egg hunt at Grandma's house.

Fashion choices have changed significantly along with most other habits over the decades. Dressing up for church, especially Easter Sunday church, once involved planning, expense, and tension. Ladies bore hats. Song lyrics even referred to them: "In your Easter bonnet, with all the frills upon it." Men, even the farmers, mechanics, and blacksmiths, wore coats and ties. Little Suzies donned dresses and gloves. And little Dicky proudly pranced in his blue suit, the one with the short pants and the egg pocket.

Many folks today, churchgoers and non, still feel that attendance at a worship service, Easter or other, means dressing uncomfortably and pretentiously. On the contrary, I know of few, if any, congregations where formal dress is still expected. I am certain that God Who is worshipped in those churches does not impose a formal dress code. After all, in the Old Testament, God informs us that He looks on the inside, the heart of a person, not the outside (1 Samuel 16:7). In the New Testament, He warns against church folks showing favoritism toward the well dressed. (James 1: 1-4) As Robert South, English churchman, wrote three centuries ago: "God expects from men that their Easter devotions would in some measure come up to their Easter clothes."

Putting on "Sunday-go-to-meetin' clothes" may demonstrate sincere effort to give God the best a person has. No doubt, God admires that attitude. I, to a degree, share it and implement it personally. Donning fancy clothes can sometimes, however, constitute an attempt to show off, to fake piety, to fool others as well as oneself. Such hollowness doesn't impress God.

Bottom line: lack of finery need not prevent folks from attending worship services. A corollary: attending in superior clothing should not delude the wearers into believing that they have worshipped in truth. Samuel Johnson, British man of letters, wrote, "Alas, sir, a man who cannot get to heaven in a green coat [work clothes] will not find his way thither sooner in a great one [dress clothes].

Easter carries deep theological truths. Here is one, expressed in common language: "God doesn't care how many flowers a gal has in her bonnet or how many 'eggs' a guy has in his hip pocket. God came to earth via the death and resurrection of His son Jesus to receive and rescue all who will come to Him, whether they be wearing sweats or gowns, jeans or tuxedos."

This Easter Day may we all focus not on the expectations of those around us, but on the great God who created the eggs, the clothes, and all of us.

November 26, 2015

A Life Lived in Gratitude is not Wasted

Thanksgiving morning: the only day of the year my dad and I hunted. Our family eked out a living on a small farm Dad sharecropped with Doc Yaple, the landlord. So little Richard spent lots of time in the fields with Dad planting, tilling, harvesting, and spreading fertilizer, less politely known as manure. But this day was different.

Dad showed bravery, allowing me to carry a loaded long gun and marching along beside me. Being a cautious man of good sense, he probably actually trailed behind me, out of the line of fire. PETA would have been proud of me. I am sure I bagged neither hare nor pheasant, but that wasn't the point for me. Dad took the time to take me hunting. Thanks, Dad.

This Thanksgiving morning, although they are long gone, 1981 and 2010 respectively, I realize that I owe thanks to my parents for the many things they gave me. Some were tangible. The basics of life: food, shelter, and clothing. Like most children, I took these for granted and without special gratitude. At this juncture, however, having raised two of our own children, I know that these basics of life are not a given even in our great country. Looking back, I now see that my folks had to strive mightily to put vittles on the table, to keep a roof over the table, and to stash sufficient drawers in our dresser drawers. My parents, Dad, by working the farm and later driving a bulk oil delivery truck; Mom, by working in town at the A.S.C.S. office, and together, by clerking auctions on Saturdays, met the needs of a family of five.

Other provisions were intangible. These were probably the more important ones or, at least, more permanent ones: industry, independence, integrity, endurance, and such. Wayne and Nina worked hard. (See above herein). They did not rely on others to provide what they could, with effort, provide for themselves. They valued honesty and insisted upon it in themselves, in their family, and in their close circle, sometimes distancing themselves from friends or associates who treaded the crooked path of dishonesty. And they never gave up. Severe medical problems, lost employment, family disappointments, and the many difficulties life brings did not cause them to throw in the towel in frustration.

I fear I learned their lessons only partially and followed them rather imperfectly, but today I am grateful to have had the chance to observe them making these kinds of footprints through the snowy fields of life.

On this, my 69th Thanksgiving Day, it occurs to me, and maybe to you, gentle reader, that we owe thanks in many ways to many people for many reasons. Maybe not all had the advantage of a good childhood. If you did, you owe gratitude to those who provided it, whether it be parents, grandparents, adoptive, or foster parents. Even if not, by this time in life, we all have others we can be thankful for having protected, supported, educated, and nurtured us. Neighbors, friends, teachers, preachers, coaches, communities, government (yes, I'm sure), and most assuredly our God.

My wife often recites a saying she picked up from an author, Ann Voskamp: "Thankfulness precedes the miracle." This Thanksgiving Day, let's begin to allow gratitude for the blessings we have received from the hands of others in our lives take precedence over our selfish tendency to crave and demand more. Expression of our gratitude may well result in the miracle of contentment coming to reside in us.

December 25, 2016

Christmas all year long? Say it Ain't So

Our question for today: "Do you wish the Christmas season were shorter or longer?" The answer: "Depends."

Members of certain categories, no doubt, have no doubt. Retailers would vote to focus shoppers' avaricious attention on the offered wares every day of the year. Yuletide frenzy in April would jibe well with All Fools' Day. The entertainment industry, without doubt, would welcome the opportunity to pedal glittering holiday "specials" year around. Imagine TBS running "The Christmas Story" 24-7 365 days per year. Hallmark could add a third channel to fit in all their sugarcoated melodramatic Christmas dramas.

The food/beverage industry would rush to serve up this gluttonous gambit. Sales charts would be the color of Santa's black belt, not Rudolph's nose. Imagine office Christmas parties in June, at the lake! And, of course, credit card companies would be salivating at the prospect of all of us slobbering financial idiots continually buying all the "have to haves" at 24.9% APR. Mr. Chairman, the great State of Commerce casts all of its votes for the concept of yuletide running from New Year's morning through New Year's Eve.

Correspondingly, however, those who must deal with the consequences of the excesses predicted above probably would vote contra to continuous Christmastide. The ecstasy of the long-running fantasy must eventually yield to the agony of the inevitable realistic consequences of overconsumption. Hopelessly indebted petitioners would quickly overwhelm the capacity of the bankruptcy courts. Employers would find no employees at their stations on any Mondays after the every weekend Christmas bashes. You've come to know about Throwback Thursday; these will be Throw Up Mondays. The network executives creating the "shout news" shows wouldn't succumb to the snowflake specials without, as their emcees would say, "significant pushback." No, not all would vote, "Aye."

I wonder how the church would react. Attendance could rise if all who come out yearly for the Christmas pageants maintained their devotion to 52 such extravaganzas. On the other hand, the pastors and loyal parishioners called upon to produce those shows may become comatose from exhaustion by mid-February. Additionally, think of the poor cattle, camels, and sheep trapped for posterity in those cardboard stables!

Mostly, though, I wonder how I myself would respond to such an opportunity. As a believer in Christ, my first impulse leads me toward an affirmative vote. Yes, I begin to intone, let's celebrate the incarnation of God on Earth in the form of Baby Jesus all year, every year. But then my personal hypocrisy meter buzzes. I am supposed to have been doing that already since the day Christ entered the cradle in my heart.

Maybe I should cast a negative vote on this extension issue. On the whole, after all, the tenor of our culture's celebration of our precious Savior's birth seems to have precious little connection to the genuine meaning of His coming. I remember a little ditty I used to sing cynically to my young children: "Oh the real meaning of Christmas is to get all the gifts you can get." Why should a Christian vote for 12 months of that kind of convoluted celebration of Christ's birth? My sanctimonious self-edges toward the "no" lever.

As is often the case, though, I am settling somewhere in the muddled middle. Full-time Christmas rush madness? No way, Jose! But an extension of those delicious times each December that reflect accurately the Immanuel principle of "God with us?" That would be great with me. Yes, let's all vote with our hands, our feet, our pocket books, our minds, and our spirits to extend year around the gifts of generosity to the needy, the times of warmly hugging family and friends, the occasions of surprising neighbors and strangers alike with unsolicited good deeds, and the moments of quietly contemplating the impact of God Himself coming to dwell for a while on this planet and eternally in our hearts.

Have a merry "extended" Christmas this coming year!

April 16, 2017

Miracles Never Cease, Especially the Easter Kind

"Do you believe in miracles?" Sunday, February 22, 1980. Lake Placid, New York. TV sportscaster Al Michaels excitedly erupted with this question upon the happening of the seemingly impossible victory of the USA Olympic Men's Hockey Team over the heavily favored USSR "machine" in that year's Winter Olympic Games. Thanks to Mr. Michaels' call, the world forever will refer to that contest as "The Miracle on Ice."

As with most words, "miracle" can carry multiple definitions. Al's version matches the number 2 definition in Merriam-Webster's: "miracle: an extremely outstanding or unusual event, thing, or accomplishment." Per this definition, the utterly surprising victory of the fresh, amateur American boys over the grizzled, professional Soviet men qualified as a type of miracle. The odds makers had not prepared for such an odd outcome. Nevertheless, this miraculous outcome did not exceed the bounds of human possibility or comprehension. The mighty Soviet skaters just had a big off day. Bad ice happens. The 1 in 100 chance of an historic major upset keeps sports fans watching. (Think Mississippi State's shocking termination of the U. Conn ladies' 111 game winning streak).

"Do you believe in miracles?" Sunday, April 5, 33 A. D. (or thereabouts). Jerusalem, Judea (Israel). Adherents of Jesus Christ (Full Disclosure: I am one.) began posing this question to themselves and others upon discovery of His empty tomb on that first Sunday morning after the fatal Friday. Thanks to the voices of those followers, the world has forever since termed that event as "The Resurrection." Fans could refer to it as "The Miracle in the Morning."

Merriam-Webster's definition number 1 applies to this occurrence: "miracle: an extraordinary event manifesting divine intervention in human affairs." The aforementioned USA hockey puck hackers beat the odds, quite an unusual accomplishment. He obliterated the whole concept of odds. Through concerted human effort and by dying on Friday, but arising from the dead on Sunday, Jesus did not just beat the odds. He defied them. Little luck, the boys in baggy pants pulled out a win, a number 2 definition miracle. Through divine intervention, Jesus defeated death. Easter commemorates a number 1 definition miracle.

Of course, not everyone believes in definition number 1 miracles. Skepticism toward supernatural miracles is natural. Parents, playmates, professors, and pundits teach us that reality rules. "Smart people must rely exclusively on what they can see, touch, measure, and verify," they say. Generally that view of the world prevails, as it well should; but it is the exception that rules in this instance.

37 years have passed since "The Miracle on Ice," and many, although a decreasing number, remember that definition number 2 miracle. 1,984 years have passed since "The Miracle in the Morning," and many millions in every corner of the world are remembering that definition number 1 miracle still today. Additionally, while the active celebration of "The Miracle on Ice" has disappeared with the winds of a few passing decades, believers in "The Miracle in the Morning" continue even these centuries later not just to remember, but to celebrate in lively fashion the miracle of Christ's resurrection.

Why the difference? Simple. The impact of miracles manufactured by humans fades fast. The players get older. The team disbands. The viewers hit the remote. On the other hand, God-ordained miracles bring eternal changes. Jesus Christ is the same yesterday and today and forever. (Hebrews 13:8) We can join in and celebrate Christ's defeat of death just as joyously today as His followers did upon their discovery of the empty tomb 1,984 years ago.

Most people don't care much these days about that old "Miracle on Ice," but nearly all have had or are having a time of crisis when they direly need a "Miracle in Life." The "Miracle on Ice" led to a gold medal one game later for the USA team. The Easter miracle leads to something better than gold. Those who even today declare their belief in the Christ who arose from the dead and trust Him with their lives here on earth will one day walk with Him eternally on those proverbial streets of gold.

Mr. Michaels' complete exclamation included one more word: "Do you believe in miracles? YES!" In similar fashion, the Easter miracle doesn't lead to the "gold" without a "YES!"

December 24, 2017

<u>May You and Your Family be Surprised by Joy on Christmas</u>

December 25, 1958—a long time past. So long ago, that Elvis still could have fit into yoga pants. An ancient time when Elizabeth Taylor was working on her 2nd or 3rd of what would become 7 husbands…or 8 if we count both marriages to Richard Burton.

Little 11-year- old Dicky, there in our humble farm tenant house on Blackwater Road, happily anticipated the imminent Christmas morning ritual. Dad had completed the morning chores. Mom, er…I mean Santa, had stocked my stocking, (more accurately, my dad's larger work sock which I had conveniently borrowed for the occasion), with a candy cane of regulation size, a few walnuts in the shell, and an orange. Citrus in winter in these parts was a bit of a treat back then. I was expecting to spy a new basketball (Cool!) and maybe a flannel shirt (Not so exciting, but a mom does what she's got to do.) under the tree. Sister Janet had arisen and appeared downstairs. Everything was in its place. Well, every thing, but not every one.

For the first time since Mother Nina began "hatching chicks" in 1939, not all the chicks were in the nest on Christmas morning. Oldest chick Ruth Ann had married sailor Fred, had moved to the Charleston, SC naval base, and, for the first time ever, would not be breathing in with us the sweet aroma of our freshly cut pine tree on Christmas morn.

I confess that little Dicky had not invariably mourned her absence. As I informed Kenny at the grain elevator shortly after her wedding, "No, I don't miss her; now I've got the whole side of the dinner table all to myself." On this day, however, her vacancy cast a slight pall over the front room. Nevertheless, I volunteered to buck up and soldier on. After all, she had been thoughtful enough to employ the U.S. Postal Service, or maybe it was the Pony Express, to deliver our respective gifts. Anyway, always having subscribed to the doctrine that no good gift should remain unopened, I subtly suggested that we proceed. "Why are we waiting? He who hesitates on Christmas morning is dumber than Dasher. Let's get on with it, folks!"

At that critical juncture, we all heard it: automobile tires crunching the frozen nuggets of gravel on the driveway in our barnyard. We sprang to the frosty window to see what was the clatter just in time to observe the black Oldsmobile, caked with snow, ice, and road salt coast to a halt. Ruth Ann and Fred had slogged home, 600 miles through the snow and ice of the darkened eve, over the mountains, without benefit of the 6-lane West Virginia Turnpike all of us summer beach bums have come to know and loathe, but with the benefit of tire chains. (Kids, ask your grandparents to explain that equipment). Unexpectedly and joyously, Nina's chicks had gathered in one place once again. Where was Norman Rockwell when we needed him?

Not all Christmas mornings produce joy, but the first one did deliver. On the first Christmas morning, Luke records (Luke 2:10) that the angel exclaimed to the shepherds outside Bethlehem, "I bring you good tidings of great joy." Although neither the dictionary nor the Bible makes a clear distinction between happiness and joy, I personally sense the two emotions to be distinguishable. Author J. D. Salinger had the right touch when he wrote, "...the most singular difference between happiness and joy is that happiness is a solid and joy is a liquid." My solid 1958 Christmas gifts made me happy...for a while, but that basketball has long since burst and flannel now makes me itch. The joy produced by the surprise family reunion, our little Miracle on Ice, melted over me, continues to bring me joy, and will until I succumb to death or senility. Happiness dissipates over time; joy settles in and resides. Joy adds a dimension beyond happy. Happy is a cup of instant coffee. Joyful is a steaming hot mug of full-bodied, bean-ground, fresh-brewed Colombian.

We Delongs continue, in a way, to celebrate the day Ruth Ann and Fred came all that way just to be with us. We Christians ought to celebrate the joyful good news that Jesus, Emmanuel, came to earth just to be with us. Feeling happy about the gifts and other trappings associated with the holiday traditions of our culture is not wrong, but it is incomplete. Such a limited celebration might bring temporary happiness, but understanding, believing, and living out the knowledge that Jesus, God incarnate, came to seek and save us will bring everlasting joy. May you be surprised by Joy this Christmas.

December 8, 2019

Look Beyond the Present this Holiday Season

On a December day 50 years or so ago, I set a standard that may never be broken. The little Adelphi UMC Sunday school at which my girlfriend Beth taught needed a fill-in for the jolly man who normally filled the role and costume of St. Nick at the annual children's Christmas party. I trust that my acquaintances have judged me as a fellow of reasonably good cheer, even back then; nevertheless, my Santa impersonation at that gathering came off pathetically.

First, my athletic silhouette then didn't possess the retirement bulk it now commands. Who wants a flat-bellied Santa? Additionally, my cheeks showed no cute rosiness. . . unless that bit of late-teen acne counts as pinkish. And the pasted-on beard looked, surprise, pasted-on. My brown Bass Weejun loafers looked pretty cool on campus, but big, black leather boots would have served as a more appropriate accent for my polar ensemble.

Certainly any child without eye problems and minimally familiar with the television Santa, the Lazarus Santa, or any other legitimate fake Santa in the world must have spotted me as non-saint Dick rather than Old Saint Nick. A few of the more charitable kids may have allowed that poor Kris Kringle had just had a rough year. Maybe his sleigh had been rear-ended by a sputnik.

Besides my anemic appearance, my demeanor gave me away. I just found it impossible to get "into character." My hollow "Ho, Ho, Ho's" fell as flat as a reindeer pattie on frozen tundra. My body language silently spoke volumes: "Don't touch me and I won't touch you!" No one since has imitated the illustrious image so ineptly.

According to businessman Donald Gilmore, "There are three stages in a person's life. First, he believes in Santa Claus. Second, he doesn't believe in Santa Claus. Third, he is Santa Claus." I married that girlfriend. She bore us two great children. With the help of my checkbook, my Lazarus (Think Macy's.) account, and my Visa card, I became Santa Claus, confirming what a Mr. Holmes once said: "The Christmas season has come to mean the period when the public plays Santa Claus to the merchants." I know I did a better job of portraying Father Christmas to my kids and to the local merchants than I did to those bewildered kiddies years ago.

Entertainment magnate Hal Roach observed near the end of a good year for the American economy: "Some businessmen are saying that this could be the greatest Christmas ever. I thought that the first one was." I hope we can agree with Mr. Roach. Playing Santa well is nice, I suppose. Giving and getting gifts can produce some momentary happiness. Our challenge, though, is to resist the pressure to judge the value and success of a Christmas season, or of life itself, on how well we play the role of Santa. Someone said it well: "Don't get so wrapped up in what the world has to sell that you miss what God has to give." The genuine Christmas message is not a Target commercial. Neither Santa nor Amazon delivers it. God Himself delivered it in the form of Jesus as a baby. Emmanuel. God with us. Real, enduring joy comes only as we connect with and imitate, however imperfectly, the man/God Jesus, who came to portray the Father perfectly to us.

When we look back upon our Christmas season this year, let us hope that Evelyn Underhill's wish for us has been realized: "I hope your Christmas has had a little touch of Eternity in among the rush and pitter of it all. It always seems such a mixture of this world and the next, but that after all is the idea!"

Look beyond the present this season.

IX.   Living Life in Modern Culture (Post 9/11)

The tragedy on September 11, 2001, changed the world and all of us living in it. It's not overstatement or cliché to say that the event marked the passage from our old world to a new, more fearful, more paranoid, more cautious, and even cynical pattern of assessing individuals, cultures, and nations. Many of my pieces after that fateful day deal with the resulting conflicts and changes, both personally and throughout society. Life changes, but life continues.

February 16, 2003

War Calls for Civilian Duty, Too

Hut, 2, 3, 4. Hut, 2, 3, 4.

Monday morning. 11 a.m. September 1965. On the soccer fields south of Ohio Stadium. I, in Army green, a freshman member of the Reserve Officers Training Corps – ROTC – of The Ohio State University, marching with my platoon.

I am so old that when I attended OSU, the university compelled all male students to take basic ROTC for six quarters or substitute hours of unpleasant courses. Having played in the high school marching band, I knew I could march. Having hunted a few rabbits as a kid, I felt I could handle a firearm. Having studied hard during my high school years, I knew I could conquer the military classroom work. I elected ROTC. Although I had thought of myself as a dutiful person and patriotic enough, I confess that I did not enjoy my experience in green.

I hated Mondays, the one day we marched. I had to don my uniform in preparation for the parade grounds and had to wear it most of my class day. My problem: While in uniform, I was required to initiate a salute to all those military persons of higher rank I met on campus.

Remember, OSU contained 50,000 students even then, and many thousands were in uniform, just as I, on Monday. I could not assess the other uniforms quickly enough. I was so fearful I would miss a salute, I saluted all. I believe I may have saluted the Good Humor man twice and the library custodian once.

Military has been much on my mind again of late. Iraq, Korea and Afghanistan have become more than just geography lessons for all Americans. Then, a few days ago, the realization of our military's devotion to our country hit with an impact.

I attended the memorial service held for Capt. Adam Kocheran, deceased at age 31 years.

Adam was a child of our friends. He was an outstanding young man. He graduated West Point. He became a commander in the U. S. Army Special Forces (Green Beret). He died late last month from injuries suffered in an accident while leading his unit in training exercises in Puerto Rico.

Capt. Kocheran was not a Monday-morning student patriot. He was a full-time career patriot. He did not study and train for a grade. He prepared so he would be ready when the call came. He was ready. And so are the hundreds of thousands of young and not-so-young women and men who have left, are leaving, or soon may leave the comfort and safety of home to travel to faraway places to protect the homes, family, and friends they have left here.

Good Americans, all well-meaning, have spent the past few months arguing the merits and demerits of an attack on Iraq. Democracy will soon yield a decision. If the political decision dictates military action, the brave ones who execute the plans will do so without further debate.

Political discourse is vital – a necessary and wonderful privilege of our free society. Active soldiers, however, do not enjoy the luxury of participation in such discourse. They follow a chain of command, not a poll of the public. When the superior officer says go, soldiers do not ask, "Why?"

Like Capt. Kocheran, they prepare and they respond.

Non-military personnel, such as most of you readers and I, have the latitude to second-guess our President and our leaders. In fact, we have a responsibility to discern as best we can, with the help of a free press, whether our nation is following the right path.

But when the debates end and when the orders are given, we civilians, too, have a duty. That duty is to support our troops with all we have. We may support by paying our taxes. We may support by paying, without too much whining, the war-induced escalated prices at the gasoline pumps. We may support by giving extra attention to the soldiers' families who are left behind. We may support by our prayers.

My hitch in ROTC was not service to my country. Boys my age were then dying in the rice paddies of Vietnam when I was shining my shoes for parade practice. In reality, I was not fit to shine their shoes. In retrospect, no matter our view of the Vietnam conflict, we all now know that our failure to show respect for our armed forces of that era was shameful.

I pray that war in Iraq yet can be avoided. I pray that our troops will come home with no war stories to tell. I pray that missiles can be hammered into microchips.

But if that cannot happen. If rumors of war end in actions of war, I trust that you and I will conduct ourselves as genuine patriot-citizens who support our forces in the field. If we do less, we'll no more deserve the label of loyal citizens than I deserved the label of real soldier.

Gertie Could Teach Lessons about Fighting Terrorism

"Osama . . . meet Gertrude."

Nearly one-half century ago, about this time of year, my fellow goblins and I had to face Gertrude. We were a tough group, a really mean gang of 8- or 9-year-olds. We'd put on our gangster suits or bad guy cowboy garb and head out into the Halloween Eve night.

We growled our slogan, "Trick or treat!" We expected sweet responses. We . . . er, I mean, some of the other marauders, made the stingy homeowners hiding behind the drapes pay the price. Overripe tomatoes left from the summer gardens had to be put to use. Some of my buddies thought they looked good on house siding.

We knew what we wanted: good candy and lots of it! Nobody had better try to stand in our way.

Had we known what "mafia" meant, we would have called ourselves the Kingston Mafia. Had we known "terrorists" would one day come to define those who deal destruction indiscriminately, we would have worn the label proudly – so long as we had our disguises intact.

Only two opponents in town could back us down. Vernie lived in a cottage with weeds higher than the roof. Most of us had never seen her, but two of our companions lived beside her and swore she had six fingers on each hand. That convinced us she had more solid evil credentials than we, so we gave her a wide berth.

Gertrude presented a more troublesome presence. We knew Gertie. We saw her regularly as she gazed sternly from her pew in the village church to which our parents tirelessly dragged us. Maybe God didn't impact us much yet, but Gertrude . . . now there was a force with which to be reckoned.

We couldn't see God, but we couldn't miss Gertrude.

While we were clear where we stood with Vernie (Avoid her!) and God (Ignore Him!), we were ambivalent toward Gertrude. Maybe the modern word is conflicted. The issue at what price, candy?

Gertrude gave good stuff: maybe it was an actual, full-sized candy bar vs. the usual penny stuff or some off-brand.

Gertrude also had a peculiarly offensive protocol, especially for young pirates. She would not give up good stuff until the beggars revealed their identities and registered their names in her stenographic tablet.

Who did she think she was? I guess she knew who she was. She was the one with the good stuff, and she wouldn't budge. She'd have required the Lone Ranger himself to unmask and write his real name – and legibly, too.

We surrendered annually. Our taste buds trumped bravado every time.

Memories of Halloweens past with the nearly harmless companions of my youth prompt me to contemplate the deadly serious issue of terrorism loose in the world today. By using this metaphor, I do not mean to trivialize the very real impact and threat of the cloud of terrorism under which we have suffered and now live. Even though I am neither a military man nor a politician, I sense some parallels between the way Gertrude treated us and the way the world may choose to treat the criminal trick-or-treaters. Human nature doesn't change even though the stakes of the game increase dramatically. Review of the case of The Kingston Rascals versus Gertie moves me toward some conclusions relative to this world's current critical condition.

Identifying the Enemy Helps Neutralize the Enemy.
Once Gertrude discovered who we were, most of us became impotent. Nothing fans the flames of incorrigible behavior like the promise of anonymity does. Just knowing that she knew us immobilized all but the boldest of us.

The new federal anti-terrorist act has surely increased snooping by Big Brother.

With photo I.D. required everywhere from banks to pay toilets, the Gertrudes of government will know more of us by sight than ever before. Having been trained to revere the protection of our personal liberties built into our legal system, I fear the erosion of our freedoms. I fear more, however, the chance that our whole system may be demolished from without rather than stolen from within. At least many of the amateurs may be deterred by the searchlight of these new laws.

Notifying Those Related to the Enemy of the Enemy's Unacceptable Behavior Stops Even More of the Behavior.
Gertrude's forced disclosure didn't slow us because we thought she could stop us.

We shaped up only because we knew she could squeal to our parents. And we knew our parents could inflict pain on us.

Having identified the major terrorists, the responsible, mature citizen-nations of the world now must inform and indeed require the pretender nations of the world who support terrorism to cut it out. That's a big part of what the war in Iraq was all about.

A System of Rewards, Granted or Withheld, Convinces Many to Cooperate who would not otherwise do so.

Gertrude's treat was just too good to risk losing. When the rewards are great enough, behavior changes. One might think Gertrude's annual visitors' list would have dwindled. Not so. The payoff made the procedure more palatable.

Difficult as it may be for us to believe or admit, nations also react to rewards and punishment.

Those who oppose terrorism must stop giving good stuff to those who support or tolerate the evil ones.

Establishing a System, Publicizing the System, and Following Through on the System Assures Compliance.

Gertrude applied her system every year to all who begged. Drop the mask. Register. Get the candy.

Those nations opposed to today's terrorists must do no less. To those countries trying to stay perched on the fence, between the good guys and bad, we must say this. Declare your position. Sign on. Get the rewards.

Now we didn't keep records, but I'd guess Gertrude suffered fewer tricks over the years than did her penny candy neighbors. Her method worked.

Terrorists who are allowed to remain faceless strike often. But those who have been identified, who have been announced to the world, who have had rewards withheld and who have experienced consistently applied international sanctions on their behavior may strike less often.

"Trick or treat, Osama! Gertie's gonna getcha."

April 2005

The School Bell Tolls for Voters

Here's an idea relating to the ongoing local, state, and national education debate. I'm not sure how to translate the idea into specific actions to have a specific impact, but I've got an idea.

Nancy Franklin, writing in *The New Yorker* recently about the death of comedian Johnny Carson, noted part of his success was he always seemed to be in the prime of his life." . . . definitely an adult and fixed in a certain time when adulthood was something to aspire to, not something to be avoided." Yes, once upon a time, not so many decades ago, childhood and adulthood differed.

Children, then, wanted sooner or later to be adults. That has not changed. Adults, then, however, did not want to be children. Now, I fear, no one wants to stay adult.

While many advantages come with adulthood, many inglorious disadvantages come as well: aches, pains, hair loss (head), hair gain (ears and nose), taxes, bifocals, real jobs and responsibilities.

One of those responsibilities, which across all cultures, including ours, adults have shouldered, has been the care and nurture of the young.

Adults have worked so children could play. Adults have sacrificed so children could thrive.

Adults have starved so children could eat. Adults have taken risks so children could be safe.

Adults have even died so children could live. In short, mature adults subordinate their interests to those of children.

Even now, we disdain all who ignore this basic principle of human behavior. We all reserve a special distaste for any among us who abuse children in any way. What self-respecting adult would jump in a lifeboat and leave a child on the deck of a sinking ship? Jesus asked rhetorically in Luke 11:13: "Which of you fathers, if your son asks for a fish, will give him a snake instead?" What cad would steal a morsel of food from a starving infant, toddler or child?

Throughout history, self-respecting folks offer their best for their youngsters.

When faced with a stark choice of sacrificing to provide food, clothing, shelter or medical care to a child in need, I believe even we modern adults would still rise to the mature level and fulfill our clear and historic duties. The duty to provide a proper education, however, is a murkier one, which allows us to avoid it without the pangs of a guilty conscience. After all, what constitutes a "proper education?"

G. K. Chesterton wrote, "Education is simply the soul of a society as it passes from one generation to another." Knowing how to feed the soul is ever so much more difficult than knowing what to feed the body. A body not fed dies quickly. A soul not fed dies slowly over the period of a generation. We dare not permit the soul of our society to wither, do we?

I do not claim the experience, expertise or plain sense to prescribe "The Solution" to our ever-worsening predicament, to-wit: how to impact a suitable education to our young-uns without bankrupting our citizens and over government.

I do know, though, the children of this world, including our community, look to us to be adults.

I know my parents fed, clothed, sheltered and educated me whether convenient or inconvenient.

I know education is essential, and children cannot educate themselves. Children cannot teach children. It may or may not "take a village," but one thing it does take – a group of adults willing to find a way, even if uncomfortable, to educate the youth of their community.

So, I have an idea. I know it's sketchy, half-baked, and lacking in particulars, but at least it's a start.

Here's the idea: We adults should grow up and act like adults, assuming the responsibilities of adulthood, including educating our young.

In this one area of our lives, let us adults quit impersonating kids with all the short-sighted, self-directed, selfish and immature characteristics that come with youthfulness, and instead, grow up, act like adults, work together, and discharge our responsibilities to our younger generation.

Maybe we need to elect legislators who will tackle this problem, not avoid it like a pancake at an Atkins party. Forty-nine other states are grappling with this same issue. What have they done?

What's worked? What hasn't? If Ohio's system ever worked, it is clearly failing now.

Legislators – please try something!

Maybe we need to elect school board members who will fiercely institute efficiencies in a manner that will not cripple the delivery of basic educational services.

An aside: I applaud all those brave souls serving now on school boards. I believe nearly all serve because of their love of kids, not for money or recognition.

Maybe we need to step forward and volunteer a few hours or some materials for our school systems.

Maybe we do need to pass another tax levy, comfortable or not.

I hear the bell. Time for school!

June 30, 2006

Justice, Mercy Duel on Immigration

"Great taste!" "Less filling!" "Great taste!" "Less filling!"

A few years ago a beer company grabbed attention with its ad campaign contrasting two groups of its beer's proponents. One set of drinkers touted the beer's flavor; the other bragged on the beer's lightness. I couldn't referee that shouting match, but today a more serious dichotomy presents itself and demands the attention of all concerned citizens.

"Justice!" "Mercy!" "Justice!" "Mercy!"

The opposing horns of justice and mercy are gouging Americans concerning our current illegal immigration dilemma and what we should do about it.

Some shout, "Justice!" "Catch the illegal invaders," they say. "Arrest them. Deport them." Not to do so, they claim, would make a mockery of our system of laws and would work an injustice both to the earlier immigrants who have obeyed the laws and achieved citizenship the hard (and legal) way and to all the existing citizens who will be forced to pay the financial and social costs of integrating the illegal immigrants, to-wit: education, welfare, medical, and other public services.

These justice seekers would equate the illegals with the defendant Abe Lincoln once described: "He reminds me of the man who murdered both his parents and then, when sentence was about to be pronounced, pleaded for mercy on the grounds that he was an orphan." The immigrants enter our country illegally, then complain that they're not being treated as guests. Justice givers shout that the border breakers' own illegal actions have placed them in their disadvantaged position.

Others shout, "Mercy!" "Don't lay a hand on these unfortunate aliens, strangers in a strange country. Feed them. Clothe them. Educate them. Protect them. Hire them." Not to do so, they assert, would dishonor our national tradition of being the melting pot. Give us your huddled masses yearning to be free. This group reminds us that the rest of us, except the Native Americans, achieved citizenship only because of our immigrant forbearers. These mercy bearers believe the social costs of assimilating the immigrants pale in comparison with the costs to our collective conscience of mistreating any of God's children, no matter their illegal status.

Of course, the point of the old beer commercial was that the recommended beer was both better tasting and less filling than any other brand. Can a response to our immigration problem be found which contains both justice and mercy? The current Administration and several other politicos believe so. They propose a policy requiring the illegals to meet certain requirements to become citizens and gain permanent residential status (justice) while allowing those persons to stay here as guest workers (mercy).

I have experienced first-hand neither beer nor immigration issues. Stuck here, happily, in south-central Ohio, I cannot imagine anyone less qualified to offer an opinion on the immigration imbroglio in which our nation finds itself. The closest I have come to running the Rio Grande is buzzing through Taco Bell's drive-thru in a rainstorm. I can, however, remind ourselves of a guiding principle or two.

I have been taught that ours is a nation of laws, not of men. A culture based upon whim and not law invites anarchy. This suggests that those shouting "Justice!" must be heeded if we are to maintain an orderly society. Edward Young, in Night Thoughts, wrote, "A God all mercy is a God unjust."

On the other hand, the Good Book tells us, "Mercy triumphs over judgment" (James 2:13). A culture based upon strict law enforcement without allowances for mercy sometimes ignores common sense and the common good of its members. Wisdom requires taking into account unusual circumstances. Those shouting "Mercy!" suggest that the nation's lack of a sincere effort to prevent 11 million unauthorized entrants over the past years forfeits the right to demand deportation now.

I'm not sure of each ingredient Congress will need to include in this new batch of immigration law that it is brewing, but I do suggest it will need to include both a measure of justice along with at least a dollop of mercy. Only that kind of just, yet merciful law can fully satisfy the thirst for righteousness that all Americans share.

May 5, 2007

Beware the Sticks you Throw Don't Become Boomerangs

"Sticks and stones can break my bones, but names will never hurt me."

At least, we grade schoolers in the 1950's spouted that back to those who would dare attack us by hurling nasty names at us: sissy, baby, teacher's pet, and the like. Of course, in reality, we would much rather have endured being marked by a rock than branded with a name. The rock's mark fades in time, but the name's brand might never leave.

A few months ago, within the space of a few weeks, this newspaper's readers branded its staff a couple of times. If you're not a regular reader of the *Gazette* or if you're a member of the F & S Club (i.e., funnies and sports only) let me just say that the writers of a couple of stories used words attempting, no doubt, to illuminate. Instead, the words inflamed. Feelings were justifiably hurt. Apologies were necessarily and genuinely offered, but the effects will linger. One who has lighted a match cannot unlight it once its flame meets gasoline.

My friend, John Fraim, whose words once graced these pages, I believe ofttimes quoted both Rudyard Kipling and William Shakespeare. Allow me to do the same.

Kipling said in 1923, "Words, of course, are the most powerful drug used by mankind."

In Act 3, Scene 3 of Hamlet, Shakespeare's King Claudius said, "My words fly up, my thoughts remain below; words without thoughts never to heaven go."

Who among us has not experienced the truth of the impact of words spoken or written without forethought? As an attorney and a former English teacher, I have contemplated words and their impact for decades now. I would not claim expertise, but I do claim experience.

The *Gazette*'s problem, I am convinced, stemmed from a little inattention, brought on by the urgency of the daily publication deadline and the need to phrase stories in an eye-catching, thought-provoking way. Carelessness often begets misery. Proverbs 12:18 says, "Reckless words pierce like a sword, but the tongue of the wise brings healing."

Our society has been based on the freedom of speech guaranteed in the First Amendment to the U. S. Constitution. This allows citizens generally to say what they feel or think...to a degree. Defining that degree is the trick. One may yell "Fire!" at a wiener roast, but not in a crowded theater. One may openly challenge another with opinions, but one may not use "fighting words" in the face of another.

So, what's one to do? Stop communicating all together? No, but communicating on a delayed basis, <u>after, not before</u>, thinking, could be helpful. My secretary tells me about her old, country pastor who repeatedly insisted that his parishioners "engage brain before speaking." I understand that radio stations broadcasting live, call-in talk shows over the airwaves have some kind of six-second delay mechanism allowing the station to bleep inflammatory or inappropriate comments prior to their release to the public. My daughter has a program attached to her TV which somehow bleeps out words which the tender ears of my grandsons should not receive. I imagine some prime-time shows have more bleeps than words. Simply put, we should think before we speak.

Many problems stem from the fact that words carry both denotations and connotations: the literal meanings (denotations) versus the excess baggage that comes with the word (connotations). The careful writer or speaker gives forethought to the connotations his or her words may convey to a receiver of these words. The careful communicator anticipates what feelings those connotations may conjure up in a reader even though the writer may not have intended that reaction at all.

The problem with public discourse today: the speakers are actually intending to inflame. The more offensive the word and the more combative the tone, the higher the ratings. Successful business dictates giving people what they want. Unfortunately, people today must want the basest of things. This has not really changed over the centuries. The Romans wanted to see blood and death live in the coliseum. Today's public wants the <u>Ultimate Fighting Championship (UFC)</u>. Not surprisingly then, the listening public wants words used as weapons . . . the epistle as missile.

But how, the astute reader may ask, can we be effective in our communication without peppering in some poison to get attention? I can only testify as to those folks I've known who have accomplished much without ranting and raving. Bob Knight exemplifies the modern, successful basketball coach, but I remember a gentleman who had a very successful coaching tenure at Paint Valley High School in the 1960's named Oral Crabtree, who conducted himself as in a perfectly gentlemanly manner. Mahatma Gandhi took the non-inflammatory route to lead India to independence. My own father, a farmer, and my own father-in-law, an attorney, each accomplished much in his own way, but neither resorted to verbal attacks. And think how many grandmothers have conveyed their love and motivated their families with gentle nudges versus caustic comments.

So, the problem may not be "in your set." The problem may be that we who are receiving actually desire words with mean, rotten connotations. We'd rather feel than think...unless we feel our own ox being gored. Then, we fire off our own letters to the editor.

People, both public figures and private individuals, are hurling injurious words at an alarmingly increasing rate. I fear that the cuts from verbal sticks and the bruises from written stones may be permanently scarring our body politic.

Watch out when you tune into the shout shows on TV tonight, but also beware of what sticks and stones you may be throwing at your loved ones, friends, neighbors, and even enemies. Some sticks become boomerangs. Just ask Don Imus.

January 31, 2008

A Lesson from a Friend

Got a minute? I'd like to introduce you to my friend. Well, actually I'll just have to tell you about my late friend. He died last week...but not before teaching me a lesson.

Marcel Hundziak was a most unlikely acquaintance of your countrified correspondent. Born in Poland in 1923, young Marcel was imprisoned by the Nazis from 1942 until his escape in 1945. He didn't share lots of detail, but I did glean from him enough to reveal that his captivity in no way resembled a country club. The club part, however, did apply and was applied.

Marcel had reason to live out his life in bitterness. Instead, he chose to devote himself to the service of others. He earned his medical degree, emigrated to the U. S., became a citizen, served in the U. S. Army, attaining the rank of captain, and then, in the private practice of psychiatry, served children and adolescents until his retirement. Instead of seeking a dividend of revenge, he sought to invest his life in others.

I met Dr. Hundziak and his wife in connection with some real estate transactions. His story startled me, but his presence enthralled me. In his early 70's then, he was a paragon of personal gentleness, compassion, thoughtfulness, and manners. A case in point instructs.

My job involves representing my clients and their best interests vigorously. Client Marcel made that task challenging. Once I worked months to obtain an eviction order for him, the landlord. Thereupon, the good doctor arranged through friends and his church for the truck and labor to transport to Cleveland the household goods of the defaulting tenant at no expense to the tenant, thus sparing the tenant the shame and loss of the sheriff setting those goods out on the road. Justice prevailed, but mercy triumphed.

Interesting, you may think, but what's this got to do with life and the world today? Much, I submit. As in 1942, still today the world contains a great deal of...what word shall I choose? President Bush chose "evil" (Remember the axis of evil?) and was excoriated. I hate excoriation, especially when I am the excoriatee. So, I'll choose "ungood." Yes, much ungood exists. The question then becomes, "How can one stand for what's right, against what's ungood, and still not be excoriated as being an arrogant, intolerant, ungood clod?"

Dr. Hundziak's life's experiences and choices light the way. "Does ungood exist?" was not a philosophical question for Marcel. He suffered in its grip day after day for years under the unrighteous ugliness of Nazi Germany. Could anyone have faced him and suggested that Nazism was just another way of viewing the world and that he should not expect to impose his worldview on those who honestly held these admittedly different, yet not necessarily ungood values? After escaping the clutches of the ungood, Marcel eventually served in his adopted nation's armed forces in an attempt to assist the right and suppress the wrong.

While discharging his duty to support his government in challenging the forces of wrong, Marcel did not sacrifice his spirit of personal charity. In matters of his personal rights, he was ready to yield to the interests of others' good, but in matters of public justice, he recognized the importance of applying collective power for the common good. Dr. Hundziak's life supports the principle that good, kind, and gentle individuals can and should stand together to fight for good and against ungood. No inconsistency exists between extending grace and compassion on a personal level and joining in a government or institutional policy of using all means, even forceful means, to resist the destructive forces of ungood.

This autumn (only 9 more months thankfully) our nation will elect a new executive leader. She or he will set the tone and execute the policy of our government relating to the momentous issues of our time. As commander-in-chief, that person will need to recognize the ungood in this world and lead forcefully in rejecting and throttling it even if to do so brings allegations of intolerance. As Jefferson said, "Rebellion to tyranny is obedience to God." Protecting our borders and our interests demands it. On the other hand, the great leader tempers the steely determination needed to guard our citizens and our freedoms with the milk of human kindness, the hallmark of individual American citizens and American culture throughout our history.

No less authority than the New Testament authorizes the same dual approach. St. Paul stated that God has ordained all authorities, even those of secular governments (Romans 13:1). Jesus said to render to Caesar what is Caesar's (Matthew 22:21). The purposes of civil government are valid. Yet Jesus also taught that loving our neighbor as ourselves is evidence that we love God (Matthew 22:39). "With malice toward none and charity toward all" – that's how Abraham Lincoln put it. Dr. Hundziak demonstrated in his life an ability to cling to the institutional value of advancing right, even forcefully, against wrong, while retaining the personal virtues of gentleness. I know God helped him to do that. May God guide us in the U. S. A. to do the same.

November 16, 2008

Lenders Will Have to be Accountable...Settle for Klein Bars

"Put it on Dad's bill." Around 1959, as a 12-year-old seventh grader, using these magic words, I bought a lot of candy bars, one at a time, at Targee's Red & White grocery store just up the block from my school in Kingston. Of course, the normal candy bar, a Snickers or a Hershey, cost five cents then. When Dad was "buying," I ordered the best.

When I was on my own, I was a bottom feeder. I looked for bargains. At Jum Buchwalter's grocery, way on down the street, Dad didn't run an open account. When the chocolate fit hit and I found myself in that part of town, I had to pay cash. Often, therefore, there I opted for the Klein bar, an inferior Hershey's imitation, but which cost only three cents.

Dad's two cents worth made all the difference. On the Buchwalter days when I had only three cents in the pocket of my little denim dungarees, I had three choices of conduct open to me: 1) buy the less satisfying Klein bar, 2) postpone my purchase until I could get to the Red & White store, or 3) defer the gratification of my sweet tooth until I could actually afford the good stuff.

I didn't keep score, but I doubt that I chose alternative number three very often. Most days a Klein in the hand was worth a Snickers up the street. And the theory of waiting to satisfy my appetite until I could pay for that process myself was foreign to me.

While Dad was by nature a generous giver, I knew to observe reasonable limits in my use of his credit. I may have been a junk food junkie, but not a credit junkie. I did not join the Red & White candy bar of the day club. Five cents now and then didn't seem to disturb the balance of trade in our household, but I surely did not try to milk this chocolate cow every day of the week. Five days a week, every week, and I'd have added more than a dollar a month to the liability side of Dad's precarious balance sheet. I knew better than to go down that road. I knew Dad would talk to Hoke Targee and "cut me off." I knew if I became addicted to credit the way I was addicted to chocolate, one day I'd have neither credit nor chocolate.

Today on the national scene, the consumers of the USA are that 12-year-old, wanting the best and wanting it now. That's normal. The lenders, i.e., banks, credit card companies, mortgage companies, and retailers, are the Red & White, anxious to lend and sell, expecting to receive the profits as rewards. That's normal, too.

The government is Dad, but not really. Dad arranged the credit, but had the resolve to put on the brakes. If I had overused my credit opportunity, I would have been eating Klein bars the rest of my childhood. If the clerk at the store had encouraged me to abuse the account privilege, neither Dad nor I would have been dealing at the Red & White in the future. Overextension brought consequences.

Kids crave candy; people need houses and want luxuries. Grocers sell sweets to kids for a profit; lenders loan money to purchasers for a profit. Parents monitor the candy buying process and interrupt it when appropriate; prudent government regulates credit processes and intervenes when necessary to prevent abuses.

Now what would have happened if Dad had become a shareholder in the Red & White? If he cared more about the store making a buck a month from sales of Snickers to me than about maintaining the integrity of his own bank account, he would have encouraged the Red & White to sell me all the candy it could – on credit. And Dad would have created one spoiled, candy-bloated child.

I submit that the government, apparently having learned nothing from the Savings & Loan crisis, has become a shareholder, figuratively and now literally with the recently proposed bailouts, buy-ins, workouts, or whatever you choose to call them. By its lax regulation and maybe by its tacit encouragement, the U. S. government has become the prime shareholder in a bankrupt lending apparatus and has, in the process, created a country full of spoiled citizens bloated by the artificially sweet deals of the government-subsidized lenders. Fannie and Freddie wanted and received Snickers bars every day.

Daddy government needed to put on the brakes years ago. It didn't, and now it's going to have to pay the bill for the premature satisfaction of the unrestrained appetites of its children; hence, the $700,000,000,000.00 credit card bill just found in the national mailbox.

Here's where the analogy breaks down. Unfortunately, the citizens, we the people, are not merely the consumers; we are the government, too. We kids who were allowed to satisfy our appetites fully by saying, "Put it on Uncle Sam's bill" now have discovered that we ourselves must pay the bill.

And we only have three cents in our pocket. I guess we will be eating Klein bars for a long while.

May 8, 2011

Certain Values Should Be Timeless

Good night! My goodness! Has it really come to this? Just turn on your TV and see what now passes for news and entertainment!

The "news" programs have become shouting matches. Attempts to convey information and facts have yielded to folks, including the supposed journalists, choosing up sides and hurling insults against each other in an ugly tug-of-war. More and more I believe these correspondents would fit better on the World Wrestling Federation channel, if one exists. The British essayist G. K. Chesterton had it about right: "The modern world . . . has no notion except that of simplifying something by destroying nearly everything." Tearing down must build up ratings.

And the entertainment! Oh, boy! Not having seen, let alone followed closely, the survival-themed shows such as Survivor or the reality-based ones such as Jersey Shore, I am not qualified to render an expert opinion; nevertheless, I shall ask a question. What does our national preoccupation with these themes tell us about ourselves as a nation and as individuals? When did even cooking become a death match? If it's entertaining to watch teenagers act like teenagers, with their pettiness, shallowness, and self-obsessions, and to watch grown adults act like teenagers, then we're in a tarnished Golden Age of entertainment.

Can you imagine life without a constant diet of this type of diversion? If you have cable, dish, or whatever, (With all the technology available, you can probably get TV reception on your fingernail.) you don't have to. Our children think we are regressing toward senility, but instead of consuming the news at 11:00 and instead of laboring through the inane pseudo-realistic competitions all evening, my wife and I have become regular viewers of *The Waltons* at 8:00 on INSP.

A couple of months ago I accidentally took flight from the screaming heads of Fox/MSNBC, from sit-coms depicting men as airheads, and from the un-reality shows, and landed upon *The Waltons*. I had missed the original presentation of the series since I was busy in the 1970's, but after a few minutes that evening, I was hooked. The first, brief visit was refreshing. A winter's worth of viewing has been reinvigorating. We have actually worn the dust off the scream screen, a.k.a., the boob tube.

For your information, just in case you are young or forgetful, *The Waltons* was a weekly series in the 1970's depicting the trials and triumphs of a nuclear family of eleven, including Grandpa Zeb and Grandma Esther, trying to survive the Great Depression of the 1930's on the family farm in the mountains of Virginia. What could be more irrelevant, you may say! I beg to differ. Even though we never see John-Boy texting while riding Blue the family mule or view the family gathered around the kitchen table filled with multiple Styrofoam McDonald's containers, every episode's content relates well to modern life.

Allow me to highlight some values regularly exhibited: devotion to family (Can you imagine Jim-Bob being voted off the mountain?); humor and light-hearted fun even in dark times; sense of community and neighborliness; selflessness; sincerity; integrity; truth; honesty; generosity; charity; sense of self-reliance; responsibility and discharge of it, including by father John; respect for vegetation and animals (pre-green even); love of and loyalty to the U. S. A.; respect for the law; and respect for other people and their property. Are we so jaded that we cannot commend advocating these values once considered basic to good character? Surprisingly, the show even tackles some controversial, even inflammatory issues: war, peace, Nazis, and Native Americans.

The parallels between the 30's and today are striking: financial collapse, foreclosure epidemic, international wars, the proper role of the U.S.A. in the world, and the competing philosophies of U.S. government to be applied to these domestic and foreign problems.

Call me Grandpa Zeb if you want, pining for the good old days. I'll admit that the Walton's farm of the 30's resembles the Delong rented farm of the 50's. I well knew the inside of an outhouse until I was 12 years old. My bathtub had "Wheeling" written on its metal exterior and had handles for carrying it around. My childhood did not know pizza or MRI's. But I am surely not endorsing *The Waltons* because I'm glorifying the past. I like the conveniences of the present much better than the difficulties of the past, the Waltons' or my own. Nor am I suggesting watching more TV. I think less is surely better. And I certainly am not claiming I have attained some higher level of behavior than anyone else. If I took off my shoes, you'd see my feet of clay. I merely suggest that certain values are, or should be, timeless and that we ought to honor with our attention those behaviors, not the more base traits, which seem to be overrunning our society and our good sense.

Have we become so sophisticated that the plain expression of preference for these attributes is ridiculed as old-fashioned and provincial? I submit that it would be better for ourselves, our families, our community, our nation, and our world if we revisited these principles more often. As St. Paul wrote in the fourth chapter of his letter to the Philippians:

". . . (w)hatever is true, whatever is noble, whatever is right, whatever is pure, whatever is lovely, whatever is admirable – if anything is excellent or praiseworthy—think about such things." Let's all sleep on that.

Good night, John-Boy.

November 20, 2011

I Hope You Feel Better Soon, Uncle Sam

Dear Uncle Sam,

I hear you've not been doing so well lately. You're not as young as you once were, but I don't consider you to be ancient yet. When I think back to some of your ancestors, I recall that many of them lasted for centuries. You're a mere 235 years old - - just a kid by some standards. Remember Cousin Roman? He lasted over 500 years. Before that your ancient Greek cousins endured 7 centuries or so. I trust you're just getting started.

Maybe you've just been having a little mid-life crisis. Would it cheer you to remember some of your previous victories? Think about how you flexed your baby muscles to get out from under that mean old Great Uncle George III. Then you worked for years with that other George, (Washington was the family name) and his friends to "grow" this new land.

It's not always been easy. That big family feud in the 1860's broke your heart. Doubt existed that you'd even survive that time of brother against brother. Even though you're still finishing the healing process, you did survive. Then a few decades later, you were forced to go overseas, not once, but twice, to defend our cousins against evil aggressors. Those meanies would have taken over our families, farms, and factories if you hadn't stuck out your chest and your neck to do the right thing. Thanks. The last few decades, though, you seem to be in a little funk, to have lost your mojo, and to have departed from your groove. Pardon me for saying so, but you just don't seem to be yourself lately.

Maybe you're too self-conscious about your faults. You're not perfect, you know. Take the matter of your faltering work ethic. You had always been a strong worker. "Nobody could outwork that Uncle Sam," they'd say. And, besides, working like a dervish, you were always thinking up new and better ways to do things. Not so much lately.

And I've noticed a little slippage recently regarding your financial stability. You had always encouraged us to pay cash for what we bought. What's this I hear about old Samuel running up credit card debts like some college kid with his dad's VISA?

While hoping not to offend you, I want to mention another thing. You seem to be scared of your own shadow lately. You've been the toughest guy on the block for a couple of centuries now, but since that awful day in September a few years back, you seem somehow less sure of yourself, maybe a little paranoid even. One thing I've always admired in you was your willingness to be fair to everyone. Sometimes you would punish or subdue a wrongdoer, but you had always followed a fair process before you delivered them their just due. You seem so jumpy now that you occasionally go off half-cocked.

While I'm at it, let me address something else I've noticed. Uncle, you've always welcomed newcomers into our family. Oh, sure, in-laws were always a little suspect in your mind for a while, but once they were in, they were no longer out. If they aspired to and met our family standards, you eventually accepted them. Now, you seem schizophrenic. One month you're inviting everyone in, no rules of admittance. Next month, you won't let anybody in. Why not just go back to your old method: 1) Have a rule. 2) Give an incoming in-law the chance to comply. 3) If that person complies, accept that person. 4) If that person does not comply, don't let that person stay. Seems that would save you lots of sleepless nights.

Ol' Sammy, I'm writing at this juncture because I know you're conducting another national election next year. By the way, that's another of the things I like about you. You do your darnedest to be sure everyone feels that they "have their say." I'm just sad that during these election periods, your family acts like a bunch of spoiled brats: "My way's best!" "No, my way's the only way." I just wish you could convince us all to share our views, choose our leaders, and do our best to help them succeed in their leadership roles.

One more thing and I'll shut up. I haven't seen you in church much lately. I suppose everyone is entitled to sleep in on Sunday once in a while, but you may be overdoing it. I don't expect you to become a preacher and connect every single act you take to your religious beliefs; however, I must frankly say that when you were attending services more regularly, you seemed more "with it" and "together" all week. Maybe, like the old days, you would lead better if you based more of your decisions on a private, but solid spiritual foundation . . . the way you used to.

So, Uncle, I hope you believe me when I say I'm writing to help you. I don't believe for a minute that you have lost your mind, but you may be a little forgetful about what has made you so great. Neither do I believe you have lost your might. You may have allowed yourself to get a little flabby lately, but there's nothing wrong with you that a little discipline wouldn't cure. Apply yourself and I'm sure your muscle tone will reappear soon.

Finally, let me prescribe one more thing: a dose of moderation. "Moderation in all things," it has been written. Maybe you could stop lurching to the left berm and then back to the right berm, but just steer your buggy of state straight down the middle of the road. After all, that's the path that brought you where you are now. Uncle Sam, I pray for you every day and hope you soon will be feeling on top of the world.

Your loving nephew

December 16, 2012

Good Ol' Days had Some Bad Parts, Too

Faithful readers (maybe all three of them) of my recent columns may fairly criticize me for spending too much space pining for the good old days. As a response, I now pay honest homage to my memories of the bad old days. Having recently passed the threshold of the House of Medicare, I have reached an age at which I can recall plenty of the not-so-good old days. Here's a partial, painful listing of things I once had to do with that I'm now glad to do without.

Outhouses

Until I reached twelve years of age, the tenant house in which my farm family and I resided contained no water closet. The path to the outhouse was watered with my tears and possibly other liquids. Neither summer's heat nor winter's cold could keep me from my appointed rounds, but I never grew to enjoy the wait, the walk, or the . . . well, you know what.

Unpleasant understates the conditions under which the little white house out back served. Bees were no respecter of my needs. Darkness attended the toilet's interior, day and night. The landlord had not been thoughtful enough to install an exhaust fan. Modesty precluded the inclusion of a window or a screen door. Glade had not been invented yet, so let's just say that the ambiance was not inviting.

The only positive of a dozen years of such torture: even today I have no trouble making it to the next exit on the Interstate. Practice made perfect.

Inferior Highways

Want to take a cross-country trip? Be prepared to spend most vacation days driving there and back. Two-lane terrain led to nowhere in a slow way. Even short ten-mile trips were an adventure. From our farm near Kingston to downtown Chillicothe was an hour round trip. No Adena Regional Medical Center campus or Kenworth facility existed at the intersection of State Route 159 and U.S. Route 23. Instead, at "the Y," S. R. 159 simply dead-ended into U.S. 23, the two lanes of which then poked south past Hopetown, through Vaughan's dairy farm, passing Miller's Motel, across the narrow, rickety metal bridge into the First Capital at Bridge and Riverside.

Now it's ten or twelve minutes to the Bridge Street malls, five minutes of shopping, and back home in a half an hour from start to finish. Truth to tell, though, my wife and I often choose the backroads to Columbus when out for a weekend trot. Could that betray a secret yearning in my heart for those bad old days?

Buildings without Air Conditioning

Nothing was air conditioned in the bad old days-- not the house, not the car, not the office, not the school, not even the outhouse. I've often said that clean water is the last luxury I'd give up, but air-conditioning is a close second. I remember sleeping in my own sweat and lying on the floor beside the screened window sucking for air in the summer. The upside: electric bills were much lower.

Party Line Telephones

In rural areas, no private line options were available for our phone service. We hicks had to share a party line with at least one set of neighbors, maybe more. Besides the problem of availability, if you had a talky neighbor, you needed to interrupt her filibuster to get access to make even an emergency call. On the other hand, with no Facebook, Twitter, or other social media, listening in on a neighbor's conversation was the best way to catch up on local happenings. Unfortunately, the vice versa doctrine reminded us that nothing we said on the phone was private . . . sort of like the Internet today. Oh, and if traveling, the public telephone booth was the only hope of communicating back home. Many nights as I traveled to law school from Kingston to Bexley in the 1970's I possessed in my wallet only one thin dime, there for one emergency call. Today, when I'm on the road, I have the security of my cell phone . . . if I remembered to bring it and if I can figure out how to use it.

Antiquated Office Equipment

Imagine a keyboard without a monitor. Imagine typing a message that went nowhere but the page of papyrus before you. And no spell check. Make a mistake and pay a permanent price. Using a typewriter eraser was about like using a moderately sharp rock to perform surgery. The corrected symbol stuck out like a sore digit. Just start over . . . for the nineteenth time! And, if miraculously, you got it right, you could not copy it. We had no photocopiers. It was carbon paper or nothing!

Disease

Joking aside, those times were bad days when speaking of illness and disease. For example, I was just on the good side of the borderline between prevalent polio and prevented polio. I remember being carted down the road with my little chums to Kinnikinnick to our neighboring Centralia school for our first polio shots. I did not understand the threat against which our loving adults were protecting us. I dreaded the certain, short-term pain more than the obscure, unknown suffering which awaited a significant number of us if Sabin and Salk had not devised this miracle vaccine. Later, as I watched an aunt of mine limp through life, I could appreciate that the pain of prevention was well worth the polio prevented. Ditto for smallpox.

Politics

We moderns who think of ourselves as mature and sophisticated like to carry on about how uncivilized our political system has become. Admit with me that you have said something like the following in the past year: "I'd love it if those running for office would stop mudslinging and just tell us what they'd do to solve our problems." Hey, at least now they're just slinging muddy words, not shiny bullets. Ever hear of Vice President Aaron Burr and his political opponent Alexander Hamilton? Their d-word wasn't debate; it was duel. They disagreed. Burr shot and killed Hamilton. Debate over. The polls didn't matter. The projectiles did. Do you call that the golden era of polite politicians?

So, you get the picture. When you hear me waxing eloquently of how great were the old days (e.g., families intact, churches filled, morals intact, integrity unimpeachable), I invite you to gently remind me: "Richard, old boy, much as you hate to admit it, these good now-adays beat those bad old days in many ways." But, just be prepared to forgive me when I respond by telling you how good the bad old days really were.

March 3, 2013

Rational Discussion of Violence Needed

In 1956, my older sister took me, eight years old, to "the show." We country folk called movies "shows" back then. Some of our acquaintances called their automobiles the machines, too. Showing that night at the Moonlight Auto Theater, a drive-in movie theater on East Main Street in Chillicothe: "The Day the World Ended." Some things children ought not see. The world didn't end that night, but a big part of my childhood inner peace and innocence did.

We would now call this movie a sci-fi horror flick. Its premise can be succinctly stated. Nuclear war happened. (Remember, the atomic bombs had fallen on Hiroshima and Nagasaki only eleven years earlier). Radiation poison had caused some humans who survived the carnage to mutate into giant, hideous, monster-like creatures. The villain man-monster pursued our heroes and heroine. Of course, the good guys eventually won, but the graphic way in which the bad guy was portrayed stuck with me long after the thrill of the victory had faded.

The mutant monster pursued with an unrelenting, vicious style. None were safe from his mad crusade. I vividly remember his hands: no fingers, but three claw-like prongs enabled him to snare, hold, and kill his prey.

For months, maybe even years thereafter, in the still darkness of night, in my small, slant-ceilinged bedroom under the eaves of our little farm house, in my mind's ear I heard the claws of that mutant crunching into the wooden clapboard siding as he was making his way toward my window and then. . . .

My head knew better in the daylight. After dark, however, my irrational heart trumped my rational brain. Fear gripped my little being. Oh! No! My world was ending again!

My parents unwittingly made a mistake by allowing me to see a movie for which my young psyche was not prepared. We elders today are making mistakes, too. We allow our youth to see and experience, or have not been successful in preventing them from seeing and experiencing, scenes and events for which they have not or cannot be prepared.

All right-thinking people everywhere lament the murders at Newtown, Connecticut's Sandy Hook School. And all seek to pinpoint causes and to find solutions to the nightmarish scenes of violence the U.S. has been experiencing. Just call the roll: Columbine, Tucson, Aurora, Chardon, and now Newtown.

Many sincere folks propose near absolute prohibition of private gun ownership. Only trouble is: prohibition of anything almost never succeeds. Our nation tried unsuccessfully to halt alcohol abuse by outlawing alcohol. Use of liquor was leading to problem and often violent behaviors. It still does. The number of people killed in the U.S. annually because of alcohol-related motor vehicle events roughly equals the number killed via firearms homicides. But no one suggests outlawing liquor again. That was not and is not a fix.

I am not a member of the NRA. I used to hunt a little and did learn to use a rifle in ROTC class as an undergraduate student at OSU in 1966. I am not a drinker. My only drink may have been as a partaker of Holy Communion as a guest at a wedding ceremony at a church of a denomination that took the terms "bread and wine" literally.

I do have friends and relatives who own and shoot guns and ones who drink liquor. Sometimes I worry about some of them, too. But I do not suffer under the illusion that outlawing guns or liquor will stop the use of either.

Neither do I believe that simple tinkering with the manner in which we diagnose and treat people with mental illnesses will alleviate this problem quickly. Changes do need to be made. I am glad the experts are revisiting the protocol and procedures for helping and regulating treatment of folks with these illnesses. Assisting in the diagnosis and proper treatment of folks who are victims of mental illness will provide more safety for all who inhabit our communities.

Of course, no course can turn around this regression towards uncivilization quickly. I humbly submit, however, that a good place to begin a turnaround is to take action to prevent our children, our grandchildren, and the youthful members of our society from seeing and experiencing things they should not see and experience at their age.

Note, I did not say legislate a prohibition or invoke heavy censorship. That will not work. The only way to achieve an effective curb is to take an actual interest in the children and teens around us.

In loco parentis is the Latin for the legal doctrine, once popular, that allowed those in charge of minors to act in the place of a parent if no parent was around. The theory presupposes two truths: 1) that parents would always have the best interest of their child in mind if they were on the scene; and, 2) that surrogate parents would recognize and honor that interest, too. Reinstituting that practice in our culture presents problems. First problem: Parents, today, especially often the fathers, are no longer truly present in the lives of their own children. Second problem: We adults are no longer comfortable exercising control over other parents' children. We seem to have lost the common, accepted norm of what's good and proper for children to do, see, and experience.

Nevertheless, could we start by agreeing that children should not be inundated with violent images and sexual images on television, computers, hand-held games, or, for heaven's sake, in real life? Could we agree to allow adults, whether parents, relatives, teachers, or neighbors, the latitude to interfere when juveniles are engaging in conduct obviously not suitable for such young-uns? For example, dare we allow a teacher to lay hands on pupils to break up a fight? Might we allow an adult in a public place to change the channel on a TV televising an especially adult-oriented (Jerry Springer) program without risking a federal case? Maybe we need a law parallel to the Good Samaritan Law by which those who in good faith attempt to assist those who have been injured are not subject to the risk of liability for their efforts. Call it a Good Adult Law.

Many days I fear that the world has gone crazy and that the way back to common sense cannot be found. I cling to the hope that our leaders will find some large levers to push to begin that return journey to sanity. In the meantime, I pray that I and each of us will awaken to the reality that in our own little ways in our own limited spheres of life, we will recognize and discharge the need to protect those around us, young and not so young, from seeing and experiencing what will steal their peace and innocence. After all, the world did not end in 1956.

April 21, 2013

Small-Town Life Growing on Collegiate Set

Finally, the world is according us some respect. We rural folks have lived and labored in obscurity for centuries. The intelligentsia has considered us the weak end of the traditional dichotomy of town and gown. At last, now, at least one bastion of higher learning recognizes that those of us residing in townships, hamlets, villages, and small towns serve a purpose in our culture beyond being the butt of the humor of the sophisticates.

Kenyon College, situated in the Village of Gambier, Knox County, Ohio, population sans students of 2,391, has just completed a week-long series of events to explore and advance what it calls "rural sustainability." I guess that means keeping alive the country culture, especially the society and the soil upon which we non-urbanites live and, not incidentally, support the very physical existence of the urban types.

How striking that Kenyon has taken up the mantle of savior of the soil and soil types. Its tuition is among the highest in this nation. Kenyon prizes its reputation as an exclusive liberal arts college, devoted to the usual positions and policies liberal arts institutions espouse these days. The school is well-endowed. Terrific examples of classic architecture line the campus grounds. The place looks like Ivy League West.

Yale University, however, a true Ivy League School, sponsors a Sex Week on its campus. (Don't ask. Look it up on the Internet if you have a strong stomach.) Yale's website states, apparently with a straight face, that the week is "designed to pique students' interest" in the topic. I am approaching elder stage, but I have enough memory retained to believe that college students need precious little outside motivation to pique their interest in matters sexual. After all, I never met a pig I had to coax to wallow in mud. Kenyon has designed its "Rural by Design" week instead. I appreciate that.

By the way, I also appreciate that Kenyon has retained its designation as a college. Educational institutions from tech schools to kindergartens have taken to tacking "university" onto their names. Maybe Kenyon is coming around to some genuine rural ways. Country folk do not feel the need to attach high-falutin' sounding names to their own just to impress others.

The syllabus for the country week at Kenyon included, among other offerings, a talk by the Director of the Ohio Department of Agriculture, a local food brunch, a barn dance (held in a barn but maybe not a traditional square dance), and a concert with Appalachian music. My wife and I attended a lecture by a Holmes County farmer, bishop, and writer, David Kline, for that day BAOC (Big Amishman on Campus).

I have often said, and still hope and believe, that a person does not necessarily have to have a small mind just because that person lives in or near a small town. David Kline certainly exhibited a wonderfully facile mind; yet his gracious style and understated wit disarmed any in his audience who may have intended to attack him as somehow small, backward, or intellectually inadequate. The millions who live in the cities, though, have not often concurred in the view that country mice can run and keep up with city mice. Instead, we who live outside the metropolitan limits seem still fair game for the arrows of insulting humor slung by the media. Jokes ridiculing folks for their race, gender, sexual preferences, and religion (other than Christianity), have been mostly banished from public utterance; and I believe that is a good thing. But bashing us "hillbillies" continues to be a national sport for most of the media.

History recommends rural life. One of my sometimes heroes, Thomas Jefferson, made a statement in 1781 with which I can agree: "Those who labour in the earth are the chosen people of God, if ever he had a chosen people, whose breasts he has made his peculiar deposit for substantial and genuine virtue. It is the focus in which he keeps alive that sacred fire, which otherwise might escape from the face of the earth." Rack up one vote for the rural life. (Of course, don't ask about Jefferson's time in Paris, France).

The Good Book also votes for agriculture in Proverbs 10:5, "He who gathers crops in the summer is a wise son, but he who sleeps during harvest is a disgraceful son."

My point: urban chic does not deserve its preeminent place in our culture. Stereotypes die hard. Let's be realistic. The millions of metropolitans will not soon generate lots of higher regard for those of us who by choice or necessity exist here in exurbia. In actuality, though, we have our self-respect, which has come by keeping our heads high, our hearts humble, and our hands occupied.

I salute Kenyon College for getting its feet on the ground and its head out of the academic clouds hovering around the ivory tower. Thanks for devoting a week to rural issues. That's diversity for which we country cousins have been waiting.

August 16, 2015

Lamenting the Lost Art of Whistling

Am I alone in noticing a significant decrease lately in the frequency of a certain pleasant activity? In former days, I heard this pursuit regularly. As a kid, I heard my dad do it every day. I employed a paralegal who performed this at her desk frequently and to a very positive effect. A client friend of mine engaged forcefully and happily in this pastime nearly everywhere he went. Yet today the habit of personal whistling is vanishing.

Most who whistle do so as a sideline, a diversion from whatever presently primarily occupies their minds and bodies. Whistles spill out nearly involuntarily. Through pursed lips, Dad's rendition of "I'm Forever Blowing Bubbles" often accompanied the drudgery of his daily farm chores. Kathy's compositions overflowed while she resolutely plowed through piles of professional papers. Don could be playing softball, sitting in my waiting room, or just walking down the sidewalk when a happy tune bubbled up and out from his satisfied soul. Whistlers seem oblivious to their own whistling. The tones slide out naturally, without conscious effort. The song "Whistle While You Work" fits them well. They just whistle while they work or play or walk or rest. How pleasant!

The melodies emanating from whistlers' tonsils nearly always uplift. No one whistles a funeral dirge or a heart-wrenching blues tragedy. No television producer would have suggested a dark, stormy Wagner symphonic piece as the theme song for The Andy Griffith Show. Instead the upbeat, relaxed, all-whistled ditty that was chosen perfectly introduced each episode portraying the simple life in Mayberry. "Whistle a Happy Tune." Whistlers nearly always possess sunny dispositions and outlooks. Dad, Kathy, and Don all filled that bill.

I find no empirical evidence to buttress my opinion, but personal experience convinces me that whistling has gone the way of public pay phones, halo light TV picture tubes, and transistor AM radios. I don't wonder why. First, with streaming music available at nearly everyone's fingertips and ear buds at nearly everyone's ear tips, whether working or walking, waking or sleeping, who needs to entertain oneself? Furthermore, modern songs do not often lend themselves to being whistled. Dad could whistle "Pretty Bubbles." I could whistle the Beatles' sonorous "Michelle, My Belle." I just cannot imagine, however, my grandson Adam whistling a version of "Bang Yer Head," a song (and I use that term loosely), in the screamo subgenre of hardcore punk. Additionally, rapid-fire interruptions so constantly badger folks today that a whistler would choke mid-whistle trying to finish one stanza. Notifications, bells, buzzers, and, dare I say, whistles, emitting from smart phones, iPhones , iPads, computers, TV's, household appliances, and automobile dashboards render fluid whistling impossible.

Does it really matter, this whistlelessness? I suppose not really, not in any profound sense. If the world loses all the bee pollinators, we've got a problem. If all antibiotics become ineffective, we've got a problem. If nobody whistles, nobody whistles. Big deal, huh?

The demise of the whistlers, though, may be symbolic of a sad passage occurring in our nation's culture. Walt Whitman penned a poem in 1867 titled "I Hear America Singing." His masterpiece was a paean to the spirit of a growing, surging America, working away, confident of its future. Whitman's tone identified the USA as a nation of work, but all the while with a carefree, optimistic, forward-looking temperament. America whistled while it worked.

America is neither singing nor whistling these days. Sour people do not sing. Pessimistic people do not whistle. Politicians attempt to ratchet up confidence by simply declaring that "America's best days lie ahead." Unfortunately, the populace seems to be singing a different tune. The troubles and sorrows of this old world have stolen our whistles, both collectively and individually.

The next presidential election cycle has begun. We must endure fourteen months of bombast until our next Hobson's choice, an apparently free choice, but one to which no real alternative exists. Your humble correspondent would not dare suggest what candidate you and your party should nominate or for whom you should eventually vote. I do observe sadly, however, that no present candidate yet exhibits to me an ability to get America singing again. Instead, all the potentials appear just to be whistling past the graveyard. I await one who can inspire us together to whistle a happier tune than we have for many decades. I fear, though, I may just be whistling Dixie.

September 27, 2015

<u>The Times are a Changin'…Well, Maybe</u>

Time flies. Things change. My heart memory estimates "about 5 months ago," but my brain certifies that fully 50 years ago this month, at the tender age of 17 years, I fled the friendly confines of Kingston (pop. 1200), migrated 42 miles due north, and matriculated at The Ohio State University (pop. 50,000 or so). In the raucous mid-1960's in his hit song "The Times They Are A-Changin'," Bob Dylan whined, "You best start swimmin' or you'll sink like a stone." Bob had a point, one applicable both then and now to me and to our nation.

First me, then. Change manifested itself immediately upon my arrival. Having qualified for a scholarship allowing me to live cheaply in a 12 foot by 12 foot windowless box built into the concrete bowels of the west wing of Ohio Stadium in exchange for working for my fellow residents in cooking our meals, washing our dishes, swabbing and waxing our floors, carrying out our garbage, and cleaning our bathrooms, I opened the door of my dorm room to encounter my cracker box companion for the next nine months. Heretofore, I had thought of myself as an open-minded, fair-thinking white teenager, sympathetic to the plight of our country's minorities and certainly supportive of the burgeoning civil rights movement…in theory. Now I was to get the opportunity to experience how racial integration worked up close and personally. Cary and I coped well, much more harmoniously than the USA as a whole.

My folks quickly completed the severance of the apron strings and headed back to Appalachia, leaving little Dicky to fend for himself there on the banks of the Olentangy. Before I could establish my equilibrium, some destabilizing news swept through our hall. We newbies secretly hoped to rely on the stable, solid upperclassmen close by to lead us on our maiden voyage through the perilous shoals of our university experience. Well, one of those would not be on board to assist us. One upperclassman had hanged himself in his room just before our arrival. That report did not generate confidence in us rookie sailors.

More reminders of mortality would follow. A few days later, two fellows died in an auto accident just yards from our dorm entrance. On another fine, fall afternoon, as I returned to the stadium after class, I came upon workers flushing some reddish fluid down the sewer drain at the base of the southeast tower of the Shoe. A student had leapt to his death. Campus life included lots of campus death, a big change from my protected high school days back in good ol' Ross County. Mr. Dylan was right: swim or sink.

Mixing with new cultures firsthand furthered my campus culture shock. Targee's Red and White in Kingston had not had a kosher food section. Novels, movies, and TV had created my mind's narrow notions of a Jewish mother: loud, outgoing, emotional, and overprotective. When I met the mother of my hall mate, Jerome Kauffman, from Cleveland, I had to add a new adjective: thoroughly delightful. My education was broadening my horizons in unexpected ways.

Next, the nation, then. The 60's loosed pervasive, destabilizing changes. The civil rights movement necessarily wounded the nation's fabric. The expanding war in Southeast Asia fractured the populace into hawks and doves. The British music invasion threw Elvis into the back seat of his Cadillac. The sexual revolution opened our eyes. Continued assassinations clouded our eyes. Traditional politics imploded before our eyes with the 1968 Democratic Convention morphing into a riot. The nation was drowning. All the while, this country boy was just trying to pass accounting.

After half a century, some conditions really have not changed much. Racial strife still chafes our nation's neck. Our proper relationship with Israel stumps us as surely as matzoh crackers did me. Wars abound. Terrorists hound. Public battles regarding formerly private sexual matters embarrassingly occupy our attention. Popular music mystifies me the way the Beatles' did my dad.

Lots, however, has changed on campus. $178 paid my first quarter tuition. This year's annual tuition tops $10,000. Course offerings have expanded, too. Bar-B-Q Science appears as a course this quarter. Whatever happened to Western Civ? Free speech that thrived on campus in the 60's is giving way to speech codes and political correctness. Then, far left speakers and far right speakers could share a stage. Now, faculty and activist students veto prospective presenters who could offend sensitive ears. Should I be surprised that a recent survey of college graduates revealed that 10% of them identified Judge Judy as a member of the U.S. Supreme Court?

Burton Stevenson, world-famous anthologist, librarian, and one of Chillicothe's favorite sons, listed an applicable old French saying in his <u>Home Book of Proverbs, Maxims, and Familiar Phrases</u>: "The more things change, the more they stay the same." "Carmen Ohio," the beautiful alma mater of my alma mater, contains the line "Time and change will surely show." Yes, I admit they are both showing on this old boy. Furthermore, from a pessimistic perspective, Stevenson's old proverb confirms that the banes of humanity never seem to fade. War, prejudice, greed, and death march on. To the contrary, however, neither does the good ever completely vanish: peace, love, charity, and life itself.

Time does fly. Things do change. But, one ingredient can sweeten these somber truths. Another old proverb reminds: "While there's life, there's hope." In the Good Book, King David, under the weight of distress, illness, and attack, affirmed to God, "No one whose hope is in you will be put to shame" Psalm 25:3a. As long as we live, hope does exist that things can change for the better for each of us, our families, our neighborhoods, our nation, and even our world. Time for a change?

September 17, 2017

Dissent, with Respect, is Always Worth It

Do any of you feel this way? For the past little while, I have been noticing a hesitancy occupying my tongue. I harbor plenty of opinions about multiple subjects, some even foundational: government, religion, art, modern culture, sports…even food. Lately, though, I am having trouble pulling the trigger to spout my wisdom.

My part–Germanic genetic heritage led me, in my formative years, to adopt positions and then to hold them stubbornly, without thought of abandoning them, even in the face of withering and often reasonable opposition. My professional training as an advocate reinforced my natural inclination to take a side and cling to it like lard sticks to arteries. Nature predisposes me and nurture instructs me to: 1) gather facts; 2) draw a conclusion; 3) announce the wise conclusion to family members, friends, neighbors, enemies, strangers, the court, and anyone else within range, whether or not they are interested; and, 4) vigorously champion that point until I could honestly declare victory or until the bitter taste of the humble pie of defeat at last touched my brain.

I have had my share of verbal victories, but, not surprisingly, also of humbling defeats. Not all of my family has agreed to vote as I have so astutely recommended. Not all of my college dorm mates in our late night bull sessions accepted my well-reasoned mini-sermon that Jesus is the Way. Not all of my friends have applauded my superior preferences in artwork, in movies, in TV, or in sports activities. And, as a few former clients could confirm, not every judge rewarded my brilliant legal arguments.

Here's the difference between then and now. Formerly, I felt generally free to "let 'er rip." I knew that even when political arguments erupted over the main course, the family or dinner guests could end the meal laughing over dessert. The college chums who had so hotly belittled their mates' dwarfed intellects would be slapping hands a few minutes later over a cool bottle of something. Friends didn't unfriend friends just because their tastes differed. And just because I occasionally lost a battle, my professional colleagues did not surmise that I was an eternal loser, incapable of winning on another day.

In today's combative atmosphere, however, I don't believe most people are operating on the scriptural proposition that "love covers a multitude of sins" (1 Peter 4:8). Ironically, in a society where tolerance is held up as the principal virtue, the intolerance people usually exhibit toward those folks around them who hold even slightly different views on even non-essential issues is becoming sadly shockingly prevalent.

Express a non-conforming political opinion and watch the dinner party dissolve into a UFC finale. Put forth even the most delicate dissent to an accepted theological tenet and prepare to be bedeviled. Gently suggest that a heretofore warm acquaintance may be mistaken in any behavior and expect to receive a cold shoulder forevermore. Reliance on antisocial, er, I mean social media, where we needn't communicate face-to-face, no doubt increases the incidence of rude and relationship-breaking responses. I still contend that the frequency and intensity of downright hateful reactions is increasing no matter the form of communication.

I cross the border this month into my 70's. Forgive me for singing the "good old days" tune, but a better way did once exist. A case in point. My parents differed in their political party alignment. Their votes for POTUS nearly always cancelled each other. I learned that FDR was either "God's great gift to us working people," OR "the fraud of the century." This distinct and obviously heartfelt difference never interfered with my folks' ability to cooperate to accomplish the important chores of their lives together: raising children, working their jobs, tending to their marriage, enjoying friends, worshiping God.

Can you agree with my notion that we have become a nation full of overreactors? I do not suggest that we become a pack of chameleons, changing our colors just because the blinding light of public opinion shines brightly on our thin skins. Some hills are worth dying on. I cannot envision changing my mind on the existence and supremacy of God, no matter the uniform popularity of any opposition. Nevertheless, having and holding to certain non-negotiables does not require one to kill relationships with those camped on a different hill.

Courage of one's convictions indicates maturity. Rejecting all who dare disagree shows immaturity. The person who insists that only those who agree in every jot and tittle can remain in the circle of friends should not prepay for a large funeral room. One who unfriends others so easily will likely be unfriended in spades before this life ends.

There! My tongue has been temporarily loosed. Gee, I hope I don't lose any friends over this.

September 2005

Responding to Hurricane Katrina

"Get 'em out of the Manor and take 'em up to Kingston."

This could have been the cry of the emergency workers in January 1959, when the flooding Scioto River ravaged its valley. With no floodwall and no control system of lakes and dams upstream, many residents around the First Capital rapidly found themselves residing below river level. Their dilemma: get out fast, leaving all possessions behind, or risk drowning.

Some of the flooded folks from Chillicothe Manor and other areas north of Chillicothe found themselves washed up on the shores of Kingston, the miniscule municipal corporation next north of Chillicothe. The school gymnasium became their refuge. My dad, a member of the school board, invited one family to bunk with us, in our humble tenant house on the farm we rented outside Kingston, until the riparian rapids receded. We didn't have an abundance of space for our own family before the addition of the evacuee family of four or five (I can't remember), but we weren't lacking food. Dad always had laid in plenty of meat and produce to see things through the winter, and Mom could cook for nine as well as for four.

Besides food, shelter, and clothing, we provided some medical services. Father Evacuee had some sort of heart attack during his stay with us. The old Chillicothe Hospital on Chestnut Street being inaccessible from Green Township during the flood, Dad took the now twice-victimized Mr. to Dr. Lightner, the general practitioner in Kingston. I don't know what Doc did during those pre-catheterization days, but it must have worked. The man lived to say good-bye to us and head back down State Route 159 to resume residence in his freshly-watered Manor manor.

I am grateful that this has been my only opportunity to observe close-up and personal the devastating and dispossessing effect that Mother Nature can visit upon the inhabitants of our fragile, man-made habitat on this often vicious and unforgiving planet.

"Get 'em out of New Orleans and take 'em up to somewhere…anywhere."

That's been the rallying cry since crafty Katrina ripped through the Big Easy on August 29. The winds blew, the rains came, the levees broke, and a hydraulic Hades of H_2O presented tens of thousands of the old city's inhabitants with a more urgent challenge than even the '59 Manor residents faced: climb up fast or drown.

The game of assigning blame for the less-than-perfect handling of the emergency has already begun. I'll leave that to those more inclined and talented in such dart-throwing. The essential activity for now is assisting: moving people, sheltering people, feeding people, clothing people, treating people. Even if we cannot shelter people in our own school gyms and even if we can't take people into our homes, we can and should help by contributing our money or our time to the reliable emergency associations and church organizations which will be ministering in tangible ways to those in dire need.

These micro issues demand our early attention, but pale in comparison with the macro issue: "Can New Orleans and its environs be rebuilt and repopulated and, if so, is the cost of doing so a proper expenditure?" In other words, can the cost to the nation be justified by the expected results? Shall we base our long-range view of this matter on simple, harsh economic realities? Should our willingness to invest in reconstruction be dependent upon the guarantee of a good return on our investment?

Jesus seems to have said, "No." He said, "If someone wants...your tunic, let him have your cloak as well" (Matthew 5:40). That doesn't sound very practical, but pure charity is often impractical. On the other hand, the Apostle Paul advised that one must first take care of his own family. "If anyone does not provide for his relatives, and especially for his immediate family, he has denied the faith and is worse than an unbeliever" (I Timothy 5:8). So, does this mean that we ignore the needs of our neighbors?

In 1959, we Delongs could help out by sheltering and feeding a few of our neighbor Manorites for a few weeks, but we could not have afforded to rebuild their home had it been lost. To attempt to do so would have bankrupted our family. After taking good care of the micro details of saving and protecting victims, our government, and of course that is we, must now determine to what extent the Gulf Coast is "our family" as opposed to "just neighbors."

I believe most of us as individuals and our nation collectively want to be charitable. Good sense, however, requires drawing a line on the far side of thoughtful generosity and the short side of bankrupting extravagance. We would like to teach the world to sing and buy everyone in it a Coke, but where does duty end and senselessness begin? At the city limits? At the township line? At the state boundary? At the Mason-Dixon Line? At the nation's edge?

Whether it's New Orleans or Yellowbud (that local hamlet that suffers repeated floodings), universal health care or Iraq, the old economic quandary of "guns or butter" continues to nag us. What part of our limited, finite resources do we dedicate to hardware and infrastructure to protect life and what part to food and perishables to support life?

Even though we do not have the resources to buy all the guns and butter we would like, I pray that we as individuals and as a nation will be able to find a way and have the fortitude to relieve generously the sufferings of all our brothers and sisters, domestic and foreign.

November 3, 2019

People Can Find Acquaintances in Unexpected Places in Life

One needs a search party to find advantages to aging, while disadvantages march right to your door. Illness, decreasing income, residence changes, and losses of spouse, family, and friends join the parade day after day.

Psalm 90:10 informs: "The years of our life are threescore and ten [70] . . . they are soon gone and we fly away." If my life were a ballgame, I'd be in the first overtime period. If I could turn back the game clock, I would call my mom for help with a recipe, my dad for advice on whether to trust a local business, my father-in-law for his take on our crazy political scene, and my friend Jerry for a good-humored pat on the back. Alas, it will not be; yet, I'm not willing just to play out the clock. Samuel Johnson put it plainly: "If a man does not make new acquaintances . . . he will soon find himself left alone."

Recently I have found delightful unexpected acquaintances. They cannot replace old friends, living or departed, but they do open new avenues of joy, love, and learning. Age is no barrier. My additions range from age 3 to 103. Young Jacob, a condo neighbor, is exceptionally inquisitive, noticing everything. He once inquired, "What other names do you call your garbage pail?" In only the opening minutes of his game, Jacob has taught me to observe carefully. And he's so cute and happy I can't help feeling better after a visit. No wonder Jesus ordered, "Let the little children come to me...." (Mark 10:14)

Centenarian Lucille doesn't act her age. She charms visitors. She engages each person in her presence. She thinks. She studies. She exercises manners, never failing to call thanks to my wife for a greeting card. She laughs, heartily. In quadruple overtime, Lucille has taught me to live vibrantly no matter my life expectancy.

I bumped into John, nearly literally, in a local coffee shop. A shade older than I, John exuded an air of classic gentlemanliness. He deflected my inquiries about him with his questions about little old me. At home I googled his name. John served years as CEO of a multibillion dollar consumer company, as chair of probably your favorite global entertainment firm, as trustee of an Ivy League university, and as volunteer leader of dozens of charitable projects. He centers on others in a nearly miraculous fashion. At 81, John has entered life's second overtime.

I wrote John, praising his humility. He surprised me with a reply, and we have completed a few rounds of pleasant correspondence. Although I haven't interacted with people of John's stature, I can recognize him as an exception to the stereotypical egocentric celebrity executive. John has taught me already that reaching the pinnacle of worldly success need not personally poison the participant.

I met Bill at Adena Hospital. His wife of nearly 70 years lay very sick. We chatted. We prayed for Hazel. We parted friends. Hovering around their 90's, in their third overtime, Hazel first and then Bill have passed. During our months of percolating companionship though, I soaked up lots of wisdom, history, camaraderie, and love from Bill. Think Huck receiving from Jim as we rafted along on Bill's kitchen table.

I interrogated Bill to extract stories. He and I had inhabited the same corner of the world, but our experiences were a world apart. I shall never forget his gentle telling of his situation in the early 1950's. Bill recounted without rancor: drafted to fight in the Korean War, sent to Fort Knox, Kentucky for basic training, and forced to cross the Ohio River to Indiana to make a weekend phone call to his family. Deemed worthy to risk his life on foreign soil to defend the USA, he was judged unworthy of using a public telephone in Kentucky. Bill taught me the value of forgiveness and the example of hard work (three simultaneous jobs) and devotion to family, even when the world says, "Move to the back."

I never took the Carnegie course on winning friends. I am neither especially magnetic nor, for sure, irresistibly attractive. I do, however, subscribe to Dan Schantz's conclusion: "It's hard to be interested in people and afraid of them at the same time." Feeling lonely? Don't fear, but take an interest in children, super seniors, and folks who have started, lived, or finished differently than you. You may have lots of friends you just haven't met yet.

Education

He completed eighth grade. I completed twenty years of schooling; yet, I never got smarter than he. Better educated? Yes. Certified for service in the professional fields of education and law? Yes. But innately smarter? Fuller of common sense? Definitely not.

Having arrived into the arms of his tenant- farming parents down on Richmond Dale Pike in 1912, Dad's lot was not to include lots of formal education. Readin', writin', and 'rithmetic would be aplenty of book learnin' for Wayne. Once having attained the size and strength to manage a team of horses and to tote those bales and the stamina to do so daily from sunup to sundown, school was out, literally. Family cannot eat algebra and biology. Charles and Goldie needed Dad at home to help with the farming. One might say that's when Dad's real, practical education began: the original "home schooling."

Dad may not have had much classroom education himself, but he did value it. He served as president of the Kingston-Union district's board of education. He and Mom supplied all the material and motivation my sisters and I needed to complete our twelve years at Kingston. My folks and other parents and citizens like them in our little farming community took seriously their duty to hire effective teachers, coaches, and administrators to instill in us the knowledge, habits, attitudes, and values we needed to successfully navigate the world.

As teachers across the USA have made a recent push for better compensation, I have been reflecting on the current status of K-12 education systems. I am certainly not eminently qualified to opine on the total condition of education in the USA. I did teach middle school many years ago. My wife was a certified teacher. My daughter-in-law has taught first grade for eighteen years. Three brothers-in-law served as administrators. Many of my favorite people teach or have taught for a living. My sympathies lie with the schools; but, still, my random and partial thoughts on the subject merit no special respect. Feel free to disagree as I address only a few of the issues, which bear on this subject.

---MONEY: While I have never voted against a proposed school tax, I do not believe that money alone makes the crucial difference in the quality of the educational experience. I have no idea of the per pupil expenditure in my Kingston school. I am sure it was paltry. Our library was smaller than the modest-sized laundry room in my condominium today. Our curriculum included just two years of one foreign language: Latin. The State of Ohio pulled our charter the moment I graduated, supposedly on account of the lack of resources. Despite rumors, it was not because of the poor quality of the recent graduates.

Our little 1965 class of 22 students produced a dentist and lieutenant colonel in the U.S. Army; a pilot and a bank president; a Ph. D. in computer science from UCLA; a dietician who headed the Texas State Dieticians Association; an agricultural economics degree holder who has farmed in a most modern way with techniques acquired from around the world; teachers; and, most notably, good solid parents and productive citizens. Oh, and one pretty average kid managed to pass the Ohio bar exam.

Money spent did not directly generate these results. Per pupil spending has skyrocketed in the past half century. Upper Arlington paid me $5,950 for my first year of teaching. This year's starting salary there will be $45,293. I support proper compensation for school personnel. I support generous funding, assiduously handled, for schools. But I know that well-paid teachers and classy classrooms did not spell the difference for me and my mates. Truly dedicated, talented, and loving teachers here and   there   did.

---ORDER: If merely devoting more money to public education cannot cure the system, what can? Of course, no single cure exists, but I suspect that a little more order, i.e., discipline, might help. Dad told me that teachers directed misbehaving students at his old Liberty Fractional School to march to the bank of Dry Run Creek, cut a branch off a tree, and return that switch to the teacher, which switch that instructor would apply without tenderness to the hind quarters of the offender. Dad's alma mater did not possess erudite textbooks, smart boards, or computer labs, but apparently did maintain clear lines of authority. (Please relax, gentle reader. Although tempted, I do not subscribe to the overly simplistic theory that   we   should   reinstitute   corporal   punishment.)

Order alone, without excellent instruction and adequate facilities, will not produce optimum results; however, as 18th Century British poet Alexander Pope wrote, "Order is heaven's first law." And, the Good Book informs that fear of God, (translated: respect), is the beginning of wisdom (Proverbs 9:10). Teachers and administrators, backed by the home and community, need to make clear that students must dance to the teacher's fiddle and that failure to do so will result in negative consequences. Discipline   is   the   beginning   of   learning.

---FAMILY: Now, the crux of the matter. Honest thinking leads to the realization that no matter how well financed the schools are, no matter how talented and dedicated the teachers are, the disintegration of the family limits the successes of the school systems. Even a student with perfect attendance spends 1200 hours per year in school. That leaves 7,500 hours outside school. Certainly, some students beat the odds, but chances are great that the child living in a dysfunctional home environment will not perform   well   at   school.

Conclusion: "Money can't buy me love," the Beatles sang, nor a perfect public education system. Reestablishing more order in the schools is a step in the right direction, but unless the family institution can be fixed, educators will continue to fight a losing battle. Isn't that right, Dad?

Flying Hammer

I narrowly missed dying in a round barn on a hot day 54 summers ago. No, I was not looking for a corner to . . . well, you know the joke. As a rather bumbling summer employee of a small roofing/plumbing business, I that day found myself stationed at the base of a silo 50 feet or so tall which was and is located inside the unique Maxwell Farm round barn situated along State Route No. 180, a few miles east of Kinnikinnick.

I may have bumbled, but co-worker Howard fumbled and nearly terminated my life at the 17-year stage. Howard worked atop the silo. He dangled a rope to me. He yelled for the relevant tool. I fished the tool from the toolbox and tied it securely to the line. Howard reeled the apparatus skyward. Screwdriver—check. Crescent wrench—check. And so the routine mindlessly proceeded . . . that is, until the claw hammer!

I harnessed the hammer into its noose. The hammer rose heavenward. I stood inertly at my post, no doubt staring absentmindedly at the floorboards of the barn, daydreaming about lunchtime, quitting time, girlfriend Beth, basketball, golf, supper at Mom's table, college in the fall . . . until Howard's piercing scream shook me from my youthful reverie. "Look out!" he bellowed. I jerked my eyes up and spied the heavy hammer hurtling directly toward a numskull who would soon have a numb skull, me. A single thought, in capital letters, instantly obliterated the jumbled ruminations, which immediately heretofore had been aimlessly swimming in my cranium. The message: "I'M GOING TO DIE!"

All this happened in a flash. Thanks to the law of gravity, a two-pound claw hammer travels from the top of the barn to the head of the somnambulant dunderhead below in a split second. With zero time to react, I was a sitting, no, a standing duck.

Clunk! The onrushing metal masher struck a 2"-by-12" timber that, providentially for me, jutted perpendicularly from the silo wall about 10 feet above my dumb head. That heavy board deflected the missile just enough that it sailed a few inches past my brow and clattered loudly, but harmlessly to the ancient hardwood floor of the barn, coming to rest just below my trembling knees. (About then, I probably was looking for that proverbial corner.) I lived to see another quitting time.

I hadn't thought much about death when I was 17. Now, though, at 71, I more often engage in morbid thoughts. Of course, that's natural. Robert Louis Stevenson wrote, "Old and young, we are all on our last cruise." I can add, "Yes, but for the young the port of departure is just fading from view behind them, while for the old the point of destination is coming fast into view just ahead."

We adults often advise young folks to enjoy their youth, ideally a time of fewer commitments and responsibilities. While this is sensible advice, I recently read an exclamation uttered by a character in Marilynne Robinson's novel "Gilead," which awoke me in a way similar to Howard's flying hammer experience: "Adulthood is a wonderful thing and brief. You must be sure to enjoy it while it lasts." Adults, including yours truly, need to hear and heed this advice.

Many hammers come flying at us as we endure the years. Illness, poverty, loneliness, family discord, abuse, addictions, hatred, and, to be sure, death stalk all humans. "I'M GOING TO DIE!" Sometimes we are sitting ducks, having done nothing to deserve our bad luck. Sometimes it's just the fickle hammer of fate. We seem unable to move quickly enough to avoid the impact of life's devastating blows. Vicissitudes occur.

Your humble, old correspondent would respectfully suggest that now, before the hammer flies your way, you seek out your 2"-by-12" and position yourself under it. My faith has served as my shelter, my deflector. Psalm 91 (The Message) promises: "His [God's] huge outstretched arms protect you—under them you're perfectly safe . . . ." While I heartily recommend seeking the solace God provides, I fully understand that others and I can and should seek additional refuge elsewhere, too. Family, friends, neighbors, community, physicians, public safety officers, mental health workers, recovery experts, and others can help protect us from life's misfortunes and help restore us after unanticipated or unavoidable stumbles and injuries. We must check our position and move toward help if we are to fully enjoy our brief adulthood.

And fumbles happen. I don't blame Howard for my near-death experience. Had I stayed watchfully alert rather than standing there with my teeth in my mouth and my elbows halfway up my arms, the falling projectile would have created only a minor threat that I could have evaded easily. Our problems may be initiated by another in our presence, but our mindfulness about our circumstances can help us avoid catastrophic damages.

I am not naïve. I do not really believe poet William Ernest Henley who wrote, "I am the master of my fate; I am the captain of my soul." I am only suggesting a little practical lesson for all: Keep your eyes open and your "head in the game!" And as for those of life's difficulties that cannot be anticipated or sidestepped, be sure you have positioned yourself under a good, solid 2"-by-12".

April 5, 2020

Pandemic of 2020

I wish I could offer fresh advice for best behavior during this Pandemic of 2020. Solitary confinement weighs heavy on us tender elderly and on the health-compromised among us. Even the young and fit throw fits at the necessary social deprivations: no dinners and drinks out, no movies with butter-drenched theater popcorn, no bracket-busting March Madness weekend beer and pizza extravaganzas. Alas, I can offer only warmed-over bromides that our parents first gave us and that our government and health department now gives us as The Law.

---Wash your hands! (And don't just run water over them).

This farm boy questioned that command. Dirt ruled. In it, we grew our crops and table vegetables. I admired and enjoyed it. But I guess Mom knew what Dr. Fauci only now reminds us: microbes exist beyond our vision. No wash--no supper! Okay then, I'll wash up!

---Keep your hands off your face!

Jabbing at the sore will make it worse. Rubbing your eyes will infect them. Putting your fingers in your mouth is impolite. Stop picking your...well, you know. My imperfect response: "If God didn't want our hands to touch our faces, why did he make our arms so long?" I lost. Mom, predecessor to Dr. Amy, prevailed.

---Stay as far away from those kids as you can get!

Mom hadn't heard the term "social distancing," but she definitely believed that bad company corrupts good character. My protest that everyone else was going to be there fell on deaf ears. Today's advisers modify the principle to tell us that even too much good company encourages the bad germs. My folks had to drag me to weddings, reunions, and commencements. Wouldn't we love to attend a few about now!

---We don't go to the doctor or hospital for every little thing!

The ancient reasoning differed from today's. No medical insurance existed. No deductibles. No co-pays. Just all-pays: the patient paid all, always, all ways. No urgent care facilities existed. Most rural hospitals had no ER. If Doc Lightner wasn't in or couldn't handle it, no emergency squad came with lights and sirens. The undertaker transported emergencies in the hearse. Ironic, isn't it, that if in these dire days telemedicine diagnoses a patient with COVID-19 symptoms the patient must avoid medical facilities until the last minute. Sensible, but ironic.

Other habits common to my 1950's family sound familiar. We didn't eat out. Few restaurants existed, and we couldn't afford them anyway. Occasionally I accompanied Dad on Friday to the dusty, smelly, quite non-sterile lunchroom of Scioto Livestock Sales. We did not fly or take long trips. The daily farm responsibilities along with the scarcity of disposable income kept us close to home. We've come full circle. Who would have thought that taking the garbage to the curb would become the travel highlight of our week?

Many resent these current governmental edicts as heavy-handed and intrusive. I sympathize. My wife and I have already inscribed the words of Psalm 46:10 on our gravestone: "Be still and know that I am God." I just chafe a little at practicing that on this side of the ground. Yet as a member of the corona target group, I admit that good sense dictates compliance with these tried-and-true dictates. Otherwise, I may be utilizing that gravestone prematurely.

Not being designed to stay home, we all anxiously await restoration of our freedoms. That's natural. As 19th Century theologian William Shedd explained, "A ship is safe in harbor, but that's not what ships are for." He neglected to mention that only a ship of fools would sail from port directly into a storm. Although stale, some food items continue to be useful. Old bread makes great croutons and tasty stuffing. Old or new, this counsel is true. Continue to make sensible sacrifices for a while now in order to assure better days ahead.